W9-DBU-559

A
STRAY
CAT STRUTS

· · · · ·

My Life
as a
Rockabilly
Rebel

.....

A STRAY CAT STRUTS

Slim Jim Phantom

Riverhead Free Library
330 Court Street
Riverhead, New York 11901

THOMAS DUNNE BOOKS
St. Martin's Press
New York

THOMAS DUNNE BOOKS.

An imprint of St. Martin's Press.

A STRAY CAT STRUTS. Copyright © 2016 by James McDonnell. All rights reserved. Printed in the United States of America. For information, address St. Martin's Press, 175 Fifth Avenue, New York, N.Y. 10010.

www.thomasdunnebooks.com

www.stmartins.com

Title page and chapter opener art © Revoltan/Shutterstock

Designed by Kathryn Parise

Library of Congress Cataloging-in-Publication Data

Names: Phantom, Slim Jim, author.
Title: A stray cat struts : my life as a rockabilly rebel / Slim Jim Phantom.
Description: First edition. | New York : Thomas Dunne Books, 2016.
Identifiers: LCCN 2016001232 | ISBN 9781250076915 (hardcover) |
    ISBN 9781466888876 (e-book)
Subjects: LCSH: Phantom, Slim Jim. | Stray Cats (Musical group) |
    Rock musicians—United States—Biography.
Classification: LCC ML420.P4876 A3 2016 | DDC 781.66092—dc23
LC record available at http://lccn.loc.gov/2016001232

Our books may be purchased in bulk for promotional, educational, or business use. Please contact your local bookseller or the Macmillan Corporate and Premium Sales Department at 1-800-221-7945, extension 5442, or by e-mail at MacmillanSpecialMarkets@macmillan.com.

First Edition: August 2016

10 9 8 7 6 5 4 3 2 1

For TJ, Christy, and Madison

Contents

• • • • •

A
STRAY
CAT STRUTS

• • • • •

INTRODUCTION

I love watching television. I've always loved it. The fruits of my labors are the afternoons spent changing the channel thirty or forty times an hour, keeping up with all major-league baseball games, vintage TV shows, the Game Show Network, any live concert performance being played, and the news of the day. I travel all over the world doing gigs to hustle up the rent and keep coming home to the premium cable TV package and my pals who enjoy our eclectic way to pass the day. I'm not alone in this. I read early on that John Lennon and Elvis Presley were well-known TV addicts. This knowledge only helped justify my life choice at a young age. I won't name all the names, I don't click and tell, but most of the time, any number of other household names in pop culture are on the other end of the line watching with me. As Harry Dean Stanton likes to say to me, "Don't just do something, sit there!"

Today was an especially gratifying TV day. I had just gotten back from my first visit to Buenos Aires. I had gone very far this time to pay the cable bill. It was a reminder that it's hard to make a living as a living legend. Being a member of the Stray Cats, I helped launch a thousand ships—not all of them are yachts, but it has enabled me to keep it all going in a relatively hand-to-mouth lap of luxury. We really created a new breed of rock fan that has continued to transcend the comings and goings of countless trends. We will outlive many, many bands that sold more albums than we did but will never reach the souls of these kids in the way we have.

Argentina was a classic example. I played for 200 kids, and 175 of them had a Cats' head tattoo. The other twenty-five were children and will get one the minute they are old enough. Their parents will take them to get the tattoo. The people who have chosen rockabilly as their 100 percent lifestyle are uninterested in any other facet of pop culture. The children were all dressed in different incarnations of me from past album covers and photos. There were kids in little leather jackets with red bandanas around their necks. There were kids in little rockabilly cowboy suits. There were kids wearing little baggy pants, fleck jackets, and black-and-white shoes. There are twenty-seven hot rods in all of Argentina, and they were all in the dirt patch parking lot behind the roadhouse-style gig. Big tough guys in the front row were holding their women and shaking, a few of them crying with joy during "Runaway Boys." These people have based their entire lives on the influence they've gotten from the fact that me and two guys from school rediscovered, retooled, reworked, and ultimately saved American rockabilly music from extinction and made those classic records during the 1980s. We call it Rockabilly World.

In 1979, if you had told the eighteen-year-old version of me that thirty-five years later I'd be traveling the globe, playing the drums, and introducing brand-new kids every day to all things rockabilly in exchange for my soul, I would've signed on the dotted line. I fell hard for the whole thing, all the way, when I heard Elvis Presley and then Gene Vincent, Eddie Cochran, and Carl Perkins. It was all we thought about, and we never looked back. Rockabilly music and style and how to earn a living through it was our crusade in life. If meeting and befriending most of my childhood influences, the feeling of true equality with any band that's ever done this, and having adventures along the way were also part of the devil's bargain, I would've signed in blood. It's still a huge underground movement, and I'm confident I've done my part to keep it alive. The only thing you can hope for in rock and roll is to make up your own lasting original character. Can someone draw a cartoon of you? Can someone draw a cartoon of your whole band? The Cats have achieved this part of the game in spades. This part cannot be contrived. This must develop honestly and organically. I think I've succeeded, but to do that you do sacrifice any normality your life may have had. I'm that Slim Jim guy, the one who always looks cool, wears odd socks and plays the drums standing up, and always has a superhot chick with him. It is the only way of being that I've ever known.

I've had similar experiences in Japan, Australia, every country in Europe, and all over the USA. As I'm playing on this tiny stage with a couple of locals who have learned the songs and play fine, my mind wanders. The classic devil-on-your-shoulder argument begins:

"I can't believe I'm here having to do this to hustle up the bills."

"Shut up. You're lucky to be here. We created this fantastic thing that brings true pleasure to all these people all over the world."

"Yeah, but if the other two guys are with me, it's for five thousand people, not two hundred."

"You have no control over that; everything's cool. I need this gig!"

"Imagine just being the drummer in a band that no one ever recognizes but sold twenty million records, living off royalties—what's that like?"

"We saved rockabilly; if it wasn't for us, it would have died."

"It's gotta be worth more than this!"

"So what? Play the next song!"

Before I know it, it's over—I'm on a plane back to the friendly confines of Beverly Glen in Los Angeles.

So I'm happily changing channels the next day. In between innings at the Yankees game, I hear "Rock This Town" over the PA. That's cool. Johnny Ramone would approve.

I change over to the live music channel, and it's showing a live Stones gig from the '80s. Bill Wyman is wearing a Stray Cats pin on his jacket. Wow! We're onstage with the Stones.

I click over to VH1 and then MTV. Every guy in every band has a tattoo, and in one video the guy is standing up and playing the drums. I think yours truly was the first musician to do these things at the same time.

I click to the hockey game; "Rumble in Brighton" comes on before a face-off.

I'm on a roll; I gotta keep going.

On the action movie network, they are showing a Bond film, *The Man with the Golden Gun*. My former wife is there on the screen dodging bullets in a bikini.

Over on the oldies TV channel, my former girlfriend is playing the nanny on *Growing Pains*. On the Fashion Network, my current girlfriend and love is living in a house with a bunch of models.

I can't help thinking that this must be worth something.

Maybe Time Warner will give me a month's free cable? Maybe I'll write it all down, do some talk shows, and get some easier, higher-paying gigs? Maybe I'll get my own show about world-famous TV addicts? We could all do it together.

Maybe the guys in the Cats will all get along, and we'll go out and do all the top-dollar, primo gigs we should be doing and finally cement our place in the Rock and Roll Hall of Fame. I hold out hope for this but never hold my breath.

I do know that if I stick to my five rules of rock and roll, I'll be okay:

1. Face reality.
2. Show gratitude.
3. Always be with the hottest chick in the room.
4. Always wear at least one thing around your waist that has nothing to do with holding your pants up.
5. Continue to listen to and be awed by Elvis Presley's *Sun Sessions* record.

In telling my story, I've tried to stay away from the tiresome rock bios that are in airports and on the racks in the few remaining record stores. Most rock bios I've read are loaded with braggadocio followed by a chapter of remorse or just a scorecard for how many chicks and empty bottles the writer has acquired, like a horror story where the dead bodies just pile up. I've tried to take a subtler approach and entertain you with less blood and guts. It's all about entertainment. As is true of my approach to the drums, rock and roll, and life in general, I've tried to take a slightly different approach.

Early Moments of Clarity and the Luck of the Draw

As far back as I can remember, I always wanted to be the guy in the band. I never gave anything else much of a thought. I didn't have that Beatles on Ed Sullivan moment; it was something I just knew early on in my life. It was more of a slow burn. I liked music on the radio, and anytime a band played on television, I watched with awe and curiosity. The musicians seemed to be mythic figures. It seemed like a different world. The only thing I knew about it was that I wanted in.

I loved the whole idea of living an alternative lifestyle and traveling with a gang of guys doing something that was fun and exclusive. The Boy Scouts seemed square and regimented. I knew about baseball but couldn't be good enough to get past Little League. I still follow the game closely today. Even during the crazy years, with only the USA papers three days old in a European airport, I always knew what was going on with the Yankees.

I played trumpet in the school band but was always attracted to the drums. I played the drums on the side and took basic lessons at the local Massapequa music store. Brian took lessons there, too. The guitar, piano, and saxophone seemed too unreal to me. I couldn't imagine possibly being good enough on them to be a professional. I could relate to the drums; I thought I could do it. I was pretty good at drumming naturally, and I just kept at it. I hung around with a few of the guys who played in my class. Someone had a guitar, someone had a keyboard, and everyone had a garage or a basement. There were a lot of pretty good musicians in our town. I was very serious about it and was always the guy hustling up the jam sessions, school dances, or backyard parties. I liked the feeling of being onstage and also the way it enabled me to be alone in a crowd. I straddled a few fences with all the different types in school. The guy in the rock-and-roll band can get away with being a bit of a book reader and a baseball fan, as long as you can rock out at the keg party and keep everyone entertained. It was a way to fit in without having to give too much of yourself away and without engaging too much. It allowed me to be involved and still slightly detached at the same time. I really dug being part of a team, and as the drummer I could steer in a friendly way.

I've always had a love affair with the drums. I'd save up to get *Modern Drummer* magazine, cut out pictures of drummers, and pin them on the wall behind my bed next to pictures of my favorite ballplayers. I'd send away for the free catalogs from Zildjian cymbals, Gretsch drums, and Vic Firth sticks. I thought the old jazz cats were supercool. The English guys were even more exotic and didn't seem like real people. I'd study the different ways drummers set up their kits. The fact that forty years later I'm in those catalogs and speak to and have been endorsed by Fred Gretsch, Armand Zildjian, and Vic Firth still turns me on. All drummers will tell you this. Having your cymbal setup in the Zildjian catalog is just as important as getting your picture in the paper. More than any other type of musician, drummers are just happy to be here. Without a good drummer, no band of any kind can progress.

I started out with a practice pad and a pair of sticks, then graduated to a used kit, and finally, after I proved to be serious, a real drum set. I saved money from birthdays and lawn-mowing jobs and raised a couple of hundred dollars. In a very positive memory, I went with my father to Forty-eighth Street in New York City and came home with a four-piece black-chrome Slingerland kit with all applicable hardware.

I began taking lessons from a jazz legend who lived a few towns over. Mousey Alexander had played with Benny Goodman, Red Norvo, Billie Holiday, and Clark Terry, among others. I took the Long Island Rail Road a few stops and walked the rest of the way to Mousey's house, where he had a little studio with two drum kits set up in his basement. He was a real cool cat. He had a goatee, wore white shoes, and spoke in jazz lingo. Mousey was the real deal. He had toured with these jazz greats all over the world in the 1950s and 1960s. He told me of a tour he did with Benny Goodman in the Far East. The idea of touring Japan and Hong Kong with a band was beyond my comprehension, but I knew I wanted to do it more than anything. He stressed rudiments and syncopation, and he really helped me get comfortable with swinging on the drum kit. My natural feel, which I call rocking swing, really came out under Mousey's instruction. In Mousey, I found an actual person who did these things I thought were just dreams and wishes. He proved it was possible. If I had a chance to travel the world playing music—and, when I got old, settle down and teach the drums—that sounded like a good life.

There were quite a few rock guys in our school and neighboring towns who could play faster and harder than I could. None of them had any fashion sense or a dream to travel off Long Island. I've always felt that there are a few aspects to the type of musician I wanted to be. You had to have a look as well as a musical style. I always felt I had a certain style to my playing, and I worked on it. I also liked to dress in some style that combined a rock look with some vintage piece of clothing like a hat or old sweater. I'd look in the back of one of my father's or uncle's closets for something they didn't wear anymore and mix it with jeans and a T-shirt. I'd continue to take the train into the city and hang out at Manny's or Pro Percussion on Forty-fifth Street, taking three hours to buy a pair of sticks. I'd test cymbals and compare the different sounds with the different sizes. I'd roll the sticks on the countertop to make sure they were straight. The cats working in the store were always cool with me. They sensed I was serious, and I did always buy something, even if it was just a pair of sticks. I thought it would be a great job to work at a place where you talk about drums all day and have sticks in your back pocket. I once saw Louie Bellson hanging out in Pro Percussion. I thought then and still do that being a respected drummer is the best possible job in the world. If you can squeeze out a living at it, more power to you. I took little neighborhood jobs like gardening and dog walking to save up to replace a cheap cymbal with a Zildjian every so often. All the while, I was taking lessons and practicing along to any records I had or could borrow. There was a Hank Williams record around the house, a Burt Bacharach, the first Beatles, and a Roger Miller album. Later I would save up, stash a little pocket money from aunts and uncles, and use Christmases and birthdays to get a few records I wanted. I had to turn up the headphones as loud as they went to hear the record over the sound of the drums. There was an hour a day where everyone in the house and the neighbors knew I'd be practicing. I went to any drum clinics I heard about. The guys at the newly opened Long Island Drum Center were all right. I briefly met Joe Morello, who played the immortal drum part on "Take Five" with the Dave Brubeck Quartet, and saw him do a clinic after he had already gone blind, his Seeing Eye dog sitting in front of his drum kit, never moving a muscle. I met future friend Carmine Appice at one of his clinics there. Carmine was supercool to an unknown, questioning young drummer and took me for a slice of pizza. Years later, we would remeet, and I remembered every detail and sincerely thanked him. Later still, I did an instructional drum video for his production company. These little incidents were big events for me as a young drummer with dreams of making a life out of the drums. Anytime I could meet living proof of the possibility, it fueled the fire. Most important, I lugged my drums around and jammed with as many other people as I could.

I met Leon Drucker in the fourth grade. He was in my class, and even at an early age, the serious rock-and-roll guys find each other. In our personalities, it's the classic case of "he's the bass player and I'm the drummer." Even as a kid, he was always more pragmatic and less impulsive than I was. He always thought about things a few extra seconds longer than I did. This could be good and bad. We spent hours in his parents' garage practicing as a rhythm section. He would play boom, and I would play bop. He was on the one beat and the three beat, and I played the snare on the two beat and the four beat. We were very tight as a unit and as friends. By the time fate weighed in, we were ready as a rhythm section. We wrote songs together and really worked at it. We played with a few of the older guys around town at backyard keg parties, and we would sneak through the back doors of a few bars to do the gigs. We were always willing and into playing. I learned a lot of songs during that time and learned all the different grooves and beats for the various types of blues songs. It's training I still remember and use. By the end of high school, we had already formed a band, and we hustled up and played dozens of shows. In the year following school, we had secured a couple of residencies around Long Island and had written two solid sets of original songs. We augmented our songs with blues covers and were really starting to get good at it. We spent a lot of time together and knew each other very well musically and personally.

Lee was my first true pal. I'll use this phrase a number of times about a few people. I don't use this term loosely. It perfectly describes what I feel and believe about a few choice people I've known in my life. Some of them just happen to be well known. They are the people I've met in my life. In a nutshell, a true pal is someone who I'd do anything in the world for, and without my expecting it, I know would do the same for me. If any of them call at 4:00 A.M., I answer the phone. I'll listen to anything they want to talk about. I don't have to speak with them every day, but I do stay in touch with everyone I mention in this way. If you can count ten true pals in your life, you've had a success. Any adventure or life-changing event in my life between the ages of fifteen and forty somehow involved Lee.

Brian Setzer is two years older than Lee and me. Now it means nothing, but when you're fourteen and the other guy is sixteen, it's a big deal. I always thought Brian was a cool guy. He was the first one I knew that had an earring and wore snakeskin boots. He had a Bowie record and could really play the guitar. He was well known in our school as the best guitar player but was also known for not sticking with anyone. He knew what he wanted and always had the dream to be a professional musician. Lee and I were in the same class and friends with Brian's brother, who was an excellent drummer. We've all known each other since grade school. Brian and his brother had a band, and Lee and I had our band. We were the guys who were always looking for something musically different.

This was 1979, and through the right research and quest for cool, we found rockabilly music and instantly fell in love with the sound and style. I started out finding out about rockabilly through some of the older English bands. The Beatles and Stones both covered classics by Carl Perkins and Buddy Holly. The Who had covered Eddie Cochran. A cousin of mine had a copy of Blind Faith, and I heard Buddy again on their version of "Well, All Right." These types of records were easier to find than the originals. I didn't know anyone who didn't think these songs were just more album cuts by those huge bands. No one at FM rock stations pointed out that all the English groups had strong American roots and worshiped our original rock-and-roll stars. As much as we loved these 1970s rockers, they didn't invent the blues. At a certain age, all musicians should want to get to the roots of the music they like. This was our time. WCBS 101.1 was the New York oldies station that played doo-wop and big hits from the 1950s, and I found myself tuning in a bit more. I was also listening to WRVR 105.5, a jazz station, and I'd try to see any of the original cats whenever they played at the Village Gate in the city or Sonny's Place on Long Island. These guys were so good and their chops were so far beyond what I thought I could do that it helped me stay on the path, to look out for a type of sound and look that I could make my own. I'd also go into the city to see any type of new-wave band. There was virtually no place for anything like that on Long Island. Punk rock had kind of already come and gone. Even new-wave, skinny-tie, slightly left-field stuff was discouraged and ridiculed. Blondie, with one of my fave drummers, Clem Burke, had broken through, but the look had not. Elliot Easton from the Cars is a Massapequa native, had gone to our school, and moved to Boston after he graduated. He came to see us at Arthur's Bar, and there was a little talk of him producing a demo. He's still a good buddy and was another shred of proof that someone from our neighborhood could get out of town, make a record, and go on tour.

The jukebox at Max's Kansas City had some things I wasn't aware of. It had the Ramones, Gene Vincent and His Blue Caps "Be-Bop-a-Lula" and "Race with the Devil," and Elvis Presley's first few singles on Sun Records. I was ready to be exposed to this stuff. When I heard "Blue Moon of Kentucky" and saw some pictures of Elvis in his heyday as "the Hillbilly Cat," the world stopped spinning for a split second, and I knew what to do.

A couple of days later, I went to an alternative hair salon on St. Mark's Place, cut off all my hair, and had it greased and sprayed into a pompadour style. The wisecracking, downtown hipster girl doing my hair told me, "It's about time." She was right. I walked across the street to Cheap Jacks and bought some baggy, pleated, gray sharkskin pants, pointy black shoes, and a black bowling shirt. I left the clothes I came in wearing on the floor of the changing room. I walked up to Penn Station, took the train home, and just turned back up at home and acted like nothing happened. There were, of course, the stares and disbelief from family and neighbors. Brian had adopted the rockabilly look a few months before and was playing by himself with a rhythm box in a few small bars. I started turning up, and we became a two-man gang.

I encouraged Lee to get a double bass, and I started to experiment with different ways of setting up the drums. There were pictures of Gene Vincent and His Blue Caps where Dickie Harrell was standing up behind the drums. We thought this was supercool and unique. I took it one step further and moved the drums to the front of the stage and used only the basic pieces I needed to play rockabilly. Since then, I've seen pictures and heard about a few other people playing the drums standing up. At the time we formed the Cats, I didn't know about of any of them besides Dickie Harrell. He would later tell that he only did it in photos. No one had ever moved the drums to the front of the stage and stood in a line with the rest of the band. I think I may have been the first guy to stand on top of them, too. We played a lot of gigs, and that gave me time to develop the stand-up style. We always encouraged each other to push it further and experiment with the showmanship onstage. Years later, in front of a bunch of name drummers, Tony Williams, maybe the best drummer ever, said that this change was my original contribution to the world of drums.

We wanted to create a situation where we could play the music and look the part. We started to do a fun band called Brian and the Tomcats in a few bars in and around Massapequa. The established rock clubs on Long Island would not book us. It was too weird. It was still the 1970s on Long Island, and dinosaur rock and Southern-tinged, long-haired boogie was still the rage. We weren't even punk rock. It was weirder even still. Three young kids with high hair and pink jackets, baggy pants, and two-tone shoes were not the norm. We learned and played Elvis, Buddy Holly, Eddie Cochran, Ricky Nelson, Gene Vincent, Jerry Lee Lewis, and Carl Perkins covers. Each of us was in our other "serious" band that we hoped to get record deals with. We got together to play rockabilly cover songs for fun on nights we weren't rehearsing or playing with our other bands. The Cats had an instant chemistry, and it came across to the audience. The interaction onstage was good right away. There was an understanding of not getting in the way of the other guy. Everybody had the moves and knew when to pull them out. We really loved this music and felt comfortable with each other. We were still very young but had all had a good amount of experience doing gigs. We seemed to instinctively know how to pose for a photograph and really looked like we belonged together. Every great band has distinct personalities and slightly different looks but presents a united front to the outside world. Not every band translates into a bobblehead doll; I think the Cats always did. The three of us are certainly different people, and there have always been rubs, especially in later times, between the other two. Everyone has grown up a little, but each guy, me included, is basically the same person he was when we started this thing. It was a little fate and good luck that we had the pieces we needed right there in our school and that we met up under all the right circumstances. The history of rock and roll is full of these chance bits of kismet. I'm still grateful for the accident of where I grew up and who I grew up with. The luck of the draw was with us. Right away, there was a feeling that it would be us against the world. After a few months, the handwriting was on the wall. The Tomcats, our fun band, was the one everybody was coming to see, and we were packing out these little bars on Long Island in a scene we had created on our own. We started to do the Cats full-time.

Since we were so young and made such a big impact on the rock-and-roll culture at the time, it's impossible to step away from it. I never wanted to. I'm proudly the drummer from the Stray Cats and will happily have that as my epitaph. The others have tried to distance themselves more. After our initial success, I felt I didn't have anything left to prove. The trick is to keep it going, which I know now is the hardest thing to do.

Like Hyman Roth told Michael, "This is the business we've chosen."

2

Escape from New York

I had never been on an airplane before, but I wasn't afraid. I was too excited to be afraid. We were getting out; we were going to London, the place where it all happened. We were never so sure of anything in our lives. I was nineteen. We'd sold our equipment except for the basic stuff that we'd need in London. We'd bought one-way plane tickets and had the tearful good-byes with our families and small following of fans, none of whom wanted us to leave. One of the club owners said we were stabbing him in the back. We just wanted a shot. I'm not quite sure what we were expecting. We thought we knew everything; it turned out that we knew just enough to go all the way. We cut a striking figure boarding a plane with one-way tickets at JFK in 1980: three kids tooled up in rockabilly finery with a double bass in the seat next to us.

Arriving at Heathrow before we knew the game turned out to be the first challenge. It came very close to being over before it even started. We all got in the same line for immigration. Fate intervened slightly, and Lee, carrying the bass, was told to go to a different line. Brian and I were called to the desk together. The woman didn't like us right away. Luckily, dishonesty was the default defense mechanism. We told her we were on vacation; we weren't in a band and had no intention of trying to play in England. The truth was that trying to get a gig and play there was the whole reason for coming. We couldn't go back, so we pleaded and convinced her enough to where we were granted a thirty-day visa with a special notation in our passports that if we were found trying to work we would be deported with prejudice. Our first stamps were a special outlaw category, which fueled the whole us-against-them mind-set. We would cross paths with the same woman quite a few times over the next year while going back and forth to Europe. She always gave us a mean face and said she regretted ever letting us in the country. So we antagonized her any chance we got.

We had an address. Someone who had come to a few gigs in New York told us if we were ever in London to look him up. This was all we had to go on; this was the whole plan. We somehow made it there. The subway and bus ride were unlike anything we'd ever seen. The address turned out to be a huge mansion in Kensington that had been taken over as a squat by punk rockers. The walls had been spray-painted and furniture taken out, probably stolen. Trash, bottles, and cans were strewn everywhere, and the floor and carpets were one big ashtray. The story was that it belonged to a drug kingpin who had been busted for smuggling and was in prison. After the shock and initial panic about what to do, we found some floor space, stashed the luggage and instruments in a closet that wasn't being lived in, and set about the mission to become world-famous inter-national rock stars. How to actually go about this was the part of the plan we hadn't come up with yet. We were always supremely confi-dent that if we ever got a chance, we could deliver. Where's the gig? How do you get a gig?

Back in New York, we had made our own scene. The established rock clubs wouldn't hire us—American kids playing American rock and roll was too weird, too out there for New York in 1979. It was still very much all flares and long hair, Southern rock, and the Amer-ican interpretation of the English interpretation of the original American blues. So we went around to neighborhood taverns—what we called old-man bars—that were usually owned and operated by the bartender. We would promise to bring the PA and to pack the place out—they'd keep the bar; we'd keep the door. We did this for over a year, four sets a night, five nights a week in a little circuit around the South Shore of Long Island: Tuesdays at Arrow's in Bell-more; Wednesdays at the Fifth Amendment, a singles bar way out on the island; Thursdays at Arthur's in Massapequa; Fridays and Saturday at TK's Lounge in Amityville. We learned the craft at these gigs. We got dressed to the nines every night and played hard every set. We played a lot and loved every minute of it, discovering this great music as we went along. We had to do four sets a night, so we learned the greatest hits of Gene Vincent, Eddie Cochran, Buddy Holly, Ricky Nelson, Johnny Burnette, tracks from Elvis's *Sun Ses-sions,* Carl Perkins, Jerry Lee Lewis, and any song on any compilation we could find.

We developed a good following, and it was genuinely different; no New York City hipsters, punk rockers, or even new wavers. Rock-abillies had not been invented in the USA yet. Our gang consisted of just regular, slightly dirtbag Long Island types who loved us and came every night, rallying around the scene we had created. All we wanted to do was to play rockabilly music and be left alone. The term *rockabilly* had existed in the past in reference to the music but not as a lifestyle yet. The audience didn't have a name for it. We loved dressing up and greasing our hair every day. We wound up being the local eccentrics who shocked everyone everywhere we went, and we embraced it. Every trip to 7-Eleven became a potential fight. There was no template for what we looked like. If we had been dressed like a classic rock 1970s front man with boas, sequined bell bottoms, and long hair or like a Southern rock hippie, it would've been all right; the *Saturday Night Fever* disco-boy look would have been pushing the envelope in our neighborhood but would've been accepted, but our look was totally foreign. They were all threatened by it, but our little following of people stuck with us. They liked following us around and protecting us. A few of them were pretty heavy kids into some shady stuff, a few carried guns, and they all carried drugs. They had discovered us and built their own schedules, love lives, and dealing around our shows.

Brian had a tiny flat in a house on the canal near my parents' place. I moved in with him. We played almost every night, slept until noon, had late breakfast at the luncheonette, went to thrift stores, listened to records, and were generally happy. We were making a living as musicians.

There was still a certain restlessness and the deep knowledge that we had to get out. If we wanted to get this thing as big as we instinctively knew it should be, we had to travel. There was the once-a-month gig in the city with the hope of a journalist or record company big shot being in the club, but it wasn't happening fast enough for us. A few of the English weekly rock papers had found their way to the USA, and we saw pictures of a music scene, punk rockers on the Kings Road, and concert reviews. We met a few English people in New York who knew about teddy boys and told us that Gene Vincent and Eddie Cochran were household names in England. That was all we needed to hear. Within a couple of months, we sold whatever we had and bought one-way tickets for London. That was it; that was the whole plan—let's go to London; it's cool there.

We found out a couple of places to go and hang out, trying to make the scene, meet anyone who could help find a gig. We heard about a gig in Camden, which was supposed to be a happening area, by a band called Cockney Rejects in a place called the Electric Ballroom. The whole thing sounded very appealing, so we got tooled up in drape coats, drainpipes, bootlace ties, creepers, and half a tin of Nu-Nile full regalia and hit the subway. The club was a classic old ballroom converted into a venue. The band was a loud, raucous thing, and the crowd was more interested in slam dancing than anything else. This was all new; we'd seen people be into gigs before, but not on this scale. In New York City, even the punk rock gigs were a bit more subdued and not as big as the thousand kids at this one. Standing at the bar, no one really took much notice of us. In an instant, it all turned bad. A full-scale riot spilled out from the main room into the bar: pint glasses flying, a rush of bodies swept us aside, punches and kicks rained all around. We found ourselves crouched behind the bar. I picked up a bottle to use as a weapon if anyone came behind the bar. It was mayhem. I looked up to see a German shepherd attack dog attached to a leash that was attached to a policewoman. She had a look of combined pity and annoyance. "You Teds had better get out of here," she said. She didn't have to say it twice. It wasn't directed at us this time, but it was our first taste of a whole new, slightly violent world where people take the bands and the gigs and the fashion to a very serious level.

We found ourselves walking down Camden High Street. We passed by a few skinheads spray-painting a bum in front of the Kentucky Fried Chicken. Luckily, they didn't see us. I didn't understand the tribal aspect of musical tastes yet. I hadn't met enough people who went all in with their style; I still thought it was anyone with a haircut against the squares. Even against this backdrop, the Cats were about to get a lot of attention.

We quickly ran out of money. A couple of weeks, a few gigs, a few adventures, including a night or three sleeping in Hyde Park on borrowed chaise longues, sharing bites out of a burger from Wimpy's in Piccadilly Circus. A few nights of pure sleep on the floor was cheap at fifty pence a man for twenty-four hours in a XXX theater in Soho, and that was that. No one wanted to leave, to go home with our tails between our legs. It was getting grim, but we never lost the confidence that we were just one shot away.

A few people at the squat were loosely connected with the music biz. Like most big cities, once you're there for even a short while, with a little investigation, you realize that each particular scene is pretty small, and everybody knows everybody. Someone told us about a PR person he knew who represented some famous rock bands. I didn't even know what a PR person was, and the idea of anyone actually knowing the Stones and the Who was beyond my conception. I got the address and one afternoon made my own way to Soho and rang the bell. The buzzer rang, and I went up the stairs. It looked like a little apartment. There was a very beautiful girl at a desk in the living room.

"May I help you?" she asked in an accent. I had never met a girl who looked like that before, I had never been in any office before, I had never answered a girl with an accent before.

"Who's the boss?" I say in my right-off-the-boat Long Island accent.

"He's not here. What do you want?"

This type of dialogue went back and forth for a while. She had probably met a hundred guys in bands who thought they were cool, yet I'm sure I had some snappy response. I really didn't know what I was doing there or what I wanted; I really wanted someone to help me. Another woman came in. She was about four feet tall with bright red hair and had a French accent right out of a movie.

"What is all this?" she asked us both in that peeved tone that comes naturally to the French.

I was standing there in drainpipes tucked into black silver-tipped cowboy boots, smiley pocket western shirt, a Hollywood fleck jacket, bandana tied around my neck, with a greasy mop on my head. The whole outfit was dirty from sleeping in it, and I'm sure I looked hungry and tired.

"We're in the best band in the world. We're from New York. We have no money, nowhere to live. We're stuck in London but don't want to go home."

"What's the name of the band?" she asked while looking me up and down and at her watch.

"We don't really have one," I stammered.

"Where's your demo tape?"

"We don't have one."

"Where are you playing?"

"We don't have any gigs." I was drowning on dry land.

Something must have intrigued her enough to tell me to come back the next day with the others. Maybe she thought I was some insane street urchin and wanted to get rid of me, maybe she just thought I'd never turn up again—but I did turn up the next day, and I had the other two with me.

The Cats always did cut quite a striking figure. We looked young and innocent, slightly hollow from mild hunger but with a leery rock-and-roll dangerousness honed by a month of very rough living. Tattooed children who seemed a bit dodgy and lost with an undeniable obnoxious charm. We had the complete *Three Stooges*–meets–*A Hard Day's Night* act down. We answered each other's questions, had our own lingo, did impersonations of everyone we met, and generally mocked and made fun of everything and everyone. We were a version of the Bowery Boys meets the Beatles. Without really trying, we owned this part of the act. The Frenchwoman was Claudine Martinet-Riley, and the boss was Keith Altham. Without playing one note of music, we had genuinely interested these veteran music biz insiders. They said they would rent us a little rehearsal room and watch us play.

The next day we went back with the guitar, bass, and drum, and they walked us to a studio around the corner. We hadn't played in over a month but had been woodshedding at the bars for more than a year, and this was all we needed. This was the first chance to do what we knew we could. We launched straight into the act: Lee slapping and spinning the bass, me standing behind and on top of the drums, Brian playing on his knees and behind his head, singing perfectly in tune as we ran around this little room, crashing into each other while not missing a beat. We did two or three numbers, ending with me jumping off the drum, hitting my head on the low ceiling, falling, and knocking the drums over. We were very good at it, and they knew it. We had some much-appreciated lunch and beer at a nearby pub. The first and most important part of the plan had happened: we had found someone to help us get a gig. I assume they made a few calls and arranged a couple of gigs at the rock pubs on the London circuit.

We needed a name. In New York, we'd been the Tomcats. We liked Cats in the name. A few different ideas were batted around, and then Lee came up with Stray Cats. We were cats like Elvis, we had nowhere to live—the logic was undeniable. We now had a name. Coming up with a good name can be the hardest part of the whole thing, and now we had that part, too.

There was a buzz about the first gig. We had managed to meet a lot of people while bumming around. It's the type of thing that could happen in London in 1980. A few faces and word of mouth around a few clubs had turned our first couple of shows into must-see events. If nothing else, everyone wanted to see what we could do. We talked the talk; now we had to walk the walk. The audience at the first two shows was a who's who of London at the time: Lemmy Kilmister; Chrissie Hynde and true tragic pals Pete Farndon and Jimmy Honeyman-Scott of the Pretenders; Glen Matlock and Steve Jones from the Sex Pistols; Joe Strummer and Topper Headon from the Clash; Jerry Dammers from the Specials; Chris Foreman from Madness; and the London chapter of the Hells Angels. A number of these people are still my friends to this day.

This was all we'd been waiting for—a chance to play at a bar with a decent PA for half an hour in front of a bunch of rock stars and journalists with all the marbles on the line? No problem. This was where we could have a little control over our own fates. We slaughtered it.

The other two are incredible natural musicians, and we could impress anyone, anywhere. We never doubted this for a second. This exact act had never been seen before; the lineup and stagecraft was genuinely different. No one had put the drums in the front with the singer in one line across the front of the stage before. There were about ten to twelve legendary venues around London that all the bands played; the Fulham Greyhound, the Golden Lion, Thomas A Becket, Woolwich Tramshed, Dingwalls, the Marquee on Wardour Street, and Bridge House in Canning Town were the main ones. We were the opening act on quite a few, and we blew the headliners away. With each show, there were more journalists and photographers. Allan Jones from *Melody Maker* did a feature; that was a big one. Adrian Thrills did a cover story for *New Musical Express* with Anton Corbijn taking the pictures. We shared the cover of *The Daily Mirror* with Lady Diana. All of this happened without a record deal, on the strength of the live shows around London.

We had graduated from the floor of the squat to the floor of the office at 57 Old Compton Street. We slept on the floor of Pete Farndon's house in Tufnell Park. We had all this notoriety and street cred but no money. Our actual situation hadn't changed too much. Lee turned nineteen in August; he had caught up with me again. We were still unsigned and unknown to anyone outside London. We were also still very broke, hungry at times, and homeless, floor surfing and relying on the kindness of strangers. I still loved every minute of it.

We continued to play two or three shows every week around town. The guest lists were an A-list of the London music and social scene of the time: the presidents and A&R heads of every major label, a few scattered rock stars, the grooviest scenesters looking for the new thing of the moment, and genuine music fans who had found out about us, mixed in with young double-barreled-last-name Chelsea types who wanted be in the know—all made for a very eclectic crowd. We had unknowingly filled the gap of the next big thing after the end of punk rock.

We played the Marquee, the Venue again, a few shows at Dingwalls both as headliner and opening act, Thomas A Becket pub in the Old Kent Road, the Bridge House in Canning Town, and a few others, I'm sure. One night we did two shows in two different places, an early set at a pub and then we put all the gear in a van and set up all over again to play a late set at Gaz's Rockin' Blues, a fantastic once-a-week club put on by Gaz Mayall in cobblestoned, neon-lit old Soho. It was in a tiny old burlesque basement club down an alley. The whole place had a 1970s-disco-meets-red-light-district vibe. Gaz, always dressed in a '40s-style suit, big fedora, and wing tips, also deejayed. He played all '40s and '50s jump blues, and we all liked him. He introduced me to Sarah-Jane Owen from the Bodysnatchers, who would become a girlfriend. This club hosted the hipster crowd that made up the early Stray Cats audience, and it would later become a very trendy popular hangout for all sorts of celebs, tourists, and kids digging rocking blues and roots music in a nightclub setting. We were the first band to do a live gig there.

There was a gig booked as the opening act at the Venue in Victoria. The Rolling Stones came to the show and loved it. Now it was really game on. After the show at the Venue that the Stones attended, things moved very quickly. When the Stones came, it changed the game. Paparazzi pictures taken by Richard Young made the national newspapers. Anyone could tell that this was more than a photo op. Those guys genuinely got it and loved it. We weren't English guys playing '50s rock and roll; we were young Americans doing it for real, and it came across in those pictures from that night. We had been in a few of the music magazines, but this was *The Daily Mirror,* and it changed the deal. Who were these kids playing rockabilly in a London club, and why were the Stones there partying and really digging it? It must have been good if those guys were into it.

Mick and Keith wanted to meet us and discuss our being on their label. We met with Mick first at the famed Stones office on Munro Terrace. Maybe they sent a car; I can't remember how we would have ever found the address or gotten there in the first place. We may have had on the same clothes from the gig. The office was in one of those old Georgian row houses by the river that had been converted to serve as offices. We were let in and waited to be led farther in, which meant up more stairs—creaky, narrow stairs that were covered in slightly moldy, well-worn, brightly colored carpeting. I steadied myself on an old carved wooden banister. There was a big desk on the landing with a secretary behind it who seemed to have the final say of who saw and spoke to Mick. We were told to go into another room.

Mick was standing in the center of the room. He looked every inch the spectacular rock star that he was and is. When you have an audience with a guy of that reputation, you expect a certain regal formality to it, and this scene had it all. It was in the middle of the day, and he was wearing a long white silk embroidered bathrobe. He had his back to the window that looked south over the river, so he was aglow in the filtered sunlight coming through the big window on this, the top floor. The whole scene was a kind of summoning to a mythic figure. He was holding an antique hand mirror with big pile of coke on it. He had a silver straw and was doing little whiffs as he asked us to sit down. It was exactly what you would want that moment to be. The three of us sat crowded together on a couch, and Mick sat across from us in a chair. He put the mirror down on a table that separated us and invited us to help ourselves. Still nervous and trying to soak up the whole scene while looking cool, we said, "No, thanks." He shrugged and starting talking.

We talked about rockabilly and the first American rock-and-roll stars and how it had affected the early Stones records. We talked about the best ways to record this music and get the old sound and still have a new twist. The audiences had reacted to the new songs, too. We instinctively knew this, and it was good to hear it reinforced by a guy this successful and in the know. We had figured since we first started playing that the current flavor, recording technique, and lyrics blended with classic elements would work best. As much as we liked them, we knew we couldn't sound like an old record. The Stones had done this with a Buddy Holly song on "Not Fade Away" and a lot of other blues numbers. They had made it their own and made it attractive to young people. I don't recall talking too much business, though I didn't really know what business talk sounded like. It was like it was taken for granted that we would be on their label and that they would produce us.

I remember being engaged in the conversation and him being very smart, but I was drifting. It was probably a little bit from slight hunger, and I was also reminding myself that we were sitting in London, talking about rock and roll, as an equal, with Mick Jagger when about six weeks earlier we had been playing a bar in Massapequa. This was the first time we had ever met anyone famous, let alone the most famous person of all, and not only had we met him but we had met because he wanted to meet us after seeing our gig. The last few months had been bewildering, but we stayed in the moment.

We wanted to make a record before this moment in time passed. We were enjoying the attention, but we knew that we still needed somewhere to live.

There was a knock on the door, and a secretary came in and told Mick that so-and-so was on the phone and he needed to take the call. He excused himself and said he'd be right back.

We sat in silence; we gave each other the nod. I'm not sure who moved first, but within ten seconds we had all grabbed the silver straw and done a big bump off the antique mirror. The last one tried to leave a little and tidy it up into a much smaller pile to make it seem like we hadn't done all of it. We all wiped our noses and tried to look innocent.

Mick came back in a minute later and started talking again. We all listened very attentively now. At some point he must have looked down at the table and saw the much diminished pile of powder. We all knew that he noticed it, and we tensed up a little, waiting for something to give. To his credit and the reason I'll always think he's a cool guy, he never said a word.

We let loose now, all of us chirping away and being funny. Someone found a record player, and we played some albums and were there for a while longer. The secretary had brought beers in by now, and it was a really fun afternoon spent with rock royalty. We talked about getting together again after we met with Keith. We must have left at some point, probably taking the subway back to Maida Vale, where we slept, one on the floor, one on the box spring, and the big winner, by turns, on the mattress. At least we weren't so hungry that night.

3

A Little Time with the Rolling Stones

The first time I saw the Rolling Stones play live was when we opened a show for them at the Fox Theatre in Atlanta in 1981. They were, of course, the world's most famous band, but I was too young and broke to have seen them play on the tours in the 1970s. We had had a few encounters with them in the early days in London but did not sign with their label with them as producers. It was very hard to get Mick and Keith in the same room at the same time. They wanted to coproduce the album, but there was a lot more urgency on our side. We had momentum and needed to seize it. Fate intervened, and we met Dave Edmunds, who turned out to be the right producer. Since then, I had become very friendly with Bill Wyman, who had first come to see us in Nice, in the South of France, at an amphitheater built on the ruins of a Roman theater. It was a local show for him, as he lived nearby. He was our champion in the Stones camp, and I think that Bill was instrumental in securing the opening-act slots we wound up doing on the 1981 USA Tattoo You tour later that year. We hadn't signed with their label, but I suppose they were happy enough for us when it all turned out okay. We were invited up to Mick's hotel suite during the daytime. The show at the Fox was the smallest, most intimate one on that tour. It was a perfect one for the Cats, as we had played all the theaters in Europe by that point and were very comfortable in that setting. He was very gracious, and we met Jerry Hall, who looked amazing and acted the perfect rock-and-roll hostess. The Cats played great, and it really went down well. We were always confident that we could deliver the goods in a live situation; we were still hungry for success, especially in the USA, so we welcomed the high-pressure opportunities. An added bonus of the whole day was watching the Stones' set from the roped-off orchestra pit, which we pretty much had to ourselves.

The other shows were in giant enormo-domes in Midwest American cities that held fifty thousand people. The stages were much bigger than we had ever played on before, and our setup looked even smaller than usual. The stage was a series of platforms on sloping angles. We had to nail my little drum platform to the floor to keep it from sliding into the crowd. We had complete access backstage and roamed freely before, during, and after the shows. Backstage, we played pinball and Ping-Pong with John McEnroe, ate like kings, and just enjoyed being working guests on the biggest rock-and-roll tour in history. Every crew member was superfriendly, and we fit right in. We were low maintenance, so that made it even easier for everyone to like us.

The Stones had a fantastic cast of characters around them; some of them have become rock-and-roll folk legends themselves. Big Jim Callaghan was the burly, good-natured, but truly tough head of security. Nobody came anywhere near those guys without Big Jim knowing about it and approving it. He always liked us, and in later years, I could always turn up at any Stones show, ask for Big Jim, and be welcomed backstage to say hello to the guys.

Bill Wyman wore a Stray Cats pin on his lapel and came into our dressing room every night to hang out and talk before we went on. One night he was in there chatting away when Mick came in wearing his stage outfit from that tour. It consisted of bright-yellow American football pants complete with knee pads, a number 21 jersey, and white dancing shoes with long socks. He topped it off with a giant cape made from an American and a British flag sewn together.

"'Allo, boys! 'ow are we doin' tonight in Cedar Rapids, *I-O-W-A*?" he asked in that famous combination accent that's half-Cockney and half–Texas drawl.

"Hi, Mick."

"Great, man."

"Yeah, cool."

We all answered quietly at the same time. It was still a big deal when he blew into a room.

Bill had gotten a little quiet, as Mick had interrupted his talk with us, and he stood off to the side puffing on his cigarette. Mick seemed to notice Bill's annoyance and walked over to him. He reached out as if to ask for his hand in dance and started to do a mock waltz with Bill as his reluctant partner. Bill brushed him off and gently pushed him away. We all stared at this very spontaneous, very rock-and-roll moment happening in our unadorned dressing room with most of what we owned in the suitcases on the floor. Outside the door was the circus that accompanied a big rock show that was about to go on.

"C'mon, Bill, lighten up," Mick chided him. "Why did you come all the way to Cedar Rapids, I-O-W-A?"

"Certainly not to dance with you!" Bill answered in his very cool, relaxed South London accent. It was great stuff.

Mick went on to tell us to use the whole stage as much as we could and to say the name of the town as many times as we could squeeze it in. He had just demonstrated this to us in the dressing room. Maybe he was practicing a little while reminding himself of where the show was that night.

We hadn't seen too much of Keith or Ronnie in a few days. On one night, Keith looked a bit wobbly as he was being led up the stage stairs, one step at a time. I remember thinking, *He's not gonna make it. What are they gonna do?* None of the other guys in his band seemed concerned as they walked up the gangplank and put their instruments on. Charlie spun his sticks, and Mick jumped up and down, getting the blood flowing. The lights came down, and the big cheer happened. That might be the best part of any show. Whether I'm playing or watching, it's my favorite moment. When Keith hit the stage and his roadie strapped his guitar on him, he came to life and stormed into the first number. They opened that tour with "Under My Thumb"; Keith would go over to the drum riser and exaggerate the downbeats with his guitar as he and Charlie would hang on the opening riff until they all got steady on the rhythm.

Charlie came in a few times, too. Charlie Watts is truly a gentleman. He's a fine rock-and-roll drummer with a natural swing, and has been an influence on my playing. I enjoyed the time we spent together, and he has always been friendly whenever I've run into him.

The pointers Mick gave that night on working the huge stage and talking to an audience of that size was helpful. His advice was spot-on, and it still works today. Big gestures and simple stage talk always work best. In that regard, doing a club or theater is different from an arena or stadium show. We had never traveled in Middle America before; we had played in Paris but not Pittsburgh. This was pre-MTV, and we hadn't been on the radio in the USA. The success in the States was still over a year away. Since then, I've learned how much those Stones shows helped us. It added to the crazy story and legend that was building around us, but at that point, we were still unknown, still strange looking and strange sounding to the average American audience. No one knew about rockabilly, and the closest thing they knew to the blues was the Stones. They thought we were British—anything that weird must have been from England. The attitude was like the one we had left behind in Massapequa, but by the end of each show, we had won over the audience. On one of the shows, Mick led us onstage wearing his full stage outfit and announced us to the audience, telling them that we were the real deal and how this was American music and they should really give us a chance. The Eddie Cochran classic song "Twenty Flight Rock" was part of the Stones set list on that tour, and Mick dedicated it to us at all the shows that we were on. They didn't need to do that. It was another gesture of support from these guys. We still didn't have any money, and as great an opportunity as this was, we got paid virtually nothing for the actual gigs. We played a few stand-alone shows at very small clubs on days off along the way, and they have become part of the tale, too. Every town will always have a certain small number of hipsters who follow the UK music scene, and they came out for these gigs, which helped get us to the next big show.

After the Stray Cats gig on the European tour in Nice, France, we all went back to Bill's luxurious, rock-and-roll, cool cliffside mansion at the end of a winding, dangerous road. It was the first time I'd ever been to that kind of Mediterranean, real South of France rock star mansion. We partied with some of his local friends, and he showed us some rare footage of old Stones TV appearances. The lady of the house and Bill's longtime companion was Astrid Lundström. She was a spectacular, animated, beautiful Swedish model. She and I became close friends, and she treated me like a younger brother. I was really fond of her. Astrid was around a lot, and I always felt comfortable talking around her. She gave me advice about girls and being on the road in general. She spoke frankly and was there for a lot of famous events, including Altamont, where she can be seen in the well-known helicopter scene at the end of *Gimme Shelter*.

Bill had a vast film library of vintage blues and rock and roll and was eager to show us some cool stuff we hadn't seen. He was an authority on all sorts of blues, R&B, and rockabilly, and he also really understood and liked what the Cats were doing. He knew I was a bit of a fanboy for Keith Richards and would ask me what I liked about him. I didn't have a clear answer—probably something about how I thought he was cool. Bill busted my balls a little in jest then and would tell a few tales that painted Keith in a more ordinary fashion. I see now that it was meant in a way to keep me grounded, like a "drugs aren't cool" message. I myself have been in that conversation a thousand times, being on the receiving end of the "What's your lead singer really like?" question. Bill smoked and drank vodka and tonics, but I never saw him do drugs. I would go off to the bathroom once in a while for a bump, but he never did. I'm sure he was around it a lot and had his chances to get into it but never did.

There were some great nightclub times with Bill at Tramp, a famous members-only basement club in Jermyn Street, Mayfair. There were always a few people you knew there. The Italian waiters were all characters, as was the coat-check woman, Julia, who had the final say on who got in. Like most clubs, it looked pretty grim in the daytime, but at night with low lights, candles, and the right amount of boozy atmosphere and stargazing, it was a fantastic, exclusive place. The owner was Johnny Gold, gregarious, handsome, dressed up, and there every night. He had the real club operator talent of making every customer feel like a big shot while you paid for your own drinks. The club had been there from the 1960s onward and was always considered an in-the-know place. If you were a member, you had arrived. Everyone in show business aspired to hang out there. The punk rockers would have frowned a bit, because it represented old-time showbiz and rock star excess, but I didn't care. Bill put me forward for membership, and at age nineteen, for a whopping seventy-five pounds, I became a member. I went there with Britt all through the 1980s and kept the membership current until the early 1990s. I bet my name is still on the register somewhere.

Bill and I sat there quite a few times drinking until closing time. I asked a lot of questions about legendary Stones and other music history that he had witnessed and got a lot of insider answers. He knew I was genuinely interested. He was honest, and I related to his man-in-the-band point of view. Like me, he was an equal member of a famous band that had a very strong front man. I had the feeling that we shared the belief that we loved our lead singers and were happy that they were there but didn't really want to talk about them too much. We all sat in the van and shared bad road food, and once you've seen a guy naked enough times, it's hard to take him too seriously. In New York, we'd say, "What am I, chopped liver?" I'm sure there is an English equivalent. I'm sure the singers all have their own opinions on us, the humble rhythm sections. It's all part of the dynamic that makes for a good rock-and-roll band. Bill was always careful not to bad-mouth anyone and just answered the questions honestly. I still adhere to that myself; I try to never say anything disparaging about my band members to outsiders.

I was honored to play drums on the B side of Bill's solo hit single "Je Suis un Rock Star," a track called "Rio de Janeiro." It was another one of those moments when I thought it was all a bit unreal. I was in Massapequa six months earlier, and now I was in the studio recording with one of the Stones. During the dinner break at the session, Bill took the engineers, guitar player, and me to a nice French restaurant. He was a kind of gourmet rocker and ordered food and wine for everyone. A few people joined, and it was always a cool little gang around any of the Stones.

I was the youngest one there, wearing my usual outfit from those days of sleeveless T-shirt, black boots with chains around them, leather jacket, and bandana around my neck. No one ever suggested wearing a tie or batted an eye, even in a chichi place. As with a lot of things, I'd be more conscious of these types of things now. The idea of being in a fancy restaurant with the sleeves cut off my shirt is a little horrifying, but in that moment I never thought of it once. However, my upbringing in Irish-Catholic New York had provided me with excellent table manners. We were never wealthy or went to many restaurants, but my mother and nana had really stressed proper etiquette. Even if it had been learned by a jab under the table or a stabbed elbow, I was prepared for this. I may have looked a little wacky, but I was very polite and knew which fork to use for the salad and which spoon for the soup, but when the appetizers came, I had no idea of what to do with an artichoke. Bill sensed my mild panic and embarrassment. He slowly peeled off a leaf, dipped it in the sauce, and ate the bottom of the leaf. I followed his lead, and although I thought it was a lot of work for a little payoff, I really liked it. When it came to the heart, I watched again and quickly mastered the art of the artichoke. Still to this day, it's one of my favorite things to order at a restaurant, and I have Bill to thank. Like Mick in the office with the coke, Bill never let on that he knew, never busted me. It's a very admirable quality in someone. We went back to the studio, finished off the track, and had a good session. I've got my name on the record sleeve of a track by one of the Stones. One more crazy accomplishment that I never counted on.

4

LA to Tokyo

I don't know if Mick and Keith would have been able to produce the Stray Cats record as had been discussed. It seemed hard for the two of them to get to the same place at the same time, and the whole thing was moving very slowly. We eventually signed with Arista Records with Dave Edmunds producing. Dave was a well-respected singer and guitar player who had a big worldwide hit with "I Hear You Knocking." He produced and played all the instruments on his own records. He was in Rockpile with Nick Lowe. He was maybe better known in Europe but had a cool cult status everywhere. He turned out to be the perfect choice.

The record did very well, and we had lived up to all the hype. We toured the UK and Europe, Japan, Australia, and New Zealand to sold-out, rowdy crowds, and positive reviews followed everywhere. There was a strong buzz about the Cats all over the world.

We were playing a show at the Royal Court Theatre in Liverpool in 1981. This is a classic, faded-glory, old venue that has hosted every type of showbiz event, from Victorian dance hall vaudeville to punk rock shows. It definitely saw its share of Beatlemania. I was happy to be there. It was our second tour of England; we were in the charts and riding high.

The next day, at the same theater, there was to be a taping of the long-running British game show *3-2-1*. It was a typical old-school quiz show with regular couples answering questions for money and prizes. An early culture shock observation was the difference between the prizes on American game shows and UK ones. On the American ones I had grown up on, the prize could be a car or a vacation to Hawaii with $10,000 to spend. In England, the contestants were battling for a mini refrigerator, a trip to Stratford-upon-Avon, and fifty pounds to spend on the holiday. The questions on the UK show seemed harder, too. This show featured celebs of the day in little sketches between the question rounds and singers miming along to current hits. There was a TV crew there preparing for the next day's show. Everyone stayed out of everybody else's way.

The mascot and costar of the show was Dusty Bin. He was a crude robot in the shape of a garbage can that looked like the little rolling robot in *Star Wars*. I can't remember exactly, but I think he was operated by an off-camera puppeteer with remote control. I do remember thinking he was pretty lame. The fact that thirty-five years later, I'm still referring to it as "he" is definitely lame. I know now that he was a beloved character and a national treasure. Dusty arrived on our show day with his own handler and was put in one of the dressing rooms. At the time, I made fun of everything that wasn't Gene Vincent or Eddie Cochran. This is pre–*Spinal Tap*, so maybe those guys experienced a similar thing. I thought it was amazing that a large puppet had a personal roadie and dressing room. So, for a laugh, I decided to kidnap Dusty Bin. I didn't think too much about it. There was no ransom demand or terms for release. I just put him in a different room on a different floor. At the time, for me, it was a mild prank. No one was getting hurt, and it wasn't booze or drug fueled. There were no girls involved.

After the sound check, there was a big kerfuffle in the wings. I saw the TV people and theater staff standing around the tour manager. It didn't look friendly. Our whole crew and band were ordered to assemble on the stage. The old boy theater manager, flanked by two fossils in moth-eaten usher uniforms, had summoned us. He sternly stated the crime and told us there would be no show, that the police had been called, and prosecutions would arise if Dusty Bin was not immediately returned, unharmed. The theater manager was right out of central casting. He had a pointy face, had tufts of wild hair around the side of his head, wore a tweed jacket with leather patches on the elbows, and shook his pipe at us when highlighting his point. He reminded me of the mad scientist from *Bride of Frankenstein*. This was his turf. He meant business. I got it.

Everyone turned their heads and looked at me. I was busted. The prank was turning out to be unfunny and a bit risky. I quickly measured the impact of the joke and decided that this one wasn't worth going down in flames. I gave them the "Okay, okay" look and shrug of the shoulders. It was a big principal's office moment. I waited until no one was watching and took Dusty Bin down the back stairs and back into his own dressing room.

I like to imagine that John Lennon came up against this type of thing all the time and would have appreciated the rebellion against the stuffy old guard. Maybe something similar happened in this exact place. I like to think he would have thought that doing the gig was more important.

That night, we had another sold-out show of complete rock-and-roll abandon. Nothing more was ever said about it. I always liked those old theaters. They sounded good and had the perfect-sized stage for the Cats.

I hadn't thought about this one in a while, but true pal and Sex Pistol Glen Matlock told me this was a great punk rock story and that I should write it down. He would know.

On the way to Australia, we stopped in Los Angeles to do a little recording for the next album and to try to drum up some interest in the USA. Our record deal excluded the States, and we really wanted to get something going there. We had traveled a little bit in the States during the Stones' tour but not on the West Coast. It was my first time in LA, and I loved it right away. Still do. There were palm trees, convertibles, beaches, and blondes, exactly like on television. I knew that someday I would wind up there. We had a couple of shows booked at the Roxy again, mainly to keep the expenses going—although I never remember anyone talking about money or being paid, especially on those kinds of shows. The whole thing somehow just kept going one more day.

We stayed at the Sunset Marquis in the days before it was a posh place. It was a functioning rock hotel with little kitchens in the rooms and a laundry in the basement, always a plus. It was staffed with young people and older eccentrics who had seen it all. We fit right in. Over the next couple of years, we would stay there a lot, and most days there were adventures in and around the Marquis. There were always a few bands staying there, and everyone would walk up to the Strip to see other bands playing at the Roxy or the Whisky a Go Go. I had some fun times at the Marquis with the Pretenders, who were pals from London. They played a landmark show at the Santa Monica Civic Auditorium that was the talk of the town. The Clash were there, too, and we met Graham Chapman from Monty Python, who was very friendly and looked at us like we were a comedy act. There was no bar at the place back then, so everything was brought in. Everyone left their doors open for "hall parties," and someone always had a poolside room for easy access outdoors—and eventually someone was in the water, on purpose or not. There was always booze and powder, but I don't ever remember a dark vibe. There were plenty of local girls who loved hanging with the bands, so good, clean rock-and-roll fun was had by all. Brian and I would jump into the pool with our clothes on to announce our arrival, and besides a few regular customers looking alarmed, no one ever really gave us a hard time.

The night before the Roxy shows, we were taken to the Rainbow, a legendary rock-and-roll watering hole and restaurant. We were welcomed by the staff there, including Mike and Tony, the tuxedo-clad, fast-talking, friendly but intimidating Italian maître d's who were right out of a movie. The waitresses were all either California blondes or Goth girls with neon tans, who waited for nighttime and never took advantage of the LA sunshine but were rock chicks all the way. It was dark and packed with musicians and guys who wanted to be in the band who'd come from all over the world to get here, record company types, girls looking for fun, and a few shady characters for added ambiance. It was and still is a one-of-a-kind place. One night Brian and I were standing around with drinks in hand, soaking the whole scene up, when we were approached by a silver-haired, very tough-looking older guy who was a cross between Vito Corleone and Popeye.

"Are youse da two kids who's gonna be workin' for me tomorrow?"

We looked at each other a bit confused and nodded.

"Well, youse a too fuckin' skinny; come in da back wit me."

He led us past the bar and into the kitchen and motioned for us to sit at a small table. He then yelled to a cook, and in an instant, a waitress had brought us a few plates of pasta and a basket of bread.

"Eat this; I can't have youse passin' out on me. Youse got two shows for me tomorrow. Go home. Get some sleep!"

That was my first meeting with Mario Maglieri. He's one of the owners of the Roxy, the Whisky, and the Rainbow. I've stayed friendly with him to this day. He's a real tough, original old guy who's overseen a lot of stuff on the Strip since the 1960s. There is a picture of him standing with Britt, holding our son, TJ, as a baby, hanging in the foyer of the Rainbow above the fish tank, next to a hundred snapshots of all the infamous characters who've hung there over the years since it opened in 1975. It was an old Italian restaurant in the 1950s, where Marilyn Monroe had kept Joe DiMaggio waiting for two hours on their first date. Years later as bachelor boys living on the Sunset Strip, TJ and I would eat countless dinners at that same table in the kitchen. The place is an institution in more ways than one, and we've become part of the family there in more ways than one, too. This night was my first visit to a place I'd go to a thousand more times.

Another thing we didn't know then was how much of an underground swell there was in LA for the Cats and the reception that was ahead. "Runaway Boys" had been getting a lot of airplay as an import on the local indie station KROQ. There was a small local rock-abilly scene, and combined with the spins on the radio and the buzz around the band, we had sold out the two Roxy shows, and by popular demand, two matinee shows had also been added. Four shows, two a day, was the schedule that week. Nowadays, something like that couldn't happen without major consultations and negotiations. Back then, it just happened, and we went along with it. I don't know who would've arranged it or collected the money, but we did four shows in two days at the Roxy, all sold out and all with crazy enthusiasm from a new crowd in the States. It was a harbinger of things to come.

I remember arriving at the show and seeing a line down Sunset Boulevard in the afternoon. LA is hipper and more fashion conscious than Middle America; for us, it was ahead of the curve. We didn't know that we had broken through a little in the States. It was a peek into the new landscape: a post-MTV world was waiting ahead in the States; a lot of kids were dressed rockabilly, punk, and new-wave styles. Like in the rest of the world, the Cats appealed to all the different music-based tribes of kids who were looking for something different. The shows were all memorable, and we got through them without a hitch. We partied every night between the shows, too. We were young and had good stamina, but I guess Mario's plates of pasta really did help. Kids were climbing up to the dressing room window trying to get a glimpse and sneak into the packed-out gig. It was mayhem in the daytime on the Sunset Strip. I even saw Jack Nicholson rocking out in the audience and thought, *This is my life—isn't it great?*

It was also the first time I met world-class record producer Lou Adler, who is partners with Mario in the clubs on Sunset. Lou would become a longtime friend, and we'd be linked forever in an LA extended family. "Small world" doesn't even come close to explaining it. But before all of that, Lou really liked the Cats, and like the other supersmart music business veterans we'd met, he understood what we were doing. More on this later.

We landed in Tokyo, Japan, and were greeted with an airport scene reminiscent of *A Hard Day's Night*. There were kids in the lobbies of all the hotels, and we were followed everywhere we went. The record company thought it would be a good idea to walk us through Harajuku Park on a Saturday past the rockabilly dancers with the two-foot-high pompadours that everyone has seen on postcards. These were the early days for that kind of thing. The Cats had unknowingly tapped a nerve and started a huge movement in Japan. It started out with a few finger points and low talking that turned into a few kids following us, which escalated to us being chased by a frenzied mob of Japanese rockabillies and punks through the park. It was a cool adrenaline rush, and we laughed at one another while sprinting through the park, but we knew that they would have lovingly ripped us to shreds if they had caught us. We used old-school New York skills, and the three of us easily scaled a chain-link fence and dropped to the other side while the poor record company guy got crushed. We somehow got back to the hotel. After all that, I was surprised that the gigs in Japan started earlier than everywhere else—around 6:00 P.M.—and the audiences were a little quieter than you would expect. That's just the way it is, and you get used to it and do the shows accordingly. The first trip to Japan for anyone, especially with that kind of reception, is a fantastic experience.

We went to Australia and New Zealand next. More escapades followed, and we did a few TV shows that added to the legend building around the band overseas. Australia is still a good market for rocka-billy; there are genuine people there who have a strong history of their own rock and roll and who are always welcoming and appreciative when you make the trip to play there. I've been all over Australia quite a few times and have long-term, still-current real friendships with a lot of Aussie musicians, including Jimmy Barnes, Chris Cheney from the Living End (who as a whiz kid guitarist was sneaked in by his older sister), and Mark McEntee from the Divinyls, all of whom we met on that first tour.

We came back through LA, and through a bit of luck and another kind soul, we landed a TV show that would eventually be a big break for us in the States. But first there was a gig to go to. The Stones were playing at the LA Coliseum, a little gathering of one hundred thou-sand fans and friends. We landed and went to the Marquis. The Stones had sent a car for us; the only catch was that we had to leave straight away—no shower, no change of clothes, no problem. We were wel-comed and greeted backstage. It was even bigger than I could've imagined. The stadium was decorated with thousands of balloons, streamers, and banners like a national championship football game but with a rock-and-roll expectation and excitement that accompa-nies a Stones show. The backstage area had hundreds of people soaking up the sun and the decadent hospitality that the Stones always lay on. Jim Callaghan made sure that we had an extra level of access, and we went back and said hello. I spent some quality time with Charlie and Jim Keltner talking about drums. Prince opened the show that day as an unknown performer and did great under the circumstances. After a shaky first response from the giant crowd, he won them over by the end. We would have that same ex-perience. It was a memorable day, and I remember talking to people

I recognized from the movies and TV, including the late greatest-ever Robin Williams, whom I had met a few months before and hung out with a little in London. I was flattered that we were there as invited guests and had nothing to offer anyone except ourselves.

There was a newish TV sketch comedy series in the States called *Fridays,* filmed live in the style of *Saturday Night Live.* It had guest stars and a current band perform each week. Larry David was the head writer, and Michael Richards was one of the cast members. The Clash had appeared in an earlier episode and were still a little underground, but they had broken through in the States with "Rock the Casbah." We had been living in London for the past year, and no one knew anything about it. The talent booker for the show, Chuck Hull, had been visiting in London and saw us play a show there. He loved it and had followed our success and wanted to help in the States. The show was trying to be cutting edge, but it was still a mainstream show. We did not have an American record deal yet. We were completely unknown outside the few places that "Runaway Boys" was getting airplay as an import. This guy really went to bat for us to get this big opportunity. The rumor was that he had to promise to get Journey, which was the biggest band in the USA at the time, for the week after if his bosses allowed him to have us, these complete unknowns, appear on an episode. Karen Allen, who was a big movie star riding on the heels of *Raiders of the Lost Ark,* was the guest star that week. She was cool, and the cast were all nice to us.

We really stole the show. What we did had not been seen on U.S. television before. Imagine settling down on your couch in 1981 to watch a wacky comedy show with a musical guest, turning on your TV, and seeing three very young scowling guys, two of whom are covered in tattoos, dressed in black shirts with the sleeves cut off playing a revved-up punk version of American rockabilly using only a big old slap bass and Gretsch guitar, with the drummer standing up and on top of a tiny drum kit. We were deadly serious, and it showed. I had a T-shirt made up with the lettering saying "Surgery Can Help Tattooed Teenagers" in a response to some article I had seen in a newspaper. This was one of those times in life when it was all on one roll of the dice; this was live TV in the States like Elvis on *Ed Sullivan*. We knew it and were very ready, very prepared. Everybody really played great, and we did the full act: Lee stood on the bass, spun it around, and slapped it until his hands bled; Brian played his rockabilly virtuoso best while singing his ass off and looking like a true punk rock teen idol. We let it fly and nailed it. I saw the show recently; I hadn't seen it since we did it, and I couldn't believe how good it was. We really looked the part, filled with piss and vinegar, really going for it. It's pretty shocking stuff when I look back—we looked so skinny, and the tattoos were still really colorful and looked even bigger on my scrawny arms. It was one shot, winner takes all, and we did it. We also came armed with a few soon-to-be-classic songs that are undeniable hits, and that is always the most important element. The audience included a few early rockabilly hipsters whom the camera people let move up to the front, where they swing-danced and added to the whole atmosphere. A lot of time and energy goes into being an overnight sensation.

There was a party after the show at producer Jack Burns's house. I knew him from old TV as half of the comedy duo Burns and Schreiber. He was old-school showbiz, and maybe he didn't get exactly what we did, but he knew it had been special and was a complimentary good host. We all went back to the Marquis, though I probably stopped at the Rainbow first for a nightcap.

We had conquered America but weren't completely aware of it. Big success was still about a year and a hundred gigs away, but we knew it had been an important performance. For me, it was another part of the grand adventure we'd started in Massapequa. I was loving it and really proud of our band. I'm sure we had some drinks on the plane ride back to London, and I'm sure someone tried to pick up the stewardess, and I'm sure there was a scene at customs. Somehow, no one had lost his passport.

5

I Married a Bond Girl

It was June 1982, and I was living in a tiny room at the Portobello Hotel, Notting Hill, London, W10. A few weeks earlier, I had gone through a strange changing of the guard in my personal life. I had broken up with my childhood sweetheart, Laurie, who had moved to London to be with me, when I had gotten my first solo residence on Stratford Road, Kensington, London, W8.

That apartment was a cool two-bedroom pad in a good part of town; there were always people coming and going, staying over. It was on a quiet street and near both Earls Court and Kensington High Street. The hospital at the end of the street was the one where Hendrix died. I found something cool about that rock factoid and would point it out when anyone came over.

I had somehow wound up with a piranha as a pet. Some artist friend had made a backdrop of the Vatican that I stuck to the back of the aquarium, and the fish became known as the Pope. I had tried to put one of those little bubble-blowing mermaids and treasure chests into the tank with him, but he just tore them all up. He was 100 percent hunger, rage, and destruction, but he was low mainte- nance, as I could dump a dozen live goldfish in the water and he would eat them over the course of a week when I went away. I had a neighbor who liked to party and would take care of him if I was gone longer. Countless hours of enhanced heightened enjoyment were had by all, watching me feed the Pope live goldfish while we blasted rockabilly and blues records. I would feed him strips of bacon, the trick being knowing when to let go. Actually, that's a good message for the whole time period. I had the party act with the Pope down to where he would bite right up to the tips of my fingers and make a little splash as I dropped the last piece of bacon fat into the water.

True pal Joel Brun from Paris and his wife, Helen, would come and stay for a couple of weeks at a time. Joel was a cool guy, a found- ing member and secretary of the French chapter of the world's most famous motorcycle club. He was also an original French rocker; he saw Gene Vincent play in France and was the number-one biggest Stray Cats fan. We met Joel when we performed on a legendary live broadcast concert show and interview program hosted by the number-one French telejournalist and host Antoine de Caunes from the Palace in Paris. This program featured an interview segment cut during the afternoon and inserted in between the songs from the gig that night. This one show launched the Cats into superstar status in France. It was a huge break where a whole concert was shown live on national French TV. The band, as always, delivered the goods. We, of course, didn't quite realize the magnitude of the opportunity and just went out and nailed a gig and interview. We really looked like tattooed children on this one. Antoine was just starting his career, too, and he looked as young as we did. He was a true early fan and helped us a lot. He's a good guy and is now one of the biggest stars in France. Joel can be seen sitting behind us during the interview segment, just smoking and looking cool the whole time.

In the future, we would do whole tours of France; we went to every city and town and did a lot of French television. I have very positive memories of those times. If I had learned to speak French and life had turned out slightly different, I would have happily lived in Paris. The Cats were and still are a legendary, huge act in France.

Joel would travel on the road with us and learned how to speak English by listening to us talk in the backseat of the car. This was before the days of tour buses in Europe. Brian went with the tour manager and his minder in the nonsmoking car, while Lee and I traveled all over Europe, top to bottom, thousands of miles, in a big Mercedes with true pal and ex–British soldier and bodyguard/driver Derrick "Captain Apollo" Unwin at the wheel. Joel and I had hundreds of adventures together, including seeing how many days in a row we could stay up. I think we made it to nearly five, definitely three. Another involved Derrick and Joel stepping in and protecting me from an overzealous store detective in Montpelier, who pulled out a gun when he thought I was stealing a pair of socks. When the statute of limitations runs out, I will include more of those stories in volume 2.

I had hooked up with Sarah-Jane Owen from the all-girl band the Belle Stars. It was my first taste of minor indie celebrity, as her band was known and played around England and Europe. People recognized us when we went out in London; a few of the rock papers had noticed and made small mentions. We had our picture taken a few times at gigs. She used to dress up in vintage western movie, dance-hall girl–style clothes and looked good. At the time, like anyone else, I thought each of these relationships was important. Each one has a hand in shaping you, in some way, for the future.

The Cats were getting ready to come back and do our first tour of the USA. We had finally gotten a release date for the record on EMI, and our records would be available for the first time in the USA. They had previously been available only as imports, even though we were Americans. Our first record contract was what was called an "excluding USA deal"—it should've been called just "plain stupid." Even though we had just had multiple hits in every other market, there was still doubt among the brass at the USA parent company about whether this band was for real or not. It proves that even legendary record company geniuses don't really know anything.

We had just parted ways with the original manager whom we had come to London with two years earlier. I had let the lease on my apartment go, put my few things in storage, and was going to stay with Sarah-Jane until the situation was more settled. The party friend, my neighbor, had taken possession of the Pope. I don't think he cared—being a piranha, as long as he got fed, he seemed happy. Where to go and what to do were two things very much up in the air, though not much time was spent worrying about it. It was definitely the last period in my life that I could totally live for the band and be in the moment. It's also a luxury of youth to behave that way. I miss it. The most important thing was that the Cats were going to America. A band cannot truly say they've made it without cracking America. Everybody knows this, and we knew it, too. It was time to go back to the States and do it all over again from scratch.

Through circumstances that were probably my fault, although I can't remember all the details, I wound up by myself with nowhere to live—from two girls and two places to stay to no girls and no-where to stay in one move. I thought I was upset about it, but I was twenty-two years old and had been on the road, around the world, with a successful, highly visible band for the last three years, and I wasn't really paying attention to much else. Things were constantly in flux, and I just went with the flow.

I had a few weeks to kill in London, so I moved into the Porto-bello Hotel. I had stayed there before during times between rental flats in the past. It was a very rock-and-roll boutique hotel in a trendy part of town. Everyone stayed there, and you'd always see someone you knew. It had the only twenty-four-hour liquor license in town, with a little pub and restaurant in the basement. In the late hours, they didn't mind you serving yourself drinks, and I'd always remember to write it down on my tab. I have a good memory from that basement of staying up all night with Lemmy, along with tragic true pal and founding member of the Pretenders, Pete Farndon, and a few others, playing poker. The place opened for breakfast to the regular guests at 7:00 A.M., who found us still there with a tableful of empty pilsner bottles and an overflowing ashtray. Marc Almond from Soft Cell, in full bondage gear, came clunking down the steep wooden stairs at 7:05 and politely refused to sit in for a couple of hands.

From the outside, it was an old Georgian-style house, while in-side it had been converted into a hotel. No two rooms were exactly the same, and each one had unique antique furnishings. The small lobby led to a sitting room with full-length floor-to-ceiling french doors that opened up to a back garden. It had decent showers with strongish water pressure, which for England in the 1980s was a rare, welcome amenity. It was the first hipster bed-and-breakfast but had an old-world charm and seemed to be completely staffed by nice British women. I came and went during rock-and-roll hours and would just take the key from a cubbyhole behind the front desk when it was late and the night manager was taking a nap on the couch in the lounge.

I had stayed there for a few weeks at a time, three or four different times, over the past two years, but I never had a credit card and cannot recall ever paying the bill or signing anything. It must've been sent to the little office we had on Wardour Street and must've been paid because they kept taking me back. Ignorance of the way money really worked was another sentimental part about that time of my life. Besides having enough cash in my pocket to buy some drinks, a little blow, and taxi fare, I never knew of or thought about finances. When I needed an airline ticket, I called the office. We were pretty much always on the road, and it wasn't private jets, but I lived without ever seeing or thinking about a bill. This way of life comes back to bite you, but like the rest of it, it was great, youthful fun while it lasted. Until just a few years ago, I would get a Christmas card from the Portobello Hotel every year, sent to my parents' address in Massapequa. In 1982, I still used it as my permanent address because it was the only one I could remember.

This time, I was staying at the hotel because I had nowhere else to go. On a number of nights during this stay, true pal and character Michael Corby would crash out in the extra bed in the room after a night out in the clubs. There were always more or less harmless rock-and-roll hijinks going on around me. Corby founded the glam rock band the Babys and was a real rock star whom I had numerous adventures with. The hotel had given me the small room behind the front desk that really just consisted of two single beds and a bathroom. One funny side story involves Corby waking up in the middle of the night after thinking he heard something outside our door. He went out to check, and the door closed and locked behind him, stranding him the hallway. I was passed out and didn't answer the door despite his urgent whispering. He decided to sneak out to the front desk and look for a spare key. He, of course, slept naked and picked up a large potted plant to hold in front of his privates while he roamed the hall. After a minute or so of looking through the drawer and cubbyhole slots behind the desk, he looked up to see the two girls who acted as night managers quietly sitting on the couch in the little lounge, right next to the desk, watching him and giggling. One of them walked him to the room and let him in with the pass key. Corby, once the game was up, probably walked back to the room with his head held high like Charles I on his way to the chopping block.

It's funny how random people can play such huge roles in a life. A friend from LA was in town and got in touch with me. It was Roger Klein, the manager of the Roxy. He was a good guy, and I had hung out with him a lot when the Cats had been in LA in 1981. On that first West Coast visit, I had pretty much made my camp at the Rainbow, and Roger had shown me around some cool, historic, under-the-radar spots around Hollywood. He was one of those Anglophile types, friends with a lot of the English bands, but he had never traveled to London before. This was his first trip there, and he called me when he arrived. I asked him to meet me at the hotel for a couple of drinks and we'd go out from there. He asked if he could bring another friend of his who lived in London, and I said, "Sure. The more the merrier."

The friend he was talking about was Britt Ekland, who would turn out to be one of the most important people in my life.

Being the manager of the Roxy meant Roger also worked directly for the club's owner, Lou Adler. I had met him when the Cats played the Roxy the year before. Lou is a music mogul and cool guy who had dozens of hit records as both manager and producer starting with Jan and Dean and the Mamas and the Papas through Carole King and Cheech and Chong. He put on the Monterey Pop Festival in 1967 and was also a partner in the Whisky and the Rainbow. He's famously the guy with the beard and hat who sits next to Jack Nicholson at the Lakers games. In the years to follow, Lou and I would become part of what I call "an LA extended family" and hang out on many, many occasions. I got to sit in those Lakers seats a few times—there's nothing like it; if you're any kind of sports fan, it's the best thing. Thanks, Lou. I like the guy, still see him, and am happy to have known him. I had also met Jack, briefly, after he danced throughout that whole LA show and came to the dressing room after the gig to say hello. It was another one of those "I was in Massapequa High School a year ago" pinch-yourself moments.

Britt and Lou had been together in the 1970s and had a son, Nicholai, who was nine years old when we met. So Britt knew Roger, and he knew me, and we would all become very close.

I don't know if I believe in love at first sight, but I definitely believe there is connection at first sight. When Britt came down the stairs and we were introduced, I knew something was different about her. We had an immediate, deep connection. She was older than I was, but I was only twenty-two, so most everybody was older than I was, it seemed. I didn't notice this immediately. She looked like what she was—a glamorous European movie star. I have always said and still say now that our age difference was never a factor until much later. She was stunning, gorgeous—I remember she was dressed in elegant, trendy, but still rock-and-roll clothes that suggested the classier end of the Kings Road. She spoke perfect English with a Swedish accent and got things slightly wrong in translation. I had no idea who she was, just that she was a movie actress, and she had no idea who I was, just that I was a guy in a band. It was supposed to be a regular night out. It turned out to last a lot longer.

We decided to go to the Camden Palace. Roger had some other people to see in town, so he left us at the hotel, and it was just Britt and me. She had a tricked-out MINI Cooper from the 1960s and wanted to drive. I don't think I had ever known a woman who had a car before, and certainly not one like that, so the adventure was getting better all the time. The Camden Palace is a well-known old venue in Camden, London, NW1. It's been there for fifty years and has seen every type of event imaginable. I think it's still going as a dance club and occasional live venue. The neighborhood has become trendy, but back then, it was still a bit rough.

My friend and superstar scene maker Steve Strange promoted a club at Camden Palace, and when Steve did a night, it was always the best thing going on in town. Steve was a flamboyant, genuinely original character who just about single-handedly invented the new romantic movement. He was the singer in the band Visage and always looked fantastic—he took the hipster alien look as far as it could go. He ran legendary clubs—Blitz, Club for Heroes, and many others. His nights were always the place to be on any given week. I knew him very well from around club land, and he was thrilled to meet Britt. Steve Strange recently passed away, and there's been much outpouring from everyone who was around London in those years. I really cared for and tried to stay in touch with him. He really liked to party and had trouble getting away from certain behavior. He would become good friends with Britt, too, and we'd hang out every time we were back in London. Steve thought it was "fucking brilliant" that she and I were together, and it always helps a club promoter when famous people turn up together on their nights.

Another small-world part to this is that the Camden Palace was the first place that the Stray Cats had ever appeared on a stage in England. We had come to see a band called the Fabulous Poodles in June 1980. We had met them in New York City when they played CBGB and befriended them. They said, "If you're ever in England . . ." We actually turned up. They invited us to play a couple of numbers with them; it just so happened to be at this same place.

The night that Steve Strange put on this time at the Camden Palace was the best nightclub I ever remember going to. It took place right smack in the middle of the new romantic era; punk and rockabilly influence was still lingering, and this made for an eclectic mix of music and especially fashion. Everybody got dressed to the nines to come out to Steve's clubs. Some of them looked like they had been getting ready all day to come to the club that night. The girls were dressed up like a cross between Marie Antoinette and Anne Boleyn, with a little Debbie Harry thrown in for good measure. The boys were in full-on Beau Brummell–meets–Adam and the Ants gear. Again, rockabilly and especially the Stray Cats were accepted by all the different tribes. On one occasion, I remember standing in the top-floor bar with Joe Strummer, Simon Le Bon and Nick Rhodes of Duran Duran, and most of Spandau Ballet—everyone was tooled up all the way, respected each other, and was having fun. I was a little surprised to hear the Spandau guys with regular North London accents. In those new romantic outfits, I always expected to hear a posh, Oscar Wilde accent coming out of whoever was wearing it. We were all pretty friendly. I recall a girl walking by looking like Madame de Pompadour with punk rock–style makeup and Joe scoffing at her, which sent her away in quiet tears.

Steve treated us like royalty that night. There were a few paparazzi normally camped out there, and I think there are some early photos of us going in and out. We were wined with champagne and me with whiskey and beer. Everyone took turns going to the bathroom for powdered refreshment.

Sometime around closing, we decided to leave. I would get dropped off at my hotel, and Britt would carry on home to her house in Chelsea. There was never a feeling of a one-night stand here. It was more serious and felt like it was a buildup toward the inevitability of getting together. On the way back, we decided to try to find a place to eat something. While slowing down to look for a certain street address, we were pulled over by the police. The cops made us stand out in the pissy London rain while they searched the car and took us both in. Britt was in more trouble than I was because she was driving. We rode together in the back of the police van like a couple of prisoners. At the end of the day, Britt is actually very old world, and I'm sure she was mortified by this whole thing. It was happening quickly in that slow-motion way. She was led into the back of the station house in Camden; I waited in the lobby like Paul's grandfather in *A Hard Day's Night*. She was booked for driving under the influence. The car had been towed to the station by then. In an odd twist, the cops told me that I could drive her home. I had been holding a packet the whole time and was totally wasted, but they never searched my person, and I must have looked well enough to drive but couldn't imagine how. I was wearing fuzzy leopard-skin boots, a black bowling shirt with the sleeves cut, a red cowboy scarf around my neck, and a black leather jacket. I told the sergeant that I had left my international driver's license at the hotel. I of course didn't have one, but I had to say something.

In silence, Britt and I took a taxi back to my hotel. Britt had her girlfriend staying back at her house and didn't want to bring this whole scene back there at 4:30 A.M., so we each crashed out in one of the two tiny twin beds in my little room, off the lobby of the Portobello Hotel. That had been quite a first date.

The next day, we went back to retrieve the car from the Camden Town police station. On the way back to my hotel, we stopped off to have something to eat at the same place we had been looking for the previous night. Anyone who lived in and around Kensington or Chelsea at that time will remember Witchetty's on Kensington High Street, near the corner of Earls Court Road. It was a trendy restaurant that was missing the roof off the top floor. The roof garden part of the restaurant was built around the rubble. The story I had always been told was that it was bombed during World War II; I'm not sure if this was true, but the place was missing a roof. When it rained, they moved the tables inside, but when it was nice out, it was a fun place with a great atmosphere and good food. That day, my plate was too close to the edge of the table, and when I put my fork into the lamb chop, I springboarded the whole meal onto my lap. I just salvaged what I could off my pants and ate the rest of my lunch. There was no way to look cool after that. The situation was already way beyond that; we'd already been through a memorable, embarrassing adventure and had only known each other twenty-four hours. We spent the rest of the day walking around Kensington High Street and in Chelsea. She showed me her house in a cul-de-sac next to the Stamford Bridge soccer ground, where Chelsea played its home games. I was going to New York City the next day to meet the band and start the American conquest. We made some type of plan to see each other again, but I don't remember exactly how we left it. I didn't have a place to live, let alone a phone number. I think we both knew this wasn't the end of our association. I spent my last night at the Portobello alone, packed my extra pair of boots and hair grease, somehow got to the airport the next day, and went back home to the USA.

The next few weeks were very busy and hectic. We started on the East Coast and worked our way west. It was the first time we'd ever had a tour bus, and I loved every minute of the whole rolling circus of characters. We were all working for the same goal and truly thought we deserved all the success. I still do. We were playing every night; at one point, we did eleven straight overnighters with shows and partying every night. We were doing clubs, every show was beyond sold out, and it was the hottest ticket wherever we played. There was genuine excitement for the music and the band. I found the after-hours clubs and punk rock strongholds in every town. When it got too crazy in some places, I brought the party back to the hotel. We did interviews and visited all the independent-leaning radio stations that were playing us in the afternoons most days before the gigs. It was the first time I'd ever traveled in the USA with the exception of the 1981 trip to LA and the shows with the Stones the year before. I'd been to Paris but never Pittsburgh, Tokyo but never Topeka.

The real game changer had been MTV. The Stray Cats were tailor-made for it. Rockabilly and the Cats were still too weird for the FM stations of the day. No matter what they say now, most radio station program directors across America in the early '80s were still stuck in the lame parts of the 1970s and did not embrace punk or new-wave music until MTV made it safe. We had a couple of videos that we had made in England with genre-defining pioneer filmmaker and friend Julien Temple in the late part of 1980 and early 1981. The "Stray Cat Strut" video still stands up; there is a lot of charisma in that little film. Early videos were made for pop music–type programs and shown when the band couldn't make the appearance at the station. It was a way to be in a few different places at once. They had been around for years but never had a platform like MTV. I believe that Ricky Nelson had the first one with "Travelin' Man." His father made it to be played at the end of their 1950s TV show. Believe it or not, in the early days MTV needed content. Luckily, we had two excellent videos in the can, ready to go. They got on heavy rotation, and it put us on the map. Music plus images really came together in the world of early MTV. We had had both since the beginning, and now the world was coming around to our way of thinking. We were perfect for MTV and it for us. Radio followed when it could no longer ignore the popularity of this new music. We would go to the studio and go on the air spontaneously. It was a fun time but changed very quickly. Everything at some point becomes political, and MTV was no exception. I'm very happy and proud to have been there at the start of it all.

We were socially friendly with every one of the original veejays—JJ Jackson and Martha Quinn, especially, but at the time, I considered Nina Blackwood, Alan Hunter, and Mark Goodman all to be friends. Martha's boyfriend was true tragic pal Stiv Bators, singer in the Dead Boys and Lords of the New Church. Punk legend Stiv had stayed a lot with Lee and me in our crazy punk rock flat on Gloucester Terrace in Bayswater, London, W2, in late 1980 into 1981. We were close friends.

Even small towns that didn't have national cable TV had local after-school video programs. We went to every one of these *Wayne's World*–style little shows to be interviewed and then to the local radio station. *Rock video* was now a household term, and the Cats are a part of that story. We worked it every day and then did a full-on rocking show every night. We were the hardest-working, best rockabilly band ever. Anyone who was at a show on that first Cats tour remembers it; I still hear it all the time. I know it was historic good and am not shy anymore about saying it.

By the time we hit LA, it was really taking off. We were extra popular there; the *Built for Speed* album would go gold in California. After the show in San Diego, I had the bus drop me off at the Roxy while the others went to the Sunset Marquis to check in. It was already late. I was stoked to be back in LA and wanted to see if there was any action on the Strip. We had a three-night, sold-out-in-advance engagement at the Hollywood Palladium starting the next night. I rang the buzzer for On the Rox, an intimate, very small, very private club located on top of the Roxy Theatre on Sunset and was let in. When I got to the top of stairs and looked in, I was a bit disappointed. On first glance, there was nobody there. After adjusting my eyes to the darkness, I focused in, and there she was, standing right there, talking to Louis the bartender. Our paths had crossed again. After a little small talk, we drove back to Britt's house on Stone Canyon Road, Bel-Air. My life was never quite the same again.

I woke up the next day in the later part of the afternoon. I was in a beautiful Victorian bedroom in a large brass bed with art nouveau paintings and furnishings. There was a deck that looked out over a yard and pool. I had never been in a place like this before. It was Lou Adler's house, where Britt lived in LA with their son, Nicholai. It's a historic rock-and-roll house: Lou's friend John Lennon lived there during his famous "lost weekend" year in LA until he had to move out to make room for Britt and Nicholai. She had split up with Rod Stewart and needed a place to live. I made my way downstairs and met a housekeeper and two large Norwegian elkhounds. Everyone got along. Britt was out, and I needed to get to the gig. Fortunately for me, the Cats rarely sound checked. All my luggage had gone to the hotel, and I had no clothes. Britt came back, and we quickly did my laundry so I had something to wear at the gig. It was late at that point, and I was starting to worry about the gig. The others had no idea where I was. We all partied, things were always kind of loose and anarchic with the Cats, but we always made it to the show, sometimes cutting it very close. All bands want to make every gig a special occasion and want to think each one is just as important as the next, but this one really was a very important one. As a rule, shows in LA, London, New York, Paris, and Tokyo have a little extra pressure; everybody feels it.

Meanwhile, back at the ranch in Stone Canyon, we couldn't wait for the dryer to finish, and my black Johnson's zipper jeans were still damp. So I sat in the front seat of Britt's 1977 Porsche Turbo Carrera with a towel around me while holding the pants out the sunroof to dry while we drove. I borrowed a shirt from Britt and, as always, had my punk rock, standard-issue trusty Schott Brothers Perfecto leather jacket. Britt knows how to drive a sports car, and we were speeding down Sunset Boulevard, then screeched up to the stage door, and I made it to the backstage of the Hollywood Palladium for the first time, with Britt Ekland in tow.

We had an amazing show and blew the roof off the place. It was the early stages of the brief time when rockabilly became a mainstream style. It would soon be possible to buy bowling shirts and creepers in your local shopping mall. The Stray Cats and all the hard work we put into it are responsible for that pop culture moment. This is our lasting contribution to rockabilly music and style.

After the show, I introduced everyone to Britt. After a little reluctance and the suspicion that this was one more short-lived wacky thing from Slim Jim, everybody became friendly.

I went back and stayed in LA after the tour. The others went back to New York. We were constantly on the road and making records for the next couple of years. We recorded the next album, *Rant and Rave,* at Maison Rouge Studios just off Fulham Road in London. I stayed at Britt's house on Billing Street and walked to the studio every day. Brian and Britt became pretty close; I was happy about that. It was important to me that everyone got along. My connection and relationship with Britt was then and is now genuine, not a rock-and-roll stunt, and has stood the test of time. Even when we split up, there was no animosity and no ugly legal action.

When there was a long enough break in everyone's schedule, Britt and I got married in 1984, on my birthday, March 21. We set up a tent in the backyard at Stone Canyon and had a few dozen friends and family in attendance. Glenn Palmer made me a pink tie and tails. Judge Ronald M. George, the judge who had just finished the Hillside Strangler case in LA, performed the ceremony. He told me that I was about to get a longer sentence. Lee and Brian stood in as my best men, Lou was there, too, and Nicholai was my newest, closest little buddy, and he stood next to me. Britt's daughter, Victoria Sellers, acted as her maid of honor. I had three small rock star wants: a vintage Corvette, a saltwater tropical fish tank, and a pool table. I had all three at that house, where we lived for four years. People came over on most weekends, and there were always willing pool players. Then we bought and moved into our own house at the top of Doheny Drive, moving in the fish tank, pool table, Corvette, and Pepe the Spanish dog, where we spent seven solid years together, living between London and LA, having adventures along the way.

Every now and again, we'd have a spontaneous urge to just do something. A few times while living in London, we'd get into the 1965 Rolls-Royce Silver Cloud III, drive to Paris, and check into the same little hotel. Sometimes we'd go out and other times just buy easy food from a local market and eat in the hotel room. We'd go to a classic celeb-driven place like Régine one night and the next night go see a rock-and-roll show at a place like Bains Douche. We were welcome at both types of clubs. Sunday or Monday, we'd drive back to London and resume whatever was going on there.

Britt is Swedish and maintained close ties to her roots. We'd fly to Sweden every Christmas and during the crawfish season in the summertime. We'd split the time between staying in town with one of Britt's brothers and her classic Swedish seaside country house in Dalarö. A real quaint town about an hour outside the city, it's like the Hamptons for Stockholm. The house had been in her family for a very long time. She rescued it and bought it in the 1970s. I was very friendly with Britt's three brothers, and they still come to all the shows I do in Stockholm. I was especially close with her brothers Carl and Bengt and their wives and children. We would visit with and go to shows by any number of friends when they played Stock-holm and we were in town. A good in-the-know rock-and-roll secret is to go see a big band in a place that is not London, LA, or New York. The bands have room on their guest lists and are not so stressed out. The artists are usually happy to see a friendly face in a smaller setting.

We saw and hung out with the Boss at the Grand Hotel and at a few of his shows at the original Olympic Park on the Born in the USA tour. He liked the Stray Cats and had once gotten onstage at a club in Jersey and played the encore with us. Through good buddy Nils Lofgren, we've been to a lot of Springsteen shows. As part of those shows, Bruce would bring out a girl from the audience and act out a little sketch during the song. On one of the shows, the Boss brought Britt out as his foil on the number. She is a die-hard Spring-steen fan, and it was a good moment for her. He really is the Boss and does a special one-of-a-kind show. I had a carte blanche on the Tunnel of Love tour and saw five shows at the Sports Arena in LA, bringing a different friend as my plus-one every night.

One memorable show from the Born in the USA tour was at the LA Coliseum. Britt and I were in a VIP-type area in an early version of a skybox before the show. The elevator opened, and out walked Elizabeth Taylor and Michael Jackson. He was in his full 1984 rega-lia, sequined military jacket and big mirrored shades. She was defi-nitely a movie star and carried a big presence. Even a backstage room full of jaded Hollywood types stopped, quieted down, and checked it out.

I'm a big fan of both of these true stars. I may be in a minority, but I believe MJ was innocent of the charges against him. He was an odd character, for sure, but a really talented guy—maybe the best ever—and it seemed to me that he was a genuinely gentle soul, incapable of hurting anyone.

Michael Jackson surveyed the room and walked straight up to me and said in his gentle whisper, "I really like that song you guys do about the cat."

I was speechless. I think I softly croaked out a "Thanks, man."

They did a lap of the room, stopping to chat a little with a few people, and then left again. I don't think they stayed and watched the show. That was a good one.

Back in Stockholm, we saw everyone from Prince to Def Leppard play at the Globe, a fantastic venue in Stockholm that everybody likes playing at.

In 1988, we welcomed a son, my best pal ever, TJ. Britt was forty-five years old when TJ was born. She already had two kids, and I will forever appreciate her giving me a son. We continued to travel to London and Sweden, putting TJ in a cardboard crib behind our seats on the plane. The trick was to get the last two seats in the upstairs premium economy section on the TWA flight. TJ has a very strong connection to Sweden; he speaks Swedish and stays in touch with some of the gang he met there. We lived a type of gypsy, hand-to-mouth, jet-set life in a normalish way. We didn't let not being wealthy stop us. The trick of actually earning and saving two cents is one of the hardest ones in showbiz. Life of any sort is an expensive thing to keep going. There is little financial security in both the rock-and-roll and the acting professions. We lived well but were always hustling up and juggling money. To this day, we all continue to be very close.

So in just a few short months, I had gone from two girls and one place to live, to no girls and no place to live, to one girl with two places to live.

6

Our Day: The U.S. Festival

The week of the 1983 U.S. Festival was one of the best we ever had. The whole machine was firing on all cylinders; we were riding a successful record and a justified conquest of America. We had achieved a status that I couldn't have even dreamed of when we were hustling up gigs and playing around the clubs on Long Island just a few years earlier. We had set out to make a living by playing rockabilly music; my biggest goal was to have an apartment somewhere and to wear blue suede shoes to work and not have a hassle. Now, the mannequins in the front window of Macy's had pompadours and were wearing bowling shirts. This was real rock star stuff, and I loved it.

The U.S. Festival was, at the time, the biggest rock show ever. It took place over the Memorial Day weekend in May 1983 at Glen Helen Regional Park near Devore, San Bernardino, California, in an open-field venue with the world's biggest temporary stage. The event cost $12 million to put on and was organized and paid for by Steve Wozniak, one of the founders of Apple and a major music fan. The U.S. Festival, pronounced like the pronoun, was meant to be a reaction to what Steve thought about the 1970s, which he felt was the "me" generation. He wanted the shows to be more community oriented. One of the ideas behind the festival was to combine rock music and technology on a grand scale. The whole weekend drew 670,000 people, and when we were onstage at sundown on Saturday, May 28, there were over 300,000 people watching the show. All of these fun facts are 100 percent known to be true; I looked it up on Wikipedia because I couldn't remember any of the actual hard facts about that legendary gig. I do remember very clearly a lot of the other personal details and other behind-the-scenes stuff from the day that we were on, though.

I'm pretty sure that we were starting or already on some type of tour, maybe the West Coast leg of one. I was living in Stone Canyon, and the other guys were staying at the Westwood Marquis on Westwood Boulevard, the west-side version of the Sunset Marquis where a lot of other bands stayed, too. A car picked me up, stopped at the hotel to meet the guys, and then headed to the airport. The next thing I knew, we were in a helicopter flying over LA. I know it's been said before, but the first time you are in a helicopter, it really does remind you of a Vietnam-type scene out of *Apocalypse Now*. I thought about the ending scene of the Stones' film *Gimme Shelter*. It was all a bit surreal. After what seemed like a long trip, where no one really spoke but exchanged those "can you believe we're here?" looks, we were in a chopper over a giant throng of people that seemed to stretch for miles. There was a line of cars and traffic for as far as we could see. It was another one of those moments when I was too excited to be afraid.

We touched down amid a cloud of dust and were taken to a nice makeshift backstage—functional but not luxurious. Britt and Nicholai had driven and somehow were already there. I think the current girlfriends of the other guys were there, too. We all were very friendly. Britt, Nicholai, and I all had matching white-and-black cowboy suits with smiley pockets and velvet belt loops made by Glenn Palmer. I completed the whole modern-meets-classic Grand Ole Opry outfit with sterling silver, engraved boot caps, collar points, and belt buckle with a white Kentucky colonel tie. It really was an amazing suit. I've always believed that going to work in an ensemble like that is at least half the fun.

I walked around the backstage, talked to everybody, and stood at the side of the stage and watched a few of the other groups that were on before us. I was always the hangout guy in my band and really dug the camaraderie with other bands and being into the whole moment. I watched the Divinyls, which featured Chrissy Amphlett— friend and future wife of true pal Charley Drayton—on vocals and the excellent guitarist Mark McEntee. They had the big hit and great pop song "I Touch Myself." Mark and his wife, fashionista suprema Melanie Greensmith, founder of Wheels and Dollbaby clothing line and shops, are still friends today, and I see them whenever I'm in Australia or they're in LA.

I also watched INXS. Michael Hutchence was my good friend. He was a real front man and had a great voice, too. He really was that lanky lead singer who would swan into a room, trip over a chair, and make it look cool. We had the falling-down part in common. One of their first USA tours was as the opening act of a Cats tour, and we became and stayed friendly. Our paths crossed again when Phantom, Rocker & Slick returned the favor and were the opening act on an INXS tour after they had really cracked America, including a two-night stand at the Hollywood Palladium that has played such a big role in my rock-and-roll storytelling. The usual hijinks occurred when a couple of true party guys got together. We had a few good times together when he lived in Paris and the Cats' tour stopped there with a night off before the show. It was in the later part of the 1980s, and I hadn't crashed out of partying yet.

I had a Swedish relative, Blaise Ruetersward, whom I was very close with at that time. He was Britt's brother's wife's brother. He was a big male model in Paris, and he shared a flat with a bunch of beautiful people, including a model girlfriend of Michael's. Blaise is a fantastic guy who turned up and lived with us for almost a year at Doheny Drive while he was nursing a recent heartbreak delivered by an American model in San Diego. I helped him get over it by drinking a thousand bottles of Corona beer with him and letting him beat me a thousand games in a row at Ping-Pong in the summer of 1986. At last check, he was thriving as a fashion photographer in Paris.

Anyhow, I seem to remember something in a nightclub where Michael stood up on and fell off a table in a crowded place without spilling one drop of his drink. The next night at the Cats' gig, he turned up wearing his silk pajamas and bathrobe. We cemented a real bond a few years later in London. Michael had publicly started a tabloid-fueled affair complete with custody issues with Paula Yates, the estranged wife of Live Aid founder Bob Geldof. Bob and Paula's kids went to the same prep school in Battersea that TJ went to from 1994 to 1998.

I think Sir Bob is an awesome guy and really truly did something great and important for the human race under the banner of rock and roll. He's a fellow Irishman, too. He came to see the Cats play, and I saw the Boomtown Rats on their first USA tour when we were still kids. He was part of the gang at Dingwalls in the early days of my fondest memories of London in the early 1980s. I wish we had been on that Live Aid show. It was through his example that I became involved with African famine and debt-relief charitable causes. I can't say how much I respect the guy and what he's done. I bumped into him in the Kings Road right after his first trip to Africa and intently listened to his description of the horror he'd seen. I had met Paula when she was a journalist for *Record Mirror* and also when the Cats appeared on *The Tube,* a pop TV program she cohosted with Jools Holland. I liked everybody.

So it was a little uncomfortable when I would go to the school to pick up TJ and both Bob and Michael would turn up to pick up Bob's kids. There was hostility and bad vibes between them, and although I wasn't all that close, I happened to be there and to know and be friendly with both of them. A few times, I cooled Michael out and we walked around the school's gravel driveway, away from the tabloid photographers who were camped out there. The drummer guy with a slight talent for trying to make everybody get along came into play again.

In 1997, Michael was in LA making a solo record. I was already seven years sober by then. I went to visit him in the studio a couple of times; he was in pretty bad shape the last night I saw him. He did a few songs at the Viper Room. I heard about and was shocked by what happened to him just a couple of days later. The rest of the sad story is easy enough to look up.

My girlfriend at that time was Claudia Cummings, a former

Alabama beauty queen. She was gorgeous and talented, too. It was one of the few times when I've ever seen a girl and just walked straight up to her cold without introduction and told her I would like to get to know her better. The scene was the old Hollywood Athletic Club, and Claudia was the attractive spokesmodel assistant on a billiards-themed game show. She racked the balls and smiled at the camera. My old buddy Tom Salter was one of the owners of the club and had invited me over to watch the pilot and be a face in the crowd for the TV show. Claudia was also a background singer in Jimmy Buffett's band, and I used to go to the shows. His crowd and band thought I was the punk rocker from Mars. The audience was the stoned, drunk, and higher-paid professional meathead types with their ties around their heads, giving each other frat boy high fives every two minutes. Meanwhile, I was sober, the squarest guy in the room who had a babysitter watching TJ back at the ranch on Doheny Drive. One night at a gig in Orange County, they all had to stop, stare, and comment about my quite ordinary blue suede shoes. Despite that, I have positive memories about that time.

But back to 1983, when that day at the U.S. Festival belonged to the Stray Cats. Looking back on some press clippings and reviews of the show confirms this. *Time* magazine gave a favorable review to everyone and the gig as a whole and singled out the Cats' performance as the day's best. I dug the early sets and wasn't as nervous as I would be now. I was caught up in the moment and had total confidence in our band. Everything clicked for us on that set. I think that we were always the best live band on any bill, but that day stands out because of the strength of the lineup. These were all world-class acts. If you look at the day's bill now, with the Divinyls, INXS, the English Beat, Flock of Seagulls, Men at Work, and the Clash, it becomes clear, though we didn't really know it at the time, that the Stray Cats were also representing the USA in our own backyard. We had already played a lot of big shows but were very confident that particular day, as we had a hit in the USA and were household names at the moment. The timing of the day worked in our favor, too. We strutted onstage, me carrying a bottle of Jack Daniel's, to a thunderous applause from an estimated three hundred thousand people in the daylight. During the show, the sun went down and the huge lighting rig was turned on for the first time. Seeing the film now, I am struck by how cool our little setup was. We had this huge stage around us and had, by then, learned how to work it. The core of our setup, the tiny drum kit and two amps, looked very classy and retro-revolutionary in the days of big drum kits, keyboard rigs, and amplifier stacks. We didn't have to waste time convincing this crowd. We had a double platinum album under our belts. I think we opened with "Rumble in Brighton" and did "Runaway Boys" in the set. The audience sang all the words on "Stray Cat Strut," and the call and response on "Rock This Town" was the biggest noise from an audience I've ever experienced. The footage of the gig was recently on TV, and the Cats' performance really holds up; the look and the music are timeless. As the show went on and it got dark outside, the show had highs and lows to coincide with the change of atmosphere. Especially when it is very hot and crowded, you cannot overwork the crowd too early, but you need to keep the intensity level up and keep them focused and interested during the whole show. I see a perfectly played and paced show from three guys all under twenty-five. After having not seen it in a long time, I was impressed with the onstage maturity and, as always, quality of the playing. This was a wild show that ended with me jumping off the bass drum as Lee held and pounded the double bass over his head and Brian threw his prized Gretsch in the air and caught it on the downbeat as I hit the last cymbal crash. All the while, we were under control. It was wild abandonment, but it wasn't frantic. We knew where we were at all times and were very comfortable up there. We had done it—this was the peak of the mountain we had told everyone we were going to climb. We had brought rockabilly music and style all the way back and beyond anywhere it had been before.

After this show, it was a perfect time for basking; it wasn't the day for splitting right after the show. My band had just done what would be the show-stealing set; I had my glamorous wife by my side and half a bottle of Jack Daniel's left. My best pal for the day was Eddie Van Halen, who was playing the next day and had come early to hang out and party at the festival. We nipped from my bottle and chased it with tall cans of eternally cosmopolitan Schlitz malt liquor. We'd hang out once in a while over the years to come. He's one of the best musicians and coolest guys in the biz. We have always had a good connection. We took some classic backstage pictures together that appeared in a few magazines in the day and still pop up sometimes online. I look pretty tweaked; I guess I didn't want to miss anything.

The Clash was definitely one of the best bands around then. I had seen them play a number of times, including three nights in a row in 1981. They were doing a run at the grand old Lyceum Ballroom on the Strand, London, WC1. I turned up at the stage door and was welcomed by Big Ray, their security guard. I stood at the side of the stage, loved the gig, and went back the next night for three nights running. They always had a cool conceptual part to their shows. These featured a graffiti artist on a ladder, armed with cans of spray paint in crossed bandoliers and wearing a gas mask, who did a huge mural behind the band as they played. By the end of the show, there was a one-of-a-kind backdrop. I remember going into the dressing room right after the show and seeing Mick Jones sitting and eating his dinner off a plate on his lap while still all sweaty wearing his stage clothes. He was and is a supercool rock-and-roll guy whom I see when he comes to LA. I've rehearsed, played, and made a video at his studio / groovy hangout place in Acton, London, W2.

Nicky "Topper" Headon was the drummer in the band at that time and was on their best records and gigs. He played a dozen classic drum licks on *London Calling* alone, and I've studied his playing. He was my genuine drummer buddy, and we hung out, talked about drums, and partied a bit. I was lucky in that I never got into the dark side of drugs like he and a couple of other buddies from that time did. We bought the same pink suits from Lloyd Johnson and wore them when he sat in with the Cats at their legendary 1980 New Year's Eve show at the Venue, Victoria, London, SW1. I saw him a couple of years ago; he's doing okay. I'm happy to have had some quality time with him.

Joe Strummer was at a few of the early Cats shows and really helped the cause when he said some truly nice things about us in one of the big weekly rock papers. His word was respected, and it went a long way when he told the *NME* that we weren't a hype. That was one of the worst things a band could be called at that time; it suggested a lack of substance. Our rapid rise and seemingly overnight success had caused a little jealousy, and the word *hype* was floated around in an attempt to hurt us. Joe batted that down in an interview. He didn't have to do that, and I'll always be grateful to him for it.

The Cats had done our own run at the Lyceum at the end of the first English tour. We also filmed the video with Dave Edmunds for the song "The Race Is On," recorded during the making of the first Cats record at Eden Studios, Chiswick, London, W4. We did it in one or two takes. This version of the George Jones classic was a top-forty hit in England and features a perfect rhythm track from the Cats and two of my favorite guitar solos, first one by Brian and then one from Dave.

The Clash had some problems on the day of the U.S. Festival. Topper hadn't been doing too well and didn't make the trip with them. There was a replacement drummer, and he did the best he could. I think the guys were all fighting, and it famously was the last gig that Mick Jones ever played with his own band. After a set by Men at Work that was good but left the Cats' set unchallenged, I was leaning on some road cases and noticed some kerfuffle behind the stage. The roadies from the Clash, having heard how much the band was being paid for the performance that day, were going on strike and refusing to move their equipment onto the stage and set it up. They were laying down their demands to the flabbergasted manager.

That's the dichotomy to punk rock band / road crew politics, the "we're all in it together" versus "worker's rights against the boss" argument. Certain punk rockers had preached about poverty, and when they found themselves successful with a little money, they were embarrassed and tried to hide it. That's a very hard thing to pull off; it always shows through in some way. I never thought there was anything wrong with success. Unless you give it all away, there's no way to hang on to the original ethic. I've never known anyone who really did it that way. The Clash road crew were that certain breed of professional English roadies in the 1980s who had nicknames and thought they were rock stars, too. From where I was standing, it looked like they were promised more money and started setting up the stage.

Just when the manager thought he was safe, Joe came up to him with a new problem. As part of the technology theme behind this show, the organizer had arranged for a few minutes of the show to be simulcast to the USSR using some type of satellite technology. Through a Soviet/USA agreement, coupled with the wizardry of Apple, a certain weather or military satellite passed over the concert site and would be taken over for five minutes and used to beam the gig to the whole of Russia. The only catch to this experiment was that it had to happen at an exact time. Whoever happened to be onstage at the time of the satellite passing was the band that would be shown on Russian TV. That day, it happened to be Men at Work, and I suppose that the Russians who tuned in thought it was cool for five minutes to see any band from a big concert in the USA. I'm not sure if the Clash had been promised that slot and the timing of the show prevented it, but when Joe found out he wasn't going to be on Russian TV, he went ballistic. I was still leaning on a few cases, taking nips from my bottle while keeping an eye and ear on what was going on. He was screaming at the manager to get the satellites back and wasn't having it when he was told that to do that would be impossible. A few of the technical people from the festival were brought in to try to explain it. It wouldn't have mattered who the band was; once that moment passed, that was that. I guess there must have been more stuff going on in their dressing room, because they looked a bit out of sync and distracted onstage that night.

I, however, enjoyed the rest of the night. We all watched from the side of the stage and walked around the grounds a little. I drove home with Britt and Nicholai and stayed in my own bed. It was truly a special, magical twenty-four hours in my life and career.

The next day was another day on the road for us. We had a couple of other big outdoor shows in California as the opening act for Tom Petty and the Heartbreakers. These were big shows too but not quite the magnitude of the U.S. Festival. We were taking a helicopter again; we were old pros at it by now. A car picked me up; we stopped at the hotel to pick up the others and went to the airport. I got out and went into the lobby. I saw Joe sitting there by himself among a bunch of luggage. He said that they hadn't had so much fun the night before. I told him he should hang around for a few days and goof off in LA. I said we'd be back the next day and we could hang out. He told me that he had to get back to London "like my ass was on fire." I asked him why, and he told me, "To vote." There was a national election the next day in England, and he wanted to cast his vote against Thatcher. That cat really walked the walk on this one. He was flying all the way back to London from LA to cast a vote in an election that would result in a 99 percent victory for the bad guys, but he went anyway, to have his voice heard. That's dedication.

The next few days, I'm sure, were good times. The whole week of the U.S. Festival was good times. I do wish someone had offered me stock in Apple instead of the money we were paid, which I've definitely blown by now.

With TJ in 2013. *Courtesy of Alex Rocca*

Christy and me with Mick Jones at Club Nokia in LA in 2011. *Courtesy of Gerry Harrington*

Me and Bill Wyman, 1989. *Courtesy of Jeff Stein*

Britt with TJ, 1988. *Courtesy of Bobby Gilken*

Head Cat at the Cat Club. *Courtesy of Robert John*

The Stray Cats with Robert Plant at Hammersmith Odeon in London, 2004.
Courtesy of Madison Grubb

The Cheap Dates: me, Jeff Baxter, Tony Sales, Harry Dean Stanton, and Jamie James, 1995. *Courtesy of Robert Matheu*

The Stray Cats with producer Dave Edmunds at the Brixton Academy, 2008. This was the night I fell off the stage. *Courtesy of Julie Setzer*

Me, Dave Edmunds, Brian Setzer, Jeff Lynne, George Harrison, Duane Eddy, and Bob Dylan at Dave's gig at the Palace in Hollywood, 1987. *Courtesy of Robert Matheu*

Me and Bob Dylan at the Palace in Hollywood, 1987. *Courtesy of Michael Farr*

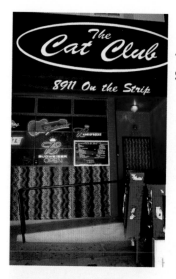

The famous awning of the Cat Club on the Sunset Strip, Hollywood, 1999.

Brian and me with the Everly Brothers at their show at Royal Albert Hall, London, **1983.** *Courtesy of Alpha, London EC2*

The Stray Cats in *Flexipop*, 1981.

Flying Slim Jim, 2007.
Courtesy of Tommy McGuire

With George Harrison at the Palace in Hollywood, 1987. *Courtesy of Michael Farr*

David Bowie, Terry Bozzio, Jeff Beck, Stevie Ray Vaughan, Chrissie Hynde, Bonnie Raitt, me, and Slash at Stevie and Jeff's gig at the LA Coliseum, 1990.
Courtesy of Gary Nash, West Promotions

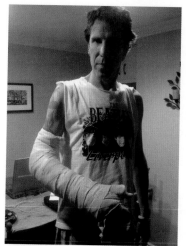

Me in 2008, recovering after breaking my arm.

With TJ and Britt in Stockholm, 2009.

At the Sage & Sound Recording Studio in Hollywood with producer Cameron Webb, Lemmy, and Danny B. Harvey in 2010. *Courtesy of Sharon Albenisius*

Christy and me with Harry Dean Stanton at the Regent Theater in LA for the thirtieth anniversary screening of *Repo Man*, 2015.

Me and Mick Jagger, 1980. *Courtesy of Richard Young*

Jeff Baxter, Britt, and me in LA, 1983.

Stephen Stills, me, Les Paul, Slash, Jeff Baxter, and Steve Vai at the House of Blues in LA, 1998. *Courtesy of Robert Matheu*

Johnny Ramone, me, TJ, and Eddie Vedder at Johnny's house (Ramones Ranch), 1995.
Courtesy of Linda Ramone

With Keith Richards at Media Sound in NYC after he played a session with us, 1987. *Courtesy of Leon Drucker*

Me and Harry Dean.
Courtesy of Jimmy Steinfeldt

At the "King Ralph" video shoot with Little Richard, 1991.
Courtesy of Jeff Stein

Me and Pete Farndon, 1981.

A rare shot of members of the Damned, the Sex Pistols, and the Clash all together: Captain Sensible, Glen Matlock, and Mick Jones with Charlie Harper and me right after I fell off the stage at Brixton Academy in 2008. *Courtesy of Gerry Harrington*

With Johnny and Linda Ramone, 1996.
Courtesy of Michael Lustig

Phantom, Rocker & Slick, with Lee Rocker and Earl Slick in 1986.
Courtesy of Frank Madeloni

At the peak of Mount Kilimanjaro, 2007. *Courtesy of Robin Wilson*

On the drum.

Halloween 2011 in Beverly Hills with Christy.

Me and TJ, West Hollywood, 1993.

The marquee at the Fox Theatre in Atlanta, where the Stones played a rare small-venue gig and the Stray Cats opened for them, 1981.

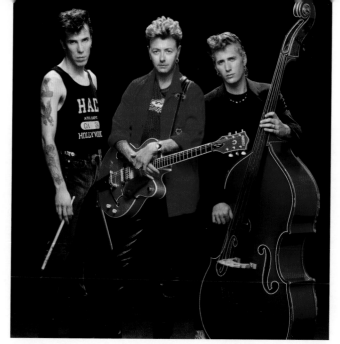

A classic publicity shot of the Stray Cats.

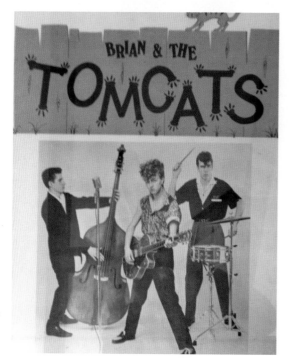

The first band picture of us as Brian and the Tomcats, Massapequa, 1979.

Me and Steve Jones of the Sex Pistols, 1994. *Courtesy of Michael Des Barres*

7

The Killer

The first time I ever met the Killer was in Beverly Hills in 1983. The scene of the encounter was at the old Beverly Theatre on Wilshire Boulevard. I'd been to see him play before at the Palomino, another legendary venue that was an authentic juke joint in North Hollywood on Lankershim Boulevard in the San Fernando Valley. As the crow flies, it wasn't that far from the Sunset Strip, but by that time, it was a different universe. Every country music artist from the 1960s through the 1980s played there. I saw many shows there featuring the original 1950s rockabilly stars, including Wanda Jackson, Carl Perkins, and bawdy rockabilly queen Janis Martin, who called me up onstage, where she was smoking a lipstick-stained, superlong cigarette and drinking a light beer, to announce me to the audience. By then, I was pretty much immune to any public embarrassment. I had already fallen off the drums and down enough staircases in nightclubs and had said enough stupid things in interviews to be thick skinned enough to take a little ribbing onstage from an old gal. In this instance, though, I did feel the back of my neck getting hot when she pulled a makeup pencil out of her handbag and wrote her hotel name and room number on a napkin. All of this was happening while I was standing on her stage with the band sitting behind me waiting to do the next number. I'll bet I still have that napkin somewhere in a box in deep storage.

"Drugstore Rock and Roll" was an early favorite record. We covered it back in the four-sets-a-night club gigs on Long Island, and we all thought Janis was smoking hot in the picture on the back of her album. The picture was from 1956, and she looked like Elly May Clampett. We didn't have any girls who looked like that in our neighborhood.

These musicians were all gracious and thankful, telling me personally that their careers had gotten a shot in the arm after the Stray Cats brought rockabilly music back onto the radio to new, younger fans and into the mainstream, where we always thought it belonged. A few of the more obscure artists hadn't done gigs since the 1950s, so for them, the new interest in rockabilly was a real blessing.

This was something that has always been very important to me and one of the things I'm most proud of being a member of the Cats. The fact that just by playing this music we were able to help these original artists that we loved and were influenced by is still a source of pride. I still get off on it. I still dig this music, those records and images, so much. The excitement I get from those original records and photos never fades away. I can still listen to a Sun Records compilation anytime, anywhere and get off on it. It will always improve my mood. I can look at the blurry photos on the album sleeve with these slicked-up hepcats in cowboy suits and the rocking songbird gals in 1950s gear and get the same rush I did when we first discovered this music and look.

Rockabilly has that elusive musical secret: it swings . . . and it rocks. That sounds easy enough, but it is deceptively simple. The beat swings, but it also needs to be aggressive and at the same time danceable. It can't be too fast, but it can't drag. It's gotta flat-out send you. The original cats—Elvis, Gene Vincent and His Blue Caps, Buddy Holly and the Crickets, Eddie Cochran, Carl Perkins, Johnny Burnette and the Rock and Roll Trio, Roy Orbison, Johnny Cash, Jerry Lee, Little Richard—all loved hillbilly, bluegrass, jump blues, and rhythm and blues, and when mixed together in the musical pot, out came rockabilly. Sam Phillips, the owner/operator of Sun Studios in Memphis, was the mad genius chef for the whole movement. Elvis Presley captured his vision, put his own stamp on it, and changed the world.

These people were mythical figures to me. The idea that I've met, worked with, and count as friends a few of these original band members is very much still with me. Being friends with Dickie "Be-Bop" Harrell, the drummer from the original Blue Caps, is to me like being friends with Paul Bunyan. This cat is a real American folk hero. He played drums and did the screams on "Be-Bop-a-Lula." There would be no Beatles or Stones without that record—just ask them.

Rockabilly should have an acoustic double bass, and in many ways, it's the one defining thing about the music. The slapping style of the double bass—Carl Perkins called it the "doghouse bass"—creates a percussive sound in between the notes that fills in the gaps. When done right, the drummer and bass player can create a big sound for the soloist to play over. Rockabilly is traditionally guitar

based, and you can't be a great rockabilly band without a great guitar player. A certain twang is the desired sound, and the truly great
ones expand on that.

I firmly believe that Lee Rocker and I are the best rhythm section in the history of rockabilly. We didn't get that way by accident;
Lee and I spent a lot of our teenage years practicing with just the bass
and drums. Being locked in with a bass player is the best feeling a
drummer can ever achieve, and I've had many, many of those moments with Lee. Brian is surely the best guitar player anywhere, and
together we invented our own style that combined these elements of
rockabilly with the excitement of punk rock and the emotion of the
blues. This music called to us. We were looking for a music that had
all these things we liked and also had an image built in that we could
add to and make our own. In rockabilly, we all found the outline for
everything we wanted to do. It was a life-changing moment when I
discovered I was hooked on this stuff.

Sadly, the Palomino is gone today. The Beverly Theatre was a very
cool original art deco theater that hosted vaudeville in the past before becoming a movie theater, and then it was a venue for small gigs
and plays. Maybe it held 750 people. I remember seeing a quite a few
shows there. It's another example of one of those LA places that was
once a grand landmark, but now it's just not there anymore. Like
many buildings in LA, if it had lasted until today, it would be vintage and antique. In 1984, it was just plain old. There is no rule saying you have to have rock-and-roll taste and vision to own property
in a good part of any town. I'd like to save the whales, live local
music, and the rockabilly architecture that is slowly fading in LA.
I've done my part for two out of three, but it's hard.

I decided to go to the Jerry Lee Lewis show that night on my own.

I saw in the newspaper that he was playing. I was just going to turn up, buy a ticket, sit in the audience, and watch the show. I didn't know him or any of his band and management. I am now and have always been a huge fan. His early recordings on the Sun label hold up as some of the hardest-rocking stuff ever put down on tape. He was one of those early alchemists to come out of Memphis who were mixing up the flaming stew of rock and roll, blues, gospel, and country that had influenced me and every other rock and roller that I admired. He always kept the music rocking and on the verge of being out of control. All the way through the 1960s and 1970s, Jerry Lee continued making great records and doing high-energy live shows, where he was unpredictable onstage. He's a true eccentric, and his personal life is the stuff of legend. He continued flying the rockabilly flag, especially in Europe, where he was hero to both the teddy boys and the rockers, causing riots at the gigs. The classic film footage of teddy boys smashing up a concert hall and throwing all the chairs onto a pile on the stage is from a gig in Germany. His 1960s records *The Greatest Show on Earth* 1 & 2, recorded at the Star-Club in Hamburg, Germany, are two of the hardest-rocking live records I've ever heard. Even when he moved to a more country flavor, I think he was just calling it country to get through to a different audience; it's still really soulful and hard rocking.

On the way to the show, I decided to ask bespoke rock-and-roll tailor and big Jerry Lee fan Glenn Palmer to join me. Glenn had seen Jerry Lee a dozen times in England, really dug it, was usually holding a little powder, and was good company. We bought two regular tickets at the box office and were in our seats talking before the show started in the mostly filled theater. A few fans said hello, but nothing crazy. I was in an aisle seat when a middle-aged guy wearing cowboy boots, a satin baseball jacket, and big belt buckle, complete with mullet and moustache that suggested he was a bit more country than rock, walked up, leaned over, and spoke to me quietly. He introduced himself as the Killer's tour manager, told me that Jerry Lee wanted to meet me, and that he was there to escort me to the dressing room. Glenn and I looked at each other and shrugged. So I followed this guy to the front of the stage, up the stairs, behind the curtain, and to the dressing room. The Beverly was an old-time theater and had a hallway backstage with numerous small dressing rooms. The tour manager pointed to one and told me to go on in. I knocked and waited for an answer. I didn't get an answer, so I knocked again.

"Come on in—it ain't locked!" I heard the distinct sound of the Killer's drawl.

I opened the door into a very small typical dressing room with a dressing table against the wall and round lightbulbs around a mirror. The Killer sat in the one chair, and on his lap sat a very big, very young rockabilly girl dressed to the nines in a big skirt with petticoats, high heels, sporting a bleached-blond beehive hairdo, Marilyn Monroe makeup, the whole thing. Jerry Lee was puffing on a big Sherlock Holmes–looking meerschaum pipe and had his arm around the corn-fed, USDA-prime rockabilly girl. He was drinking something out of a red plastic cup. When I came in, he stood up to greet me and dumped her to the floor. I was still in shock from seeing her on his lap in the first place; now she was on the floor, looking very put out and unimpressed. Jerry Lee stepped over her and came toward me. I instinctively stepped back; the wall was right behind me, and I was a bit trapped.

"Well, lookee here, boy. We got a gen-u-ine, rock-a-billy Stray Cat," he said loudly in that unmistakable Jerry Lee voice.

"Hi, Jerry Lee," I answered, still trying to take it all in. I'd seen some rock-and-roll scenes before, but this one was just plain weird.

"Call me Killer, boy," he insisted, edging even closer. There was nowhere to go in the room; the palms of my hands were against the wall.

"Mmm, I like your hair, boy," he continued in a voice like a Southern sheriff right out of the movies, all while puffing on this crazy-looking pipe.

By this point in time, I was pretty much over being nervous around famous people, especially if they were close to my own age. I wouldn't have been intimidated by anyone in the Clash, and we had met huge rock stars like Robert Plant over the years. I still felt a bit awed by the original rock and rollers. There's something about those guys that's still larger than life to me. They seem much older in a historic way. Anyone who I saw on TV in black and white earns a different type of respect.

"Thanks, Killer," I mumbled. "I use Nu-Nile on the sides and Murray's on the top, then put in a little Royal Crown to give the whole thing a shine," I continued. "Didn't Elvis use Royal Crown hair slick? I read that somewhere." I was standing there, babbling to Jerry Lee Lewis about hair grease, getting a little uncomfortable with the whole scene.

By this time, the full-figured rockabilly girl had gotten up off the floor and was sitting in the chair, filing her nails and looking very bored with us both. Jerry Lee was standing in front of me, half talking, half yelling about rockabilly music, Sun Records, Sam Phillips, and Elvis. I started to loosen up a little when he quickly reached past me and turned off the lights in the room. The next thing I heard was the girl screaming with a combination of horror, shock, and giggling glee and the Killer's demonic laugh. I felt around behind me in the pitch-darkness, found the doorknob, and squeezed my way out without ever opening the door too wide. I made my way back to the seats and watched the show.

Jerry Lee was an awesome, whirling, rocking hurricane, as always. He kicked the piano bench over on the last number and did everything he was supposed to do. After that night, I didn't have any contact with him for twelve years.

In 1996, I was living in my flat on Doheny Drive. A thousand things had happened in my life since the night I saw Jerry Lee Lewis play at the Beverly Theatre and had a bizarre meeting with him in his dressing room. I got a phone call from true pal Jerry Schilling. Jerry is a fantastic guy. He was an extremely close, inside friend and aide to Elvis Presley from the beginning but not the typical goon that seemed to surround the King. If you want a great read and some new insight into life in Memphis and LA with the King, check out Jerry's memoir, *Me and a Guy Named Elvis*. I think it's the best one. It's an honest, nonsensationalized view of life at Graceland and during the moviemaking years in Beverly Hills, where Jerry was a body double for Elvis on quite a few of those films. I had first met Jerry when he came with Priscilla Presley to a Cats show in Nashville in 1983. We've stayed pals since then. He's always shied away from capitalizing off his association with Elvis and wanted to be his own man, which is why he left the King's court and did some things on his own, including managing the Beach Boys in the 1970s and 1980s. I had been to visit him at his perfect midcentury house up on Sunset Plaza that Elvis had given him as a present in 1974.

At that point, he was managing Jerry Lee and was calling me to ask if I'd play drums for Jerry Lee on *The Tonight Show*. The host, Jay Leno, was a well-known car buff and aficionado of vintage stuff, and he knew and liked the Stray Cats. We had met him when he was doing standup comedy in New York City. I would run into him while driving my one rock star possession, my prized 1961 Chevrolet Corvette that I've somehow had since 1982, around town. He was always in a different amazing classic car and would always wave and give a honk. So when I turned up as Jerry Lee's drummer, it was a good little blast to see each other. Another good small-world moment was when true pal Jeffrey Baxter turned up as the bass player. Jeffrey is godfather to my son, and we have a long, strong friendship. He had produced a record for Carl Wilson from the Beach Boys when Jerry Schilling was managing him, so that's their connection. After a couple of run-throughs, we did a song called "Goose Bumps" that Jerry changed the arrangement for on the fly as we were doing it live on TV. I'm good at going with the rock-and-roll flow, so that part was not a big deal. There is a good cinematic opening to the performance, where the camera starts with a shot of a reflection of me in the shiny black finish of Jerry Lee's grand piano. I had the iconic Stray Cats logo on the bass drum head and that always looks supercool. After the show, we chatted a bit and took some pictures. I'm not sure Jerry Lee remembered me or knew who I was; it's hard to tell with him, but I played the drums well on his song, so all was cool.

A few months of normal life went by when I got a call from a strange woman who turned out to be Kerrie Lee Lewis, Jerry Lee's wife at the time. She explained to me that she was now Jerry Lee's manager, and he wanted me to join his touring band. I asked about Jerry Schilling and was told he was no longer involved. She told me the pay, and it was pretty good, and she said the gigs were mainly on weekends. She was insistent that the band did not drink or do drugs. This, I answered her, was okay by me. I had already been sober six years, so that part was no big deal. In fact, it was always easier and better at that point to deal with sober guys. Then she added that as long as Jerry Lee took his methadone once a day, everything was fine, and it had been for eleven years. I was a little surprised by this. I was never particularly a drug guy, but I knew that methadone was supposed to be a short-term help for withdrawal symptoms, not a long-term lifestyle choice. I needed the money, and it sounded easy enough and up my alley, yet even though I had done many gigs with other people, I hadn't really been on the road too much with anyone besides my own band. I called Jerry Schilling, and he told me, "It's a strange organization, but the checks won't bounce." I already had firsthand experience to know that Jerry Lee was a real eccentric, and the whole hiring process had been weird. I figured another adventure was right around the corner.

The first gig was in Toronto, a good city; I had been there many times. Canada can be a bit tough about immigration even though we're neighbors. The passport guy told me there was no record of a work visa and really hassled me for twenty minutes before he let me in the country. No car picked me up at the baggage carousel. I didn't know what hotel I was supposed to go to. In a flash of road genius, I picked up a copy of the local free arts newspaper that every city has and went to the back pages where the concerts and shows are always listed. I found Jerry Lee Lewis's gig listing and called the club, working backward. Luckily, they answered, and I took a cab to the gig. The others turned up together. They all came from the Memphis area, and Jerry Lee always rented a small private jet to take them to the gigs. They'd traveled in tight quarters, and Jerry is afraid to fly, so there was apparently always a lot of tension on board. This was one more reason I was happy I was coming from LA.

The band included longtime Jerry Lee sideman and musical director Kenny Lovelace and Hall of Fame guitar hero James Burton. Kenny is a lovely, faithful guy; he's been with Jerry Lee since the 1960s and is still there. James is one of the greatest guitarists of all time, having done long stints with Ricky Nelson and Elvis Presley. He's on some of the best records ever, a true rockabilly legend, and I'm honored to have worked with the cat. That's James onstage with Ricky on the original *Ozzie and Harriet* TV show when they show clips of Ricky performing at the end of the program. He was onstage with Elvis in the TCB throughout the 1960s and 1970s. There was a solid electric bass player guy who was steady and quiet. I couldn't help but think how great it would sound if we had Lee Rocker on slap bass. This wasn't my call, so I never suggested it.

The room was full, and the gig itself was going along nicely. Jerry Lee does not believe in the use of a set list; he just calls out songs or just starts playing and expects the band to know what he's thinking and follow right along. He does a bunch of Chuck Berry tunes. A few times I didn't know which one until the singing came in. On some of them, he would do the famous Chuck Berry stops every time around, and sometimes he would blow right through them. A couple of times I caught myself as my mind wandered thinking about the famous feuds he supposedly had with Chuck over the years.

Musically, I could handle it. We were playing rockabilly, blues, and rock and roll, so with that part of it, I was confident. I'd set up the drums right behind Jerry Lee as per his request. I'd been told to watch his hands for clues and cues to the tempos and stops he wanted. Sometimes he waved his hand because he wanted it faster. Sometimes he waved his hand because he wanted it slower. Sometimes he waved his hands because he wanted to stop. Sometimes he waved his hand because he felt like waving his hand. It was a bit of a free-for-all, but most of the set was okay. A few times during the set, it fired on all cylinders, and I was thinking, *This is great. James Burton, Jerry Lee Lewis, and me are all hitting it together.*

At one point, there were a few punk rock girls in the front row, and they started yelling, "Slim Jim! Slim Jim!" They started getting louder and louder. Jerry Lee picked up on this, turned around, and started glaring at me with a mean-faced, pissed-off look—the Killer look. He was staring me down like he was mad about the fact that these chicks were cheering for me. I guess he thought I was stealing his thunder. I gave him a look back that said, "What do you want from me?" I would've figured that this was part of the reason why they were hiring me in the first place. I respect my elders and all that, but I'm not some kid who fell off the turnip truck and is just happy to be onstage. I earned my stripes a long time ago.

The rest of the gig was fine. There were some amazing moments, including when Jerry Lee went into a little impromptu gospel number and we all fell in together just right, so that by the end of the song, it was really stomping. We did "Whole Lotta Shakin' Goin' On" at the end. He kicked the piano stool over and was gone out the back door while we ended the song. I went back to the hotel with the other guys. It had been a long day.

The next day we were driving to a gig that was not too far away, so we stayed in the same hotel. During the day, an envelope came through under the door. I saw it come in and opened the door to see a little guy slipping envelopes under the doors next to mine. I introduced myself. He turned out to be the infamous Dr. George Nichopoulos, better known as Dr. Nick. Any Elvis nerd, like me, will know this name instantly. He's the doctor who prescribed all the pharmaceuticals to Elvis Presley. He traveled with Jerry Lee, and the envelopes were everyone's paychecks for the three gigs we'd do over the weekend. It was Dr. Nick who paid me on Sundays before I went back home. Before checkout time, an envelope was slipped under the door with a check for the three days. He was the guy who gave us any messages about any changes about starting times for the shows and when we would come and go from the hotel to the gigs.

Since I was already out in the hallway, I decided to knock on James's door to see if he wanted to take a walk and get a sandwich. It was a clear, crisp day in Toronto, we were staying at the Fairmont Royal York Hotel, and there were some good places nearby. The band guys were all in there watching NASCAR on TV. I tried to hang and sit for a little while. None of them wanted to leave the hotel. The cars just went around and around the track. I overheard comments like "That boy can drive." I watch every Yankees baseball game on TV, no matter where I am on the road. There's no accounting for personal insanity or taste.

We did a sound check—without Jerry Lee—the next day. We were all milling about on the stage; I was adjusting the drums when I caught a whiff of something familiar. I picked up a nearby can of Coca-Cola from the top of an amplifier and gave the contents a better sniff. It was filled with booze. I covertly walked around the stage and checked each of the other soda cans. Every single one of them was filled with booze. These guys were all drinking and all telling each other that they weren't.

The gig that night was like the others: all pretty good, sold-out performances with a lot of personality up on the stage. There were a few moments of brilliance when James was just burning it up on his classic Telecaster; I was following Jerry Lee's left hand, and it really connected. This was a historic rockabilly happening, and I was an equal part of it. That must have been a special night for the fans—I'd have paid to see it. As a budding rockabilly back in Massapequa, if you had told me that I'd be onstage doing "Breathless" and "It'll Be Me" with James Burton and Jerry Lee Lewis, I would have signed in blood on the dotted line. The devil could have taken my soul right then and there. I wish there had been a way to explain that to Jerry Lee at the time.

After the show, there was a lot of paranoia floating around backstage because those guys were flying back home that night, and the weather report was calling for turbulence and rough skies between Toronto and Memphis. I learned that Jerry Lee is very afraid of flying and freaks out whenever the plane hits a bump. He was very upset with the pilot one time when he thought the lightning came too close. He started to pray very loudly. Maybe the Killer didn't want to meet his maker quite yet? They were all afraid to tell him about the impending storm that was expected on the ride home. I was flying commercial the next morning—one more reason to be happy about going to LA. The idea of Jerry Lee freaking out, flying in that bathtub-sized jet with the others trying to ignore it all and be quiet while Dr. Nick tried to calm him down made me grateful not to be part of that rock-and-roll moment. I guess they made it back all right. There was nothing in the papers the next day at the airport.

There were some other shows—none as memorable as those first few, though. There was a funny routine to it all that I got used to as time went by. The office would call and send a plane ticket; I'd meet them somewhere on Friday, play three shows, get the check under the door on Sunday, and come home Monday. It was always slightly disheveled, but it always came off, and those flashes of rockabilly brilliance and decent money made it worth doing.

I had some more strange conversations with Kerrie Lee Lewis and a few very nice ones with James Burton. James was understanding about my place in this off-kilter situation. He knew I was the youngest and the only guy from back east. They were all from the South and a little older. I understood this. He told me to call him if it ever got too weird and I needed to talk to someone. The band was solid, we made Jerry Lee sound good, and we all thought we should keep this lineup going.

After being told by his management that we had the time off, I went to London to play a gig at a fashion show for true pal Peter Golding. I had just arrived when I had a message that there was a Jerry Lee gig that had just come in for a place in Pennsylvania. I called the office and told them I couldn't make that show, and they told me they would find a substitute for the one show, no problem. A few weeks later, back in LA, I heard about a Jerry Lee show that I hadn't been called for. There was no reply from his people when I called. I called James Burton to get his input on it. He's never called me back to this day. That was the end of my tenure with the Killer. Nothing spectacular happened; they just never called me again. It would be another twelve years before I'd see the Killer again.

In 2010, my band Head Cat was asked to open a Jerry Lee show at the Fox Theatre in Pomona, California. The show was on Jerry Lee

Lewis's seventy-fifth birthday, so it was a cool historic event. Lemmy and Danny B. both definitely wanted to do it, and so did I. The night was a special one. We did the Head Cat album cover shoot with photographer Robert John in front of the art deco theater, with the album title superimposed on the marquee. We all went to Jerry Lee's dressing room for an audience with the Killer before his show. I'm not sure if Jerry Lee recognized me on his seventy-fifth birthday night. Again, with the Killer, it was hard to tell. I could tell it was a big moment for Lemmy, who had never met him, and at the end of the day, like me, is a fan. I think he saw Jerry Lee in England on his very first UK tour, and it was one of his life-defining moments. I could tell from the photographs that Lemmy was humbled in the presence of Jerry Lee. There really isn't anyone in rock and roll who's as gnarly as Lemmy was, but Jerry Lee Lewis is the gnarliest, for sure, no question. For the first, last, and only time, I could see the shoe on the other foot with Lemmy and another musician. Jerry Lee has that effect on cats in our game. Who else has been around and rocking for that long? We have some good snapshots from that night. TJ was with me and got his picture taken with Jerry Lee, too. A bit of a full circle from the first time I'd met him in the dressing room of an old theater in Beverly Hills. The Killer did his show that night. James wasn't in the band that night, but faithful, loyal Kenny was. He led Jerry Lee onstage, and it was good to catch up with him. He's been doing it every night for fifty years. Jerry Lee is very old now, but he still had a few moments where, if you close your eyes, you can see the original rock-and-roll wild man, the Killer himself. I remembered the good moments we had when I was playing drums with him.

8

Marbella

I went to visit Britt on a film set in Spain. She was costarring with classic leading man Rod Taylor in a Spanish production of a movie aptly called *Marbella* because it was being filmed in the resort town of the same name. This must have been in 1984, maybe 1985. I think it was in the summertime. The Costa del Sol is a fantastic place; I had never been there before, so it was an extra little adventure. This part of southern Spain has fabulous beaches and friendly people. It's got a Spanish vibe to it with a bit of North African influence, as it's across a narrow part of the Mediterranean Sea from Morocco. The town of Marbella itself is a harbor and is made up of marinas and docks that lead into the hills above the town. There were a lot of giant luxury yachts and pleasure boats coming in and out all day and night. An internationally infamous Saudi arms dealer had his cruise-ship-size yacht moored there; it was bigger than anything I've ever seen, too big to get close to the dock, so it was anchored off the shore and had its own large craft to take passengers to the dock. I don't even know if the guy was there, but there was a lot of activity, whispering, and pointing from the locals about that yacht.

Marbella is a popular vacation spot for English tourists, and there are a lot of pubs, fish-and-chips joints, and tea shops along the docks. If you want to get a glimpse of the typical British holidaymaker abroad, this is the place. The place attracts that breed of people who travel out of the country to an exotic location but still want it to be exactly like it is back home. They complain that the restaurants' and hotels' staff don't speak English, so they yell at them in the hope of getting their point across. The Americans do it, too. I had encountered this quite a bit on tour with the Cats with various crew members in all different countries who didn't go with the flow. It doesn't matter how annoyed, threatening, or loud you get; if a waiter in the middle of France, Germany, Italy, or Spain doesn't understand, "Steak well done and chips on the side!" or "Cheeseburger, medium with fries!" the first time, it's not gonna happen, regardless of how many times the put-out tourist says it. I remember a big bodyguard losing his mind and getting removed from a hotel dining room in Holland when, even after he had screamed it ten times, a waiter didn't understand what a mixed grill was. I've learned very well by now that "when in Rome" is the best way to roll in any foreign country and not to be embarrassed by a language barrier. In most countries, the natives appreciate any attempt at speaking the local tongue. I'd been around enough to see this all over the world and now found it funny to observe. I liked sitting in a pub in London and seeing Americans come in and order a beer only to get warm English-style bitter. In the same way, I enjoyed seeing sunburned Englishmen in LA who thought they could handle a full day in the sun at the Santa Monica beach on their first day of vacation only to be fried alive and unable to put their shirts on the next day. I'm an equal opportunity enjoyer of harmless hassles.

The film shoot had been going for a couple of weeks when I joined Britt. She was staying in a very nice condo-style hotel in the hills above Puerto Banús, one of the port villages that make up Marbella. Britt is the master of making any hotel or dressing room into a home, especially one that she's staying in for a few days—or in this case, weeks. Everything was unpacked but still ready to go. She always had a kettle with a few other handy amenities and was the first person I'd ever met who took things, besides booze, from the dressing room of a gig back to the hotel. Since then, I've lived many a day from the bananas and water I stuck in my bag after the gig.

On this job, she had an early call every day, so I would sleep in and take a shuttle down to the harbor when they took a break from filming and join her for lunch. There were many young people on the crew, and they recognized me from pop music TV shows and rock magazines that the Cats had done in Europe, and I practiced my rudimentary Spanish with them. But this was Britt's turf. She was very comfortable and professional on a movie set, and I liked watching her do her thing.

We had been together a few years at this point, and I was aware that in certain situations, it was Britt that everyone was interested in. I had had hit records at a young age, success in the music biz, and the Cats were always a band that was photographed a lot, so that part, I was used to. In the beginning of my relationship with Britt, it was strange to be photographed with anyone else but the other two guys, and the fact that anyone was interested in who you went out with or were married to was a new concept to me. In a similar way, in the beginnings of the band, the idea that anyone was interested in me for anything besides the music and the band was at first a strange idea, but I was always image aware and quickly embraced all of it. I was very familiar with having my picture taken on a stage, in a studio, or in a dressing room, so this type of attention just became part of life. Britt and I were genuinely together in every way, so it never felt like a staged thing. I liked being the tagalong guy; these were places I wouldn't have been going to, things I wouldn't be doing if I was just a drummer in the traditional sense—even a guy in a very successful rock band doesn't always experience this side of showbiz. I was young and always up for an adventure, but I was also a hotheaded New York sort, so it made for some funny times. I never really had too much of a problem with it. By that point, I was accustomed to paparazzi at the airports and understood that it's all theater, all part of the gig, and I just went along. Britt did teach me that if you're pissed off or annoyed, it just makes for a bad picture, and that's what some of them were after, anyway. So smile and take a good picture just to spite them. This I understood; it appealed to my Long Island view of the world. Now it's a good laugh to look back at all those photographs that pop up and to think that this was way before the Internet and reality TV, so if the press followed you through the airports, it was genuine celebrity. At the time, I was just going along day to day.

The film was a caper tale of intrigue and murder set in the gentrified world of the European yachting community. Britt was at ease with the director and all the lingo of moviemaking, every crew member liked her, and she hit her marks and delivered her lines every time. She looked amazing, very much the classic European, glamorous movie star and was respected for it.

Rod Taylor was a real leading man in the matinee idol mold. He had come to Hollywood from Australia in the 1950s and starred in *The Birds* and *The Time Machine,* did a great *Twilight Zone* episode, and even had a role in *Giant.* Being a vintage film and TV nerd, I knew who he was. He was that certain type of rugged, handsome, trained actor, an amateur boxer who chose acting as a career. He and I got along right away. I don't think he knew any rock-and-roll bands from the past twenty years, but we talked about a bunch of things, and he had met James Dean, so I had plenty to ask about. We also drank all day, every day. I started at lunch with a beer and took a break after a few hours to go back to the hotel and rest up a little before dinner. Britt and I had dinner with Rod and his quiet, exotic wife, Carol Kikumura, just about every night. We'd either stay on the set or go to a nearby restaurant, where the girls drank a little wine. Britt would go back to the hotel, but I'd stay out, and Rod and I boozed it up pretty good; most nights we closed the local nightclub. I was on vacation with nothing to do, was good at partying, and was still pretty young. Mr. Taylor was back at the set at 8:00 A.M. every morning and kept going all the way through; it was impressive. He sat in his makeshift dressing room tent on the dock and drank local red wine nonstop. When it was time for his scene, he snapped to it and delivered his lines in a professional manner, and when the director called cut, he tuned out again. I've seen certain guys who could turn it on and off, but he was the best.

The whole production was a very European thing. The producer, José Frade, and his wife were hot-blooded types who were there all the time, arguing and partying along with the cast and crew. Everything was loud and slightly chaotic but functioned well. The fact that all of this was being shot in this marina and on boats added to the mild pandemonium. After about a week, the weather turned bad, and it rained for a few days. A lot of wet crew members in raincoats scurried around trying to keep the gear and themselves dry. Since it was being filmed on the docks, this was a real drag for the production; not much could be done, and everyone was still getting paid. Five or six days in a row of straight rain started to fray everyone's nerves. Britt and Rod continued to turn up, be ready, and sit in their respective dressing rooms. I had become friendly with some of the crew and would bounce around the set between the dressing rooms and hang out and drink with Rod while he told me stories about Hollywood in the 1950s and working with Hitchcock. A few times, we would just go to one of the pubs along the waterfront and someone would come to get him if there was a break in the rain. One day, the producer stood on the dock in the pouring rain with his arms raised, his face turned to the skies, and yelled for God to stop the rains and save his movie. He was in the middle of the marina, with curious tourists carrying umbrellas walking by, wearing a yellow raincoat and screaming at the heavens to turn off the tap. His wife was yelling at him to come in the tent, that he looked crazy. All of this is better and more dramatic sounding in Spanish. That should have been on film.

Sometime during the weeklong rain delay, a few of the crew and I decided that we needed some coke. We'd just been drinking for a week straight and needed a little blow to counter the effects of the nonstop boozing. A plan was concocted for me to take the train up to Madrid and meet a friend of one of the crew who would sell me some stuff, and I'd bring it back to Marbella for all to enjoy. We took up a collection, and I probably had a few thousand dollars to spend. I've never particularly been a drug person, but it was the 1980s, I did as much coke as the next guy, and being from New York, I thought I had some street smarts. I was getting a little stir-crazy and was up for the adventure. I can't remember why Britt didn't talk me out of it; she usually reined in some of my crazier behavior and stopped me from getting a motorcycle when it was so popular in LA. Rod Taylor knew nothing about this; he was old school and wouldn't have understood the whole blow thing. So one morning, I took the train into Madrid, followed the directions, met some Spanish guy, and bought a few grand worth of decent coke. The guy who met me was a friend of someone in the crew. He recognized me in a crowded street and approached. I made it back to Marbella the same night without a hitch and divvied up the goods among the investors. I'm sure I did a little on the train to make the scenery even more interesting.

On a different night, Rod invited Britt and me to dinner at a restaurant in another town miles up the coast owned by a friend of his, a former British boxer. I don't know his name, weight class, or certification; there were quite a few of these guys who moved to Spain in the '60s and '70s—he was one of them. The place had framed posters from his fights on the walls along with signed boxing gloves and pictures of him with some famous fighters and celebrities who had been to his restaurant over the years. This guy was a real Cockney pug, and you could tell he must have had dozens of pro fights—a lot of them he must've been on the wrong end of; he was pretty punchy. He more than likely had trained and sparred in a gym behind a pub somewhere in East London. He looked like he had broken his nose ten times and carried himself like a guy who had been in the ring most of his life. He had a deep tan, wore an ill-fitting tuxedo, and bossed around his staff, who probably hated him behind his back. Rod was naturally a blustery guy, and when he got together with his boxer buddy, they shadowboxed each other, roughhoused, and were really loud and animated, all the while drinking and talking about old fighters they both knew. The difference was that Rod Taylor was a world-traveled gentleman and movie star who boxed a little and liked the sport and liked to drink; the restaurant owner was a bully type who fought for a living and retired with a little dough to open this place in Spain. He enjoyed socializing and sharing cocktails with his patrons—he regaled them with tales of the colorful world of European boxing in the 1950s and 1960s. Many of the loyal customers were also flat-nosed, tough characters who retired to Spain in the 1970s after working for various firms around London.

We had a fantastic dinner. The proprietor ordered everything, barking at his waiters and busboys the whole night. He sat with us and ate and drank the same things every step of the way. He would get up every few minutes to sit at other tables, talking very loudly, everything punctuated with air punching and boisterous, drunken laughter. Local seafood delicacies and meat and poultry dishes came and went, as did many bottles of expensive-looking wine that he ordered. Each time, he did the whole drill of sniffing the cork, telling a story of where the wine came from, and sipping a small amount before telling the waiter to bring new glasses and pour for everyone. This went on for a few hours. He barely spoke to me but tried to engage Britt and Carol in witty conversation. We all smiled and went along; it was his place. I could tell Rod was growing weary of this guy's act. After the final cakes and coffee, a special bottle of ancient brandy was brought out, and our pugilist host went on and on in his East End brogue about the rarity and pedigree of this brandy *más fina*.

Our host must have left the table again. The waiter brought the bill and hovered over the table. At some point Rod asked the waiter where his boss had gone; the waiter didn't quite understand and brought over the maître d', who spoke English. Rod was trying to explain that the owner was his friend and had invited us all to have dinner at his restaurant as his guests—there shouldn't be a bill. The maître d' was trying to tell us that his boss had left for the evening and he had been told to bring the bill after he had gone. This was getting uncomfortable, as it was becoming clear what had just happened. This old boxer pal of Rod's had invited him to his restaurant, told him to invite Britt, too, and after eating and drinking the best, most expensive stuff on his own menu and taking the photo op, skipped out on his own tab, sticking us with the check. Rod was a cool customer, but I could totally feel his embarrassment. Being a class act, he insisted on paying the bill himself. It had to have been a couple of thousand dollars at least with all that wine. Amex saves the day. He cursed the guy the whole time we waited for a taxi back to the hotel, the whole time we were in the taxi, and the whole next day. I agreed with him that the guy was a total jerk and no friend, but it was a fantastic dinner.

The weather had finally cleared up, and the filming carried on. The whole thing was behind schedule, and everyone worked pretty hard to get it all back on track. I continued goofing off around the set and hotel, going to the beach on my own, drinking with Rod, and generally having a great time while Britt worked. She had a day off, so the night before, we decided to do something fun. We got all dressed up in rockabilly-style tuxedo and evening gown, and after a good dinner, we went to a casino along the coast highway. This was a place right out of a James Bond movie, reminiscent of a Monte Carlo casino where the men wore tuxedos and gold jewelry and the women wore Dior gowns and diamonds. The whole place smelled of perfume, cologne, smoke, and liquor but, in this setting, not in a bad way; it was exactly what it was supposed to be. I think many of the patrons were the owners of the big luxury yachts moored in the marina. Now, we were never wealthy, but we always managed to have a good time, and we could hang in any circumstance from a punk rock club to this. This whole stay hadn't really been costing me much; we had an Amex card that we could get cash advances on, so that afternoon I went into the main town to the Amex office, and I signed for a $1,000 cash advance. I'm not a true gambler, but I loosely know the rules and how to play most of the games and used to enjoy it once in a while. I have a good memory of Brian and me wearing ten-gallon cowboy hats and shooting craps on a spontaneous trip to Vegas. Roulette is the most fun to play with someone else and also is the easiest game to play while partying. Not so much strategy is involved, and you can last a long time with a little money by making small bets and spreading the chips around the table. If you're there to have the experience and social part of gambling, it's the best game. We were there for a while, gambling a little, drinking, soaking up the atmosphere, and I had an "I can't believe I'm from Massapequa and now I'm here" moment, which is always a good shot.

We had been playing the number seventeen all night. The Cats had had a big hit song with "She's Sexy & 17," and it seemed like a lucky number to bet on. All of a sudden it came up. We had a stack of chips right on the number and a few surrounding it, so it paid off pretty well. We kept playing seventeen and it hit again and then again. I don't know the odds, but it came up three times in a row. There was much hooting and hollering and congratulations in a few languages; a few people had bet with us on the third time, so some good champagne appeared. I tipped the croupier and waiters—I had a bunch of new friends. I excused myself to the gents' a few times to top up my buzz. I was in my rockabilly tux. Jim . . . Slim Jim . . . it was all fine.

So I was sitting at a roulette table in a casino on the Mediterranean Sea with my movie star wife next to me and over $10,000 in chips in front of me. We had hit a couple of other times with different numbers, and it was looking good. The real trick is to quit while you're ahead. Everybody knows this, but very few pull it off. The long and short of it is that we sat there for another hour or so too long, tried to hit big again, bet too much on the spins, and gave back all the winnings plus any money we had brought with us. I asked the casino manager to borrow the equivalent of ten dollars for the taxi fare back to the hotel. He lent me the money in exchange for my promise to come back the next day to pay him back. I agreed.

Britt and I sat in the taxi on the way back to the hotel talking about where we went wrong with certain bets and that maybe we should've quit while we were ahead—$10,000 or even $5,000 would have been nice. But there wasn't so much regret and no anger. Easy come, easy go; it was a fun night. The next afternoon, I went back to the casino and paid the manager back his ten dollars. He was cool and looked much different in his street clothes. I had a beer with him in the empty, dark, air-conditioned casino while the staff got ready for the night ahead. There is a certain sadness to being in a night-club during the day. It never looks as glamorous, and it's easy to see that the illusion is done mainly with low lighting and alcohol. I still dig it.

Over the next few days, I joined the band somewhere in Europe for some shows, and the movie went on filming. We may have gotten together with Rod Taylor and his wife a few times back in LA. We always talked about the boxer who freeloaded at his own restaurant, and Rod seemed like he was still mad about it. After all, he was the one who paid the bill in the end.

On one of the last days of the shoot, the scene was in a dockside bar. A stray puppy of the Heinz 57 variety was running in and out of the shot, and the action had to be cut a few times. The director got mad, and some of the crew chased the puppy around in vain trying to catch him. Britt fell in love with this dog, bribed him with peanuts from the bar, named him Pepe after the name of the place, got all the necessary shots and paperwork, and brought him back to LA. I got home from the tour at night after she had been home a few days. I was greeted by a pair of eyes on the dark stairs and a puppy's growl. Pepe was a good dog, and he lived a long, happy life in Bel-Air, West Hollywood, and then saw out his last days in Malibu, but he was definitely from Marbella.

9

Where's Me *Pepper* Suit?

George Harrison always liked me. He was a smart, thoughtful, worldly guy. He didn't suffer fools and I'm sure was immune to bullshit, so I was pleased when I realized he genuinely liked me. There had to be more to it than my initial obnoxious charm. We hung out a number of times, and with a cat like George, you tend to remember them as little life markers.

We met in 1985 at the rehearsals for the now-legendary *Carl Perkins and Friends* TV special, "Blue Suede Shoes: A Rockabilly Session." It was a show done by Stephanie Bennett for Channel 4 in England, and it turned out be one of those rare things that you just do and it winds up having longer legs than anyone thought it could.

Dave Edmunds, longtime Stray Cats producer and influence, was putting together a band for a show honoring the musical life of Carl Perkins. With Dave at the helm a few years before, Lee and I had been the rhythm section for a version of "Blue Suede Shoes" that was on the soundtrack for the cinematic triumph *Porky's*. We did "Blue Suede Shoes" in one take. When we were finished, Carl said, "I've done more versions of that song than you boys have had hot meals, and that's the best one ever!" We wanted to believe him. The night was young, the studio was booked, the song for the movie was in the can, and the gear was there. Dave just rolled the tape all night. I have a copy of it somewhere in a giant box named "Cassette Hell." I'm pretty sure Jeff Lynne came by and played piano.

Carl was a supercool, humble, original rockabilly pioneer. We were longtime fans. He had come to see the Stray Cats a number of times in the past, and we had played together before. Once was at the Grand Ole Opry, which was a milestone for us as rockabilly kids. I remember hiding all signs of partying from Carl back at the hotel, not really knowing or understanding that he had seen it all before. So when Dave was putting together the band for the Carl Perkins TV show, he called Lee and me to be the rhythm section. We brought Earl Slick with us. He strummed an acoustic; it was good to have him be part of it.

The rehearsals and show were in London. We turned up at the rehearsal studio and watched George Harrison, Eric Clapton, and Ringo Starr file in. I had been around for a few years, had a couple of hits, and was comfortable to hang with anyone, anywhere. But this was the Beatles. I was a Beatles nerd, and this was a little different. Those guys introduced themselves and were very nice. They'd all known each other since the '60s and had all sorts of memories and shared experiences, so during the breaks, they kept to themselves in the English super rock star section of the room. I played the songs, and everyone seemed to like it. On the third day of rehearsal, I worked up some nerve to talk to George. I'm always the icebreaker, class clown, used to being the cool guy, but like I said, it was the Beatles and a little different this time. I also wasn't drunk in the daytime, so you'd think I have been a little smarter with words. So I walked up to George and said, "Hi, George. It's Jim."

"Hello."

"Whatever happened to Pete Best?"

A very puzzled look from George. "I haven't thought about that guy in twenty-odd years."

"Erm, that's cool. Great to see Carl, huh?"

"Yeah, great."

I thought I'd lost him. It was a stupid question. You had your chance, and you blew it. I didn't usually care about anything like this, but I was feeling like a fool who was trying to fight above his weight. I couldn't hang here. As I was walking away, he called, "Hey." I looked over, and he gave me the famous Beatles nod/wink with a thumbs-up. Suddenly I was in *A Hard Day's Night*. I felt much better.

I think George had an instinctual feeling for situations like that. I'm sure he's had more people say more stupid things to him than anyone. We had the rest of this day and then the show the next. I didn't want to be awkward. He knew it would've kept me thinking for two days and wanted to put my mind at ease. It was a very kind, sensitive act with just a simple gesture. I know this now, but at the time I was just relieved.

It took some years to figure it out, but meeting someone whose work you admire can be daunting. I still meet fans all the time, and I try 99 percent of the time to be just plain nice, a little engaging, and let the stupid questions roll off my back. Because it is a big deal to meet the Beatles, and on a smaller scale the Stray Cats, since both were more than just bands with a song that was on the radio; they were more meaningful to those who really dig music. I think George, like me, behind all the bluster was a little uncomfortable with it and didn't like hurting anyone's feelings. There is a softer way to suffer fools that's ultimately easier on you, too. I think he saw that in me and felt a kindred spirit and thought he could help. For him, it took two seconds and a nod/wink; without saying anything heavy or uncomfortable, we had a moment. It was a delayed lesson that I learned that day from George.

The show was a special filmed in live time. There was a small studio audience of rockabilly types who danced and sang along and listened to the quieter moments. Carl Perkins was endearing, and the songs are some of the best rockers ever. He and George did a duet that was touching; you could tell that George really loved him, musically and as a person. I've heard that George hadn't played in public in five years and was maybe a bit nervous. We did a campfire-like circle where everybody sang and played acoustics. Ringo and I shared tambourine and shakers and hammed it up. He's my biggest influence, and I should have been more intimidated, but he's a drummer, so I related on that level, and we got along immediately. Rosanne Cash was on the show and sang like a bird. Eric Clapton was his brilliant Slowhand self on rockabilly songs, too. He and George were pals, you could tell. Britt was at the taping with me, and she sat with Olivia Harrison.

After the show, everyone hung out for a while in a TV station greenroom and had a drink, and that was that. Since then, that particular show has become a classic cult favorite. It gets shown on British TV every year during the Christmas season, and I'm always asked about it and feel like I was part of another quirky, great rock-and-roll happening.

Since the show was in London, Britt and I stayed at our little house in Chelsea. About a week later, Olivia called Britt to organize a dinner. I guess they had planned it during the taping and were following through. Dave Edmunds and his wife, Leslie, joined us, too. We met at a restaurant near where they lived in Henley-on-Thames. The people seemed to know George, and it was an easy dinner. We talked about rockabilly, cars, pop culture stuff. Now that I sensed he liked me, the floodgates opened, and I asked George all sorts of questions about Beatles trivia and minutiae. He was happy to answer. I think he knew I was actually interested, but he answered in a tone that suggested, "Why do you want to know this? Why do you care?" He always referred to the Beatles as the Fabs. I thought this was amazing inside jargon.

After the dinner, he and Olivia invited us back to their house. We must have taken one car and left ours at the restaurant. Driving up to Friar Park was an experience in itself—I had never really seen anything quite like it. There were huge iron gates and a sign that reminded me of a bureau de change at an airport. It had little flags from each country with a sentence next to the flag in the corresponding language. The last one was a USA flag that said, "Get your ass outta here." We drove on a leafy paved road past a good-sized English country-looking house.

"Wow, that's a nice place," I said.

"That's the gardener's house," George answered.

We drove past another two or three houses: the swan keeper's cottage, the rose keeper's cottage, a caretaker's lodge. All of these were as big as our little house in West Hollywood. When we drove onto the gravel driveway, the main house appeared through the hedges and fog. It looked like Buckingham Palace. The foyer had a museum-quality model in a glass case of the grounds and houses. It was a magnificent, regal-looking place perfectly decorated with everything you'd expect with a cool vibe.

The girls walked around to look at the kitchen, and George said to me, "C'mon, I'm going to take you on the silly boot tour."

I gave my standard answer to George: "Erm, okay, cool, yeah, great!"

We went up some stairs to what was like an attic. The room was mostly empty except for some antique carved wooden armoires that lined the walls. I kept thinking this was what Louis XIV's closets must have looked like. George opened the first one and showed me the leather jackets that the Beatles wore in Hamburg. That led into the collarless suits from *The Ed Sullivan Show,* which led to an array of all the mod colorful "top gear" from Carnaby Street. He had all four *Sgt. Pepper* suits and a story with full-on Liverpool accent and impersonation.

"Paul calls me the other day and says, 'Where's me *Pepper* suit? 'ave you got me *Pepper* suit? I'm doing a video, and I need me suit; I can't find it.' I says, 'Paul, I've had it for twenty-odd years. A couple of more days won't hurt now, will it?'"

This is a private, never-before-heard scene from *A Hard Day's Night.* All I could think of saying was "You mean Paul McCartney?" I didn't; I just smiled and nodded, listened. I had my free swing with the Pete Best question. I was honored to be the one that first heard this story.

There were some more closets and crazy clothes. Then we came to a huge pirate's chest on the floor. It was right out of *Treasure*

Island. George got on the floor and opened it. It was filled with shoes. The ski boots from *Help!* were in there, the fuzzy Tibetan boots from the *Let It Be* era, everything. He was throwing them over his shoulders; it was raining shoes and boots. From the bottom of the chest, he pulled out an original pair of Beatles boots. They were battle-tested ones—worn out, worked in, not an extra pair.

"Here, take these," he said.

"Erm, okay, yeah, great."

"Wait. Give 'em back."

I handed them back. George produced a ballpoint pen, scribbled in them, and handed them back.

"Well, read it."

Inside one, he had written, "To Slim Jim from Fat George," and then signed his name.

In the other, he had done a perfect forgery of Ringo's signature. He told me they often signed each other's names. One of them would sign four signatures, and then it would be a different one's turn. A picture with all four different people having signed it could be rare. More inside stuff. He also said, "If you ever need money, sell them! It's just a pair of old boots."

I came home with a pair of silly boots and a few original buttons. What a night! It could have been just that, a great story and souvenir.

A few months later, the phone rang back in LA.

"Hello," I said.

"Is this Slim Jim from the Stray Cats?"

"Yes," I answered, slightly annoyed, thinking someone was playing a trick on me.

"This is George from the Beatles."

"Erm, yeah, cool, great. Hi, George!"

He was in town and called to have dinner. Britt and I met him with a few others at a restaurant and had a fun evening chatting away. This type of thing would happen every now and again over the next ten years. One time he was staying at the Bel-Air Hotel, and I went over to visit him, and we drove around in my 1961 Corvette smoking a joint. All the while not saying anything particularly heavy. I always walked away feeling like I had hung out with a pal, but then a few years later remembered something he said each time that was very wise and perhaps meant to teach me something in a nonaggressive way.

One memorable night was when Dave Edmunds played the Palace in Hollywood. Brian Setzer, Bob Dylan, Jeff Lynne, Duane Eddy, George, and I were all in the balcony watching. There is a perfect dressing room rock pic in existence of this night. Everyone is drinking a Corona and looks cool. It's not always important to have the hard proof, but in this case it's a good one.

The last time I saw George, we bumped into each other at a recording studio owned by Dave Stewart, where I was doing a session and he had an appointment. He came into the session and made it a point of saying hello to me. He picked up a guitar and strummed a little. We went outside and had a nice chat. When I went back into the session, I felt some pride and got a bit of "Wow, man, you *know* him?" from the other musicians and the engineer. "Oh, George, yeah, he's my buddy," I answered coolly. I was still feeling special. George did have that effect on people.

Then George got sick, and I didn't see him again. It's too sad, and everybody knows that story. I still get weepy if I think of it. After watching the excellent documentary *Living in the Material World*, I learned that it turns out George had a similar relationship with quite a few people all over the world. He would just call and made it seem like you were the only one he did this with. Finding this out made it even cooler to me, like being in an exclusive club where you didn't know who the other members were.

A few years ago, I went to a gig that my son, TJ, was playing drums on. He was in a band that was opening up for a band with George's son, Dhani Harrison. I watched proudly, as always, while my son nailed his gig. I stayed and watched Dhani. He sang and played great. I, of course, noticed his strong resemblance to his dad. Afterward, I told Dhani that I'm sure he hears it all the time, but his dad and I were pals in our own way. He said, "Yes, I heard him mention you." I introduced him to my son, and there's the circle.

10

Lemmy

A typical night off in London in 1981 would usually start with going to a gig. There always seemed to be a show, and I quickly got used to just walking straight in. The Nashville, Golden Lion, Fulham Greyhound, the Venue, Hope and Anchor, Hammersmith Palais, Hammersmith Odeon, Camden Palace, Dingwalls, the Lyceum, and the Marquee in Wardour Street were the main places. The Clash, the Pretenders, the Specials, Motörhead, and Madness are memorable ones. Someone you knew or wanted to know seemed to be playing every night.

We were admired and respected by all the bands in town. The Cats seemed to be the one band that everyone in tribal London could agree on. The fashion and music from the original American rock and rollers has never gone out of style, never will. A T-shirt, jeans, and motorcycle boots will always be the official uniform of cool. We were young enough to put a colorful new spin on it. The Cats had that basic look down and mixed it in with a lot of the current trends in London, creating our own style. It was embraced by all the trend-setters of the time. Since we were Americans and not bound by any official membership to a tribe, we could appeal to everybody. In the past, any attempt to revive the style and music from the '50s had come out looking corny, and I'm not sure if the musicianship was that great. No one had really nailed it. We didn't have a theory about this; we just instinctively knew it. We could all really play. The other two are natural virtuoso musicians; that was the bottom line. If you looked outrageous and did crazy things, it didn't matter if you couldn't back it up onstage and in the studio. If there was any doubt about the buzz going on around us, once anyone saw Brian play, all doubts quickly vanished. I could keep up and was doing something totally new on the drums. We also brought a few guaranteed hit songs and a louder, faster approach to rockabilly. It wasn't a rehashing of some old records. We had a very funny New York charm about us, and I ably and happily represented us on the nightclub scene. I liked and felt equal to all these musicians and characters.

After the gig, I'd usually meet Lemmy downstairs at the Embassy Club around midnight. I met Lemmy, the legendary founder of Motör-head, at one of the first Stray Cats shows, and we became fast friends. We liked all the same stuff and had a laugh right away. The Embassy, on Old Bond Street in Mayfair, was an oldie-worldie ballroom with a tragic faded-glory feeling around it. Miles of ornate, smelly carpet, thick Regency-print wallpaper, and chandeliers conjured up classic visions of 1930s prewar London. I once mentioned to a taxi driver that New Bond Street was still older than anything in my neighborhood in New York. He drove me around Piccadilly showing me all the stuff he thought I'd be into. London cabbies are an extraordinary breed. I've given them half the money I've ever earned in my life, and they've given me a deeper understanding of the city and a few shortcuts that few Americans know. They have a complete knowledge of the streets and charming personalities, and all claim to have once been teddy boys.

Everyone went to the Embassy. Rock royalty, punk rockers, drag queens, and Hooray Henry, country club types could all be seen drinking together at the downstairs bar. Drinks were pretty expensive. I never knew or thought about how anyone afforded anything, myself included. Like everything else at that time, it just seemed to happen. The place was owned and operated by Stephen Hayter, an openly gay, public school type who loved entertaining and the whole idea of celebrity. He let anyone he recognized stay after hours to continue partying. He was a bit over the top and flamboyant in a conservative kind of way. He dressed like a yuppie on his way to the golf course, but his speech and mannerisms were overtly gay. He was a character, and I liked him. I met Bowie on a quiet night there—Pete Townshend and Freddie Mercury, too.

Lemmy loved playing the slot machines. He was an expert and connoisseur. There were two at the Embassy. We'd stand side by side until after closing and pour fifty-pence coins into them. The bartender had an unlimited supply of little sealed plastic bags with ten pounds' worth of coins in each one. After each empty bag of coins and ten pounds I'd never get back, Lem and I would retire to the gents' to refuel. As I took out my bindle, Lem asked, "What's that?"

"Coke," I answered with a "What else?" tone.

"Coke is for chicks. Do this!"

I took a sniff of the crystalline powder off the tip of the buck knife he always carried on his belt. It felt like someone had shot an orange-flavored metal arrow up my nose and through the top of my head. I was frozen. I couldn't talk. I couldn't even blink. I made it back into the club on two frozen-stiff legs. Two regular-looking customers were at our machines, celebrating a big jackpot.

"Those guys got our money," Lem growled. "We can't leave the machines again!"

"What are we gonna do?" I was thinking more about all the beer I was drinking, not about the next bump. I was pretty sure that Lem's special brand would see me through the immediate future. I knew I'd have to pee way before the rush wore off. He wasn't going to lose another payout. He had a genius, tweaker-inspired, fully covert solution. He left the bag of speed open in the pocket of his leather jacket. He worked out a system where he could take his buck knife out of its sheath, snap it open, reach it into his pocket, give himself and then me a perfectly measured hit, snap it back closed, have it back in the sheath, and never break the rhythm of the pull on the one-armed bandit. It was beautiful to watch. Speed-freak ballet. Around three, we'd excuse ourselves from the club. Any girl that had come with me was long gone by now. The owner would disappear into his office with a few young men. I never wanted to see what went on in there.

Lem lived in a house in Battersea that he shared with a Hells Angel and a few other nefarious characters. There was a disassembled motorcycle in the living room, up on blocks with an oil pan underneath, and always a few passed-out bodies scattered around. It was an accidental living art installation. His room was in the basement. It was a concrete bunker with a gold record screwed to the wall with industrial bolts. All his clothes, belts, hats, and boots were strewn about with a haphazard flair and organization. Lem would dig around in a large cardboard box filled with cassettes. He always found exactly what he wanted. This time it was a live BBC show from Gene Vincent in the '60s that he had recorded by holding a microphone in front of the radio. I had never heard a few of the songs. He knew every detail about the players and the set list. We'd play a few games of chess in which he'd slaughter me in five moves. We'd have long talks about the impact of rock and roll on the culture, how it really did save our lives and gave us a chance to travel, mixed in with our shared love of the details, liner notes, and photographs from the original rock-and-roll artists.

At some point after sunrise, I'd have to split. I always found a black taxi on the main street, and with the help of an old teddy boy cabbie, I'd make it back to my place in Bayswater. The driver never complained about me paying with two handfuls of change.

11

A Few Stories with Keith

I had not become friendly with Keith like I had with Bill, but I have had a few memorable encounters with him that make for a good rock-and-roll story.

"The only thing we ever did, man, was sell your music back to you!"

Those were the first words I remember hearing Keith Richards say in person. It was perfect right away. The boozy, smoky English drawl I had heard on rock-and-roll interview shows was right on cue. We were sitting at a drinks- and ashtrays-filled table in the Venue, a nightclub in Victoria Station, London, in the later part of 1980. The Stray Cats had just played a scorching gig and had been whisked right offstage for an audience with the Stones. Mick, Ronnie, Charlie, and Keith were all there. They obviously loved the show. Before we even sat down, Keith stood up, knocking the chair over in an elegant way, and embraced Brian with genuine affection—must've been a guitar player thing. Everybody was all smiles.

We all sat for quite a while and yelled at each other in a noisy nightclub while paparazzi snapped away. I had paired off with Charlie, and we talked about our favorite jazz drummers. The whole scene was a bit of an unreality. The Rolling Stones had come and were all together at a club to see us play. That can't happen very often. We had met and hung out in the pubs and clubs with a few well-known people by then, mostly from other bands that were currently popular, but not of this level of legend and celebrity. They wouldn't have been in this joint if the Cats hadn't been playing. They had all come to see us. It was pretty flattering. We all sat around drinking and shouting about rockabilly music and how much the early Stones were influenced by American rock and roll.

They left when the other band started playing. The funny thing is that we were the opening act that night, and the headliner had the chance of swapping slots and would have had the Stones watch them before us, but they refused to switch and missed out. Too bad, guys, whoever you were—bad choice. That doesn't make for a good story thirty-five years later.

I heard afterward from people who really knew the Stones that it was the first time anyone could remember all those guys had been hanging out together, especially in a nightclub, in quite a while. I also heard that they were passing coke under the table during our set and that when I stood up on the bass drum, Charlie exclaimed, "Brilliant!" and dropped the vial. I gotta think they had more. We met with Mick at the Stones' office a few days later and talked about being on their label, and Brian went down to Redlands, Keith's infamous house, one time, but that was the last I saw of Keith until we did the shows on the 1981 Tattoo You tour. In the meantime, I had met Bill Wyman at a different Cats show in the South of France and become very friendly with him.

When we did the shows on the 1981 Stones tour, I didn't really see much of Keith. I think he was partying heavily on the part of the tour we were on. We had total all access and roamed about the backstage as we pleased. Like us, those guys didn't have any preshow ritual or band meeting; they just met by the stage stairs, walked up, and started the first number. I stood off to the side and watched them loosely gather, kind of say hello to each other, and then do the gig.

Before one of the shows, Keith was the last to arrive on the side and seemed in pretty rough shape. He was wearing an untucked white dress shirt over the same torn T-shirt, leopard jacket, and jeans from the last few days, half walking and half being dragged by Big Jim Callaghan. I thought he looked supercool but was a little worried he wasn't going to make it. The others didn't seem that concerned, and Bill gave me a little smile like he knew what I was thinking. All of this was happening at the bottom of the stage stairs while the intro music was blasting over the huge PA. The lights were down, the audience was going crazy, Mick was jumping up and down, running in place, Charlie was twirling his sticks, Bill was quietly dragging on a cigarette, and Ronnie was coolly pacing a little. They walked up the stairs, and Keith came up last, being helped and hanging on to the railing. As he hit the last stair and stumbled forward toward the stage, his roadie had his guitar waiting. In one motion, he walked under the strap, the roadie let go, Keith slammed into the opening riff of "Under My Thumb," and away they went. He was totally awake and in control as he stomped over to the drum riser and locked in with Charlie. It was truly a rock-and-roll transformation. Here was a cat that was completely comfortable on a stage. I watched the rest of the show from the side and then walked out into the audience for the last part of the set. I dug it; I'm a fan. It was a memorable Stones show with an extra peek behind the scenes.

In 1985, I was with Lee and Slick in New York City mixing the *Phantom, Rocker & Slick* record at Media Sound. We had recorded it at Capital Studios in LA in the previous weeks, and in typical, spendthrift rock star fashion, we had to go somewhere else to mix it. We might as well tack on a few plane tickets and two weeks' stay at the old haunt, Le Parker Méridien; just put it on the bill that you have to pay back, anyway. Earl Slick, longtime David Bowie guitarist and one of my best pals of all time, got a call from producer Steve Thompson to put the guitars on a duet he was doing with Mick and David. It was a cover version of the Martha Reeves and the Vandellas' Motown classic "Dancing in the Street" and had to be done quickly because it was to be put out in conjunction with the Live Aid charity concerts that were looming. Slick has a special talent where he comes in at the last minute, plays the right stuff, and saves a session that looks grim. He's done it a hundred times. As a result, we all got invited to Mick's birthday party at the Palladium on Fourteenth Street. It was a big bash. In keeping with the times, the three of us retired to the men's room for some extracurricular nasal activities. It was the 1980s, and there was nothing wrong or strange with three guys sneaking off into a stall in the gents'. I'm sure there were clubs where anything went, but we were there to do some coke. As we were crowded into the stall, passing an unfolded bindle back and forth, just a nose appeared over the side wall. It was Ronnie Wood.

"Aha!" he said. So he stepped around and joined an already

crowded stall; there was no one else in the bathroom. As we were all chatting and sniffing away, the door opened, and I heard a pair of boots clicking on the tile floor. I looked down under the stall and saw a pair of battered black suede pirate boots and knew right away who it was: it was Keith. We opened the door, and it became clear that we should all go out into the bathroom rather than trying to squeeze one more into the stall.

So we were all standing around the sink now. Slick had an eight-ball vial and was pouring out bumps onto that little spot between your thumb and forefinger that's formed when you make a fist. We were all talking, reminiscing a bit about when the Stones first saw the Cats, the gigs we were on, and how cool Gene Vincent was, when I impulsively suggested to Keith that he come into the studio while we were mixing and add a guitar on a song. We had a song called "My Mistake" that was perfect for that Keef, country rock, signature sound. I figured you cannot win if you do not play. It's the same reason the hottest chick in class has no date for the prom; everyone is afraid to ask. There was a split second of silence before he agreed. As I'm writing this, I'm wondering why I didn't ask Ronnie to play, too.

We went back into the club and had a few drinks. Keith's wife, Patti Hansen, was there; she was gorgeous and very cool. At some point during the night, I noticed that Keith and I were wearing identical black-and-white polka-dot scarves. I said something about trading, and before I knew it, I had his scarf on, and he had mine. We traded scarves; it seemed like a good idea in the moment and makes for a good story now, but at the time, Britt chided me because it was her designer silk scarf, and the one I got from Keith was cotton. I wore it on the album cover and still have it in one of my drawers.

We agreed to do the session over the next few days. We would be there for a week longer. Eric Gardner is important in this part, as he stayed in touch with Jane Rose, Keith's ultrahip, tough, New York gal manager. This was pre-cell-phone days, and I doubt Keith would have one even now. A few days later, we got a call in the daytime saying Keith would come in that night to do the track. Sure enough, he turned up that night with his longtime tech and famous roadie Alan Rogan. We had Jack Daniel's in the studio, and everyone loosened up before we got down to playing. Keith was the one holding that night. He carried a black bag. Rogan attended to tuning a white Fender guitar and Telecaster.

The session itself went along very nicely. The producers, Steve Thompson and Mike Barbiero, got along with everybody. As I thought, the song was right up Keith's alley. He picked it up very quickly, and we had multiple good takes in an hour or so. We spent the rest of the night talking, drinking, dipping into the doctor's bag, and listening to the rest of the album, which he seemed to like.

I had a leopard-skin jacket of my own, inspired by the one I had seen Keith wearing a few years before. It had velvet cuffs and collar, black silk lining, and my name embroidered in the inside pocket. A real custom piece of proper tailoring by bespoke rock-and-roll tailor Glenn Palmer. Glenn is a real artist, a Yorkshire man, straight out of Dickens. He trained in traditional tailoring in Savile Row in the 1960s and brought the legendary Kings Road clothing line Granny Takes a Trip to LA in the 1970s. He could make a suit for the Prince of Wales and then make a costume for a metal band. He makes stuff for me still today. He's the best there is at his game. Keith mentioned that he liked the jacket, and I insisted he take it as a token of my appreciation for doing the session. He, of course, hesitated, but I persisted. When he tried it on, the sleeves were too long, and there was no way he was going to take it. We had a fun rest of the night, and when he split, I knew I had just had a special night—and to prove it, I had a killer guitar track on a song that I wrote. I think Keith had a good time, too.

Lee and I started thinking about a cool way I could offer some type of payment. I didn't expect to get an invoice or a statement from the Musicians' Union, but wanted to do something to show we were thankful. I thought about my jacket and how he had liked it so much. The plan unfolded. We would get Glenn Palmer to make an identical leopard-skin jacket as a gift for Keith. A cool rock-and-roll gesture as payback and thank-you for a job well done. Glenn is a real artist, and things needed to be right. Jane Rose waited until Keith was asleep on the couch of her office and then measured his sleeve and neck size. She relayed the info to Eric Gardner, who relayed it to me; I gave it to Glen, and he started working on the jacket. He had it done in a couple of weeks. We shipped the jacket to the office and were told he received and dug it. A fitting end to a good story!

It was 1988 in Hollywood, and the Cats were making the *Blast Off* album at Ocean Way Recording on Sunset with Dave Edmunds. It was a good time, as the Cats were recording and touring; I think it may have been the time when everyone was getting along the best. We had proved ourselves, and now we were just working. Keith had just done his first solo album with his band the X-pensive Winos and was doing a tour around the USA. His excellent band included friends Steve Jordan and Ivan Neville and true pal Charley Drayton. The LA gig was at the Hollywood Palladium, a classic ballroom from the 1940s on Sunset Boulevard that had hosted all types of gigs and TV shows from the likes of *The Lawrence Welk Show* to riotous punk rock shows in the 1970s. The Stones had played there in the 1960s, and the Cats did an unheard-of three-night, sold-out stand at the Palladium as part of our first USA tour.

On the night of Keith's gig, Brian, Dave, and I took a break from the recording, walked across the street, and went to the show. We went into the raised balcony on the side and watched the show from there. I remember meeting Michael J. Fox and Woody Harrelson. Michael J. yelled at a female fan who interrupted him and asked for his autograph. They were both nice to me. Keith and his band were great; he always brings that loose tightness or tight looseness with him wherever he goes. They played a combination of songs from Keith's fine first solo album *Talk Is Cheap,* featuring super first track "Take It So Hard," some covers, including family favorite Eddie Cochran's "Somethin' Else" and a few Stones numbers. They did one of my all-time favorites, "Connection," and powerful versions of "Time Is on My Side" and "Gimme Shelter" with Sarah Dash trading lead vocals with Keith and really killing it. Charley and Steve switched back and forth between the drums and bass.

I really enjoyed the show and wanted to go backstage to say hello. Brian and Dave went back across the street to the studio. The Palladium is an old-timey venue, and there are a series of small dressing rooms behind the stage, real vaudeville style with round lightbulbs around the mirrors and small dressing tables. The headliner has a slightly bigger dressing room that has a small bathroom attached. The size of the room and the fact that it was Keith's first solo gig in LA meant that this tiny dressing room filled up real fast, and being Hollywood, everybody was somebody. It was really crowded and hard to get to the back of the room to say hello. I squirmed toward the back and squeezed myself into the mini bathroom for a badly needed pit stop after drinking a few pints out of plastic cups on the balcony during the gig. I'd zipped up and was starting to open the door back into the madness when I heard, "Everybody get the fuck out!"

There was a little murmuring and crowd whispering, and then again, "I mean it! Everybody get the fuck out! Jane, get 'em all out of here! I don't care who it is! *Out!*"

This was unmistakably Keith's voice. He'd just finished his show, had had it with the backstage moochers and scenesters who always made it back there, and had just thrown everyone out of his dressing room en masse. I heard the sounds of grumbling, shuffling of feet, fifty people complaining under their breaths all at once, and then the slamming of a door. Then nothing but silence. Everyone was gone. I understood his move, but I was in a tough spot; I was stuck in this little adjoining bathroom and had to get past him to get to the door that led out of there. I didn't want to be the last guy in this room who caught the "I told everyone to split" hell that was sure to follow.

So I was panicking a little, and I thought of Bill, who would have chuckled at my predicament. I eased the door open a crack and saw Keith sitting in a folding chair by himself in this now empty dressing room. To add to the scene, he was looking down, expertly playing with a big butterfly knife. I made my move, slowly opened the door, and eased myself out and headed toward the hallway door. Keith sensed the movement in the room and growled, "Who's that? I thought I told everybody to leave!"

"It's me—Slim Jim. Erm, hi, Keith. Great gig, man. I was just leaving, too," I answered meekly, remembering that although I had hung out with the guy in the past, it had been a couple of years since I've seen him last.

"Wait a minute. Where you going? Sit down," he said.

"I'm splitting. You just kicked everybody out; I thought you wanted to be alone," I responded.

"That's okay—you can stay. All those fuckers were making me crazy. Pull up a chair," he told me.

"Okay, cool!"

So I looked around the room that was filled with luggage, guitar cases, and an ironing board, found another folding chair, and saddled up next to Keith. We chatted away about the gig, how cool Eddie Cochran was, and our shared history with the Hollywood Palladium. TJ had just been born a few months before; I told him about that and asked about his wife and kids. All pretty normal stuff. During our talk, Keith had reached into one of bags on the dressing table and pulled out a nice, big pharmaceutical vial. My eyes were lighting up as he dumped out a healthy-sized pile onto the ironing board, flicked his big knife open, and carved out two thick lines, each the length of the ironing board. With no interruption, we chipped away at these long rails and talked for half an hour or so in backstage peace and quiet. The sounds of a rock show being torn down and packed up could be heard in the background. At some point, Jane Rose came and got him, we said our good-byes, he told me to say hello to the guys, and I made my way back across Sunset Boulevard to the studio with a fantastic story to tell the others.

In the past few years, there have been more encounters with Keith. I usually go to see the Stones when they play LA, and I manage to say hello. Rock shows in general are stricter, and the old all-access pass is rarer and not quite what it was in the past. I have a good memory from one of the shows in the 1990s of playing snooker with Keith and Ronnie before the show and seeing Guns N' Roses as the opening act. Another good show featured President Bill Clinton announcing the Stones at the Staples Center in downtown LA. I did turn up at that one with a regular general admission ticket, found the right few people, and wound up backstage talking mainly with Charlie Watts that night about how we drummers deal with blisters on our fingers. On the way back to the seats, I was stopped by and had a good conversation with Larry David. He's a fellow Long Islander and was a writer on the *Fridays* TV show that the Cats had gotten our big break on. We had apparently hung out back then. Sadly, I can't remember that one, but I'm sure it was funny.

Since the Steel Wheels tour, true pal Bernard Fowler has been a touring member of the Stones, and we always see him before the shows. Bernard is one of the best singers I've ever heard and was part of the very first legendary Cat Club Thursday night jam band. Bernard's rocking funk band NickelBag with another true pal, Stevie Salas, on guitar were doing a gig at the Viper Room a few years back, and I went along. The room was buzzing because Keith was there to see Bernard play. The place was really crowded, and he was surrounded in the booth by the stage. I didn't go over and was standing in the crowd. I got a tug on my sleeve, and it was Tony Russell, who has looked after Keith for a long time. He's a New York guy, so we get along fine. We crawled across the room, and I slipped into the already packed booth next to Keith.

"Hey, man. Why didn't you come over and say hello?" he asked over the crowd noise.

"Sorry, Keith, it's really crowded; you looked busy, and I didn't want to bug you," I answered.

He gave me a "yeah, okay, that's cool" kind of nod, and we watched Bernard's show from the booth. He left during the last number, and we said good night.

Not too long ago, I was in Las Vegas doing a gig at the Hard Rock Hotel. It might be cheesy, but I like to look at all the memorabilia from rock and rollers. I still get off on seeing all the guitars, clothes, gold records, and assorted stuff on display there. One of the glass cases on the floor had a Keith Richards display. In it was a White Falcon Gretsch guitar and a leopard-skin jacket with a brass name-plate at the bottom. It was the same jacket that we had made for him in 1985; I would know it anywhere. I don't know any of the details of how it got there, and I don't really care to; I think it's cool that this jacket is there for all to see. At the end of the day, I'm still a fan of the coolest guy in rock and roll, and I'm happy to have a connection. There aren't too many guys who are top-notch songwriters and have a look that anyone would want to emulate. This display case at the Hard Rock has both sides of that equation. It doesn't say where the jacket came from, who made it for him and why, or any other info about it. It even looks really cool on the mannequin. A fitting end, indeed.

12

Don't Worry About It, Son

The Cats were on the bill for a tribute concert to Les Paul being filmed at the Brooklyn Academy of Music. It was 1988. The guests included the one and only bluesman B.B. King; country music legend Waylon Jennings and his wife, Miss Jessi Colter; superstar, British gentleman, guitarist Pink Floyd's Dave Gilmour; songbird, old pal, and neighbor Rita Coolidge; guitar whiz Stanley Jordan; FM radio king, hit maker, and Cats fan Steve Miller; pop royalty Carly Simon; Les's legendary trio, drummer buddy Rick Marotta, leader of the house band, keyboardist, and composer Jan Hammer, and Les Paul Trio guitarist Lou Pallo; and party pal extraordinaire, guitar hero Edward Van Halen.

The good thing for story-gathering purposes about this show, like the Carl Perkins special, was that we rehearsed it for two days beforehand and all hung out a lot at the gig in shared dressing rooms.

We stayed at the Ritz-Carlton on Central Park South and drove to Brooklyn for the day and back to the city at night. Someone had the room next to Eddie's; we left the doors open between the suites and had a three-day party. The guys all had acoustic guitars, and it was a rare treat to watch Eddie and Brian play together. Lee, who is also an excellent guitar player, impressed Eddie with his ability to finger-pick Chet Atkins–style. It was another one of those times when I was proud of my guys and happy to be the party organizer.

The daytimes were spent in typical hurry-up-and-wait TV show fashion. There were a few dressing rooms below the stage where everyone hung out, swapped stories, and drank a little. Van Halen and I probably hit it a little bit harder than the others. The other Cats were party guys, but not like I was; I would drink in the daytime. I would especially go for it on a gig like this, where we only had to do a song or two. It wasn't a whole gig, and it was a very social setting, and though I tried not to get wasted before the show, I would try to keep a little glow going. I still looked at cats like Waylon Jennings as my elders and didn't imagine them partying too much. Again, my naïveté of the time is revealed in the light of modern day where we find out that those outlaw country guys partied more than anyone. They never said they didn't, but the substance use and struggles of Nashville-based country music artists didn't get as much media attention as someone like Keith Richards getting busted did. When it did, it was portrayed in a more sympathetic, everyman, blue-collar way. The general American public wanted to think that the country artists were different from the rock and rollers and didn't want to believe that all musicians, regardless of genre, behave more or less in the same way. It's all showbiz. I've since learned that the cast of the Grand Ole Opry had as much sex, drugs, and rock and roll as

Led Zeppelin, the main difference being the volume of the drums on the records.

Les Paul is one of the unifying cats. Everyone can agree that without his invention of the electric guitar, the whole music business and the evolution of rock and roll would've turned out very differently. He was a mad scientist with electronics and also helped revolutionize the recording process with his improvements and use of multi-tracking on tape. I'm not a guitar player or recording engineer, so I don't know the lingo or science of it, but I know that our entire game would not have turned out the same without Les Paul and his tireless quest for innovation.

I developed a connection with him, and I would get a call every few years to be the drummer on some event he was doing. I first met Les Paul when the Cats were the backing band on a big tribute to him in 1989. Again, it was a case of me just being open and honest with the guy, asking all the questions and being willing to sit for the in-depth answers.

A few years after this one, I got the call to be the drummer on a similar documentary about Les for *The History of Rock 'n' Roll* TV series. That one was filmed at the House of Blues on Sunset Boulevard and featured another cavalcade of guitar heroes, including fellow Long Islander and buddy Steve Vai, the Stray Cats' producer, longtime friend, and collaborator Dave Edmunds, good buddy and true rock star Slash, legendary singer/guitar player and former occasional party bud Stephen Stills, and true pal and my big brother Jeffrey "Skunk" Baxter. Jeffrey played bass on that show, and we were the rhythm section for these amazing players. We rehearsed all day and played all night for the part of the documentary featuring the electric guitar and Les's contribution. True pal Jerry Schilling was one of the producers of the series. This was a special night, and a small clip was included in the TV show, but the whole gig must exist somewhere on film. I remember an incident from this day where I had to get really tough with a waiter at the House of Blues when he wouldn't bring Les a bowl of soup. He needed the soup to take along with his medicine. There was no one else around to help him, and the waiter was being that awful type of restaurant stickler regarding the times for a certain item on the menu to be served. If I was able to get tough with him, he must have been a wimp, anyway. I told this waiter that this was the inventor of the electric guitar, that none of us would have a job without him, and the old boy needed a bowl of goddamned soup right away to take his medicine or there would be no show that night. This old guy might pass out if he didn't take his medicine, and if that happened, I was going to break the bowl over his head. The waiter brought the soup. This was somewhere between 1995 and 1996; sometimes these things come out a little while after they were filmed. After the gig, I tend to forget about them until I'm shown the end result, sometimes years later. Either way, I was definitely sober by then, but I enjoyed a good time and photo ops just the same.

I've never failed to have a good time at something like this. In last twenty-five years, I haven't let sobriety get in the way of a fun time or story. I loved to drink and do the occasional powder, but the older I've gotten, the happier I am to have quit partying when I did. It's hard, like anything else, in the beginning, but once you get the hang of the whole thing, it becomes your new reality and does make life much easier. If anything, I've learned to appreciate the moment and enjoy more the position of being viewed as an equal among all these cats whom I respect and admire. Maybe I used the booze to hide behind. It's possible; there is psychology to everything. I do know that I just plain loved it while it worked. When you're in your twenties and look a little tipsy in a photo, it's cool and cute in a rock-and-roll way. If you're blasted in a backstage photo in your forties or fifties, it's just plain sad. That goes double for any hard drugs. A rock-and-roll guy past the age of thirty who's obviously wired or nodding off is one of the saddest of all sights. That "rock till you drop" part of rock and roll is a young man's game. I've yet to meet anyone, not even the most legendary partyers, some of whom I've been privileged enough to hang with, who can carry on that way forever. It catches up to everyone. At some point, you must adjust. Look at any of the classic rock-and-roll guys and gals that are still doing quality work, and I think you'll see that no one can keep up the old pace of partying and still turn in good performances and records. The recovery time is longer and harder. Some do it better than others, and some are better at maintaining a certain image, but no one can keep up the old pace and carry on unaffected. I've done the personal research and tried every way and combination, but in the end, it was easier to bow out and keep my wits about me. Fortunately, for posterity, I've gathered a good thick mental journal of party remembrances with some of the greats and can remember enough to entertain the troops. Lucky me; a bunch of cats and a few true pals didn't make it far enough to figure this out.

Back at the Brooklyn Academy of Music, there was the usual chaos of filming a show, and everyone was hanging out in the dressing room waiting to be called to the stage for their numbers. I was making small talk with B.B. King. The man was a living Buddha. He really does bring that larger-than-life aura wherever he goes. In both a physical and cerebral way, he is truly a big man. He really is that guy, the living embodiment of the American blues.

He was very friendly. We were chatting away, and he was happily telling me stories of touring in a converted school bus in the 1950s and knowing Elvis in Memphis. There was a graceful motion to his gestures and way of speaking. Everything he said sounded like there was a life-learned, firsthand wisdom attached to it.

I asked him where he lived these days. "I live in Las Vegas, son." He answered in a polite way, but like it was a question with an obvious answer. Where else would B.B. King live? It made complete sense. I understood when he said it.

Since we were all sharing the digs, everyone had clothes on racks and suitcases in the dressing room. There was a flight case with B.B. KING stenciled on it, with his wardrobe inside. It was open, and I of course looked in. He had ten matching safari-style suits on hangers. They looked like 1970s barber suits with big hip pockets. He had one in peach, one in baby blue, one in lime green, one in white, one in lavender, and so on. He had five pairs of highly shined black patent leather shoes in a rack at the bottom of the case. It was perfect, exactly what you'd expect and want to see in B.B. King's wardrobe case.

I wandered over to the girls' dressing room to say hello to Rita Coolidge. Rita is a super-talented country pop songbird. She was in Delaney & Bonnie's legendary band, was married to Kris Kristofferson in the 1970s and 1980s, and had some hits on her own. She was close with Les, too. We had been friends for a few years, as she was our neighbor in Birdland, up on the hill above Sunset. Her then boyfriend and drummer, Tom Mooney, was my buddy, and we all hung out a lot. I'd go over in the afternoons. We'd smoke a joint, drink a beer, listen to records, and watch TV. Rita had been around many of the historic moments of rock-and-roll history. She introduced me to Miss Jessi Colter, who was Waylon Jennings's wife. Waylon is an imposing dude. He was in Buddy Holly's band on the night of the fateful plane crash and was the balladeer on the *Dukes of Hazzard*'s theme song, "Good Ol' Boys." I was a fan. Miss Jessi was a very cool woman who looked, acted, and dressed the part of the classic country singer gal. Of course, the other Cats busted my balls and said she was flirting with me and kept threatening to tell Waylon that I was trying to make time with his wife. It was a typical example of intra–Stray Cats band practical joking. During one rehearsal, Waylon and Miss Jessi were walking in front of us from the dressing rooms to the stage, and we all did the classic "Hello Cleveland" thing where you get lost on the way to the stage. We just followed them, so we're all lost together. Waylon kept yelling, "Left! Left! Left!" and after a few more wrong turns, we were still lost. He looked over at us and said gruffly in an apologetic way, "She don't do lefts."

He asked Miss Jessi which way to go, and she answered that she didn't know. When we all accidentally found the stage and were waiting at the bottom of the steps to go up, Waylon motioned toward his wife and said loud enough for us all to hear, "Goddamn it, woman! I done the drugs, and she got the brain damage!"

She shrugged and smiled, then we all smiled. I got the feeling that this was how they were with each other and it wasn't a mean-spirited thing. We walked up behind them and watched their number with Les from the side of the stage. I think we did a song with Les and then served as the backing band for the big finale, which was a version of "Blue Suede Shoes." We played the song, and one by one Brian called the guests, and they came up and started playing until it was one giant guitar solo. It's always struck me that the world's twenty best musicians sound an awful lot like the world's twenty worst musicians when they play at the same time. Sometimes the version of the show that is on the official release is not exactly what you did on the day; there were also two days of rehearsals that weren't filmed and aren't on the existing tape. There are usually a few things that for time purposes don't make the final cut, and maybe the sequence is a little different, but this encore section was a one-off.

During the day of filming, there was the usual hectic atmosphere around the theater. More people, more cameras, the press, personal guests, and the live audience all lent to the excitement of the show day. The show was running smoothly enough. I decided to use the gents' one last time before the encore section, where I tried to provide the backbeat to a bunch of the world's best guitarists, who were all plugged in at various volumes, with my usual, simple drum kit.

I was at the urinal thinking about the gig and staring straight ahead. B.B. King was standing behind me, in front of mirror at the sink, using an Afro pick on his hair, humming to himself.

"Stray Cats to the stage!" comes over the little squawk box speakers in the bathroom. I was startled; I hurriedly finished up and zipped up. I went to the sink to wash up and give my hair a final check when I saw the stain on my pants.

"Goddamn it, look at this!" I said in an overtly upset way. "What am I going to do?" I asked myself out loud.

"Stray Cats to the stage!" came over the speakers again, echoing a little off the tiles.

Now I was in a slight panic. "Can you believe this?" I asked to the almost empty room.

I now noticed the serene B.B. King watching me in the mirror.

"Don't worry about it, son. It lets the people know you're human," he offered me in a completely calm and matter-of-fact way.

It was maybe the wisest and truest thing I'd ever heard.

I thought about it for two seconds, nodded to him, and said, "Thanks." I went out and did my thing. B.B. was the second guitar player to join in the jam after Eddie. His single-note style and clean, piercing sound is, of course, immediately recognizable and unmistakable.

Every man alive has had a similar experience. It's happened to me many times since, but thanks to the sage words of an American treasure, I can honestly say that it has never upset me again.

13

Bird

I had a short-lived career as a movie star. As has been my good fortune, I worked with the best. I must be the only guy to have ever done one movie where my scenes were acted with and directed by Oscar winners. Any movie buffs and trivia maniacs out there are welcome to try to correct me on this one. Looking back, I see it might have been a thing to capitalize on, but I've never been good at that. In this circumstance, I went out on top.

Britt was about eight months pregnant with TJ, and all was pretty normal around Doheny Drive. We were somehow paying the bills and living the continued life of relative luxury in a hand-to-mouth fashion. I don't think I had a manager at the time, but somehow a call came in from the last agent that the Stray Cats had worked with. I was told it was an audition for an acting role. I had never done anything like this before, but having been on a hundred shoots with Britt, I was familiar with movie sets and the general setup—though not the actual job of acting. I went to some outer office in a trailer on one of the movie lots—maybe Universal? I had been faxed a few pages of dialogue and practiced it with her a few times. I didn't take the whole thing too seriously. Everyone said to go do it, so I did. The casting people must've liked it, because I got a message with call times and a location for the next week.

The role called for me to play a 1940s-era drummer, lip-synch a song to a playback, and then deliver some hipster banter back and forth with the sax player—all of this while pretending to cut a track in a recording studio. The film was called *Bird*. It was a biopic about Charlie Parker, whose music I knew and loved. I'd be playing his drummer and part-time pal. No problem; I could handle this. Lost on me for the moment was the fact that the sax player was Forest Whitaker and the director was Clint Eastwood.

The day came, and I made my way to the location. It was in a recording studio called Electro-Vox Studios on Melrose near Gower, across the street from the Paramount movie lot, a little mom-and-pop storefront right out of old Hollywood that I'd driven past a thousand times but had never noticed. It turned out to be the oldest privately operating recording studio in the world. It opened in 1936 and had hosted old-time radio shows and countless sessions for film scores and records. Nat King Cole and the real Charlie Parker had recorded there. It didn't seem like it had been operating lately. It was 1987, and the retro technology trend in the recording industry hadn't happened yet. It was just a plain-old dusty studio with old gear, not quite vintage yet. I'm surprised that the Stray Cats had never recorded there, because we used to seek out those old studios. At this time, the place was really under the radar; whoever did the research and scouted the location did a really nice job.

There was a lot of activity around this little one-story nondescript brick building. Trailers and equipment trucks were parked all around the surrounding side streets, and there were people milling about in front. A typical location movie shoot, that if you live in LA, you drive past every day without ever really knowing what's going on behind the scenes. I was met by a slightly frantic, clipboard-armed assistant and led to one of the trailers that was being used for makeup and wardrobe. My outfit consisted of pleated baggy pants, an argyle sweater vest, and a tie, and I had my hair slicked back, a bit more square looking than normal. I brought my own pointy shoes. A more or less classic, conservative rockabilly-style look that I could pull off and feel comfortable in.

I had become very nervous about doing the acting part of this job. It hit me all at once that I'd never done this before. I was never particularly nervous about going onstage; I'd done that a million times and always had at least another musician there to lean on. This was a first, and I started thinking that I'd gotten myself into something I couldn't do. All of it was mitigated by the fact that with this one job, I could join the Screen Actors Guild, and the pay was enough to activate the health insurance that the guild offered. Back then, it was regarded as the world's best health insurance, and it was a real coup to get it. It also meant that between Britt's insurance with the same union and my new membership, TJ's birth would be covered by our combined insurance. So the bottom line was that I had to get through this.

I had been assigned my own trailer, which helped fuel the whole loneliness aspect of the moment. The scene called for an entire orchestra with strings, and there were dozens of musicians sharing smaller trailers and being ushered back and forth from the makeup trailer to the set, which was around the corner. I would have preferred some company to take my mind off the full-blown fear that I had now developed. Anyone driving past would have seen a whole bunch of people dressed in 1940s clothes, carrying violins. I had successfully gotten dressed and was sitting in my trailer, staring at my faxed script, pacing the tiny trailer and repeating the lines in my head over and over again. There was a knock on the trailer door, and I said, "C'mon in."

It was Forest Whitaker, holding a saxophone, looking really cool, dressed in an old suit and looking like the spitting image of Charlie Parker. He had the whole hepcat vibe down pat. It seemed very natural on him. I recognized him from *Fast Times at Ridgemont High*—it's one of my favorite films of all time; it launched ten movie stars, and he convincingly played a tough, no-nonsense, slightly scary football player. He knew the Stray Cats from MTV and the radio. He said he listened to the record after he found out it would be me in the scene with him. He's a good guy, and I could tell right away that he was trying to put me at ease. He didn't display any doubt in my ability to pull this off.

We were both standing together in this little trailer dressed up like 1940s hipster musicians, about to film a scene directed by Clint Eastwood. I was nervous about it; he was not. He's a professional actor; I'm not. He would be miming on the saxophone, pretending to play; he had studied old film and learned how to move his fingers perfectly in sync with the original Parker recordings. We sat and talked a while, and I was feeling good about it. I told him I had rehearsed the lines a million times, and I asked him if he wanted to practice the script with me. He told me not to worry.

"Let's save it for the take, man," he said.

"Okay, man," I answered. I could relate to that. I still wanted to run the lines, but I didn't let on. Then he said the last thing on earth I would have imagined he was going to say.

"You wanna smoke a joint?" he asked.

I thought about it for maybe two seconds. The practical side of my brain lost very quickly. Out of habit, I simply answered, "Sure, man. What do you got?"

Forest produced a joint from his pack of Camels unfiltered coffin nails. I figured he was smoking them to help get in character. It was super old-timey and a very jazz cat thing to smoke them. So we sat in my little trailer chatting while we puffed away on a joint. There must have been a lot of smoke pouring out of the cracks of the window and door, and the surrounding area must've really smelled like weed, but we didn't think about it, and no one said anything. After all, we were making a movie about jazz musicians, and this was getting us in the authentic mood. Afterward, Forest excused himself and left to go to the set.

"See you out there, man."

"Yeah, cool," I replied.

The second he left, I knew I had made a mistake. I immediately couldn't remember my own name, let alone even one of the lines. I was overwhelmed by that pot-smoking paranoia I had heard about but had never really experienced myself. I was a regular weed smoker but wouldn't have chosen that exact moment to blaze up. It was a situation that maybe called for a nerve-settling shot of booze, but not a joint. Anyhow, now I was stoned, quietly panicking, and more than slightly regretting the whole thing when there was another knock at the door. This time, it was the production assistant coming to walk me around the corner to the recording studio set.

Now, it was the middle of the day in LA, so when we entered the front door to the studio, I was hit by the film-lit set and the hundred people crammed into this tiny room. It's a controlled bedlam like a rock show or video shoot, but in those cases, I have a little experience. This place was ancient, perfectly preserved by accident, not design. I dug the place and made a note to come back someday and poke around to look at the old gear. Linoleum covered the floors, and that old-fashioned heavy pegboard covered the walls. There were camera people, sound people, various headphone-wearing film crew, and twenty-five musicians all sitting in chairs with sheet music on stands in front of them. The film company must've used the Local 47 Musicians Union of Hollywood to cast the orchestra extras. These were real old-school session musicians, all dressed up in period suits waiting to be told what to do. Forest was standing in the middle and winked when he saw me come in. There was an ocean of wires and cables to step over on the floor. I was led to a drum kit that was my oasis. I sat down behind the drums and right away felt better, more in control of the situation.

The place was buzzing, everyone talking at once, the musicians plucking on their violins when I saw the flash of light from outside, and the door to the street was opened again. The place got real quiet like when the fastest gun in the west walks into the saloon. It was Clint Eastwood. He is quite tall and lean and definitely had a commanding presence. Most people agree that by 1987, Clint had been the coolest guy in the world for at least ten years already. Everybody knew him and had seen his movies. I've always been a fan and knew all the Sergio Leone movies inside out. I had watched *Rawhide* on reruns after school. Clint was wearing jeans, sneakers, and a sweatshirt but was every bit as intimidating as if he were in a military uniform or western gear. He stopped and talked to most of the technicians. It took a few minutes for him to make his way over to Forest to discuss the scene. I just sat behind the drums waiting for something to happen. As I understood it, there would be a playback of the classic Charlie Parker recording of "Laura," and we would play along to the track. We had done dozens of playback TV shows with the Cats, so I knew how to seem cool while making it look like I was actually playing the song. Then I would start tearing down the drum kit like I would at a real session while doing my lines with Forest. It was conversation about the song we just played and about his wife. So I had the length of the song to run over the lines in my head. The trick was to wait until the music faded before starting to talk. I was even more relaxed when I realized that tearing the drums down, unscrewing the wing nuts off the tops of the cymbals stands, gave me something to do that I felt comfortable doing, and the lines came out more like conversation with another musician than a movie script.

We rehearsed the track a few times. It's a pretty long song, and they played the whole thing on every take. A couple of times, the scene was stopped before the song ended when Clint called "Cut" and a light was adjusted or a microphone moved. After a few more rehearsals, Clint told the musicians to take five but not go far while the crew moved the camera to set up for a different angle. This time, we'd go through the whole thing and do the dialogue between Forest and me after the song stopped playing. I was standing off to the side while they were moving the lights behind the drum kit. An assistant director bumped into me; I was in the way, and he was asking me to move.

"Hey, kid, can you stand over here while we're moving this stuff? What's your name again, kid?" the assistant director asked in a polite but impatient tone.

Clint saw and heard this and moseyed on over. Mind you, I hadn't spoken one word to the man yet.

"Don't you know who that is?" he said to the assistant director in his best menacing but still friendly, soft-spoken strong whisper. "That's Slim Jim."

"Thanks, Mr. Eastwood," I half stammered in a thankful voice.

"Call me Clint," he responded in that same tone, looking at me with the famous half-squinting eyes and extending a big friendly paw.

"Thanks, Clint," I answered more confidently, and I took his hand. I was now buddies with Clint Eastwood.

I was pretty confident that I could do the scene. Clint hadn't stopped me during any of the rehearsals, so I figured I was doing okay. I tried to do it the same way every time. I'd nail it when it's time to do it for real.

"Here we go," said Clint. "Let's go for a take. Action!"

The playback came on the big speakers, and we made a convincing performance of recording "Laura." The violinists were drawing their bows across the strings enough to make it look real but not loud enough to drown out the playback. Forest was moving his fingers up and down the sax, seemingly hitting all the right notes and puffing out his cheeks in all the right places where Parker would've drawn a breath, and I was playing along with brushes. It all must have looked good in the camera, because we just kept going until the end of the song. We hit the last note and let it fade. I started my dialogue with Forest. I was into the third line, and I must have been doing well because no one was stopping me. Then a squeaky voice croaked, "Cut, cut, cut."

It was not Clint's voice, and any fool knows that only the director can call "action" or "cut." The call came from a little guy playing the fiddle in the front row of violinists. He looked like Larry from *The Three Stooges* with glasses. He was tapping his bow on the music stand while calling, "Cut!" Everyone was flabbergasted. This had to be uncharted waters for a professional crew that worked with this director all the time. I was stunned and just plain mad, because he interrupted my take, and I might not get it right again. Clint walked over to him and bent over just a little to make the point.

"Yes, what is it?" he asked softly but firmly.

"Well, Clint—you don't mind if I call you Clint, do you?"

"No, go ahead," Clint answered with his steely, flinty voice.

"Okay, Clint, this sheet music says the song is in the key of G when clearly upon listening it is in the key of G flat—do you understand? The score is wrong; the music doesn't coincide," the fiddle player whined. I was waiting for him to say, "Oy vey."

"It doesn't matter; the music is prerecorded—no one will hear what you're doing here. We're just trying to make it look like we are recording the song. It's okay. Don't worry about it; just make it seem like you're really playing," Clint answered the annoying character, really keeping his cool in a measured response.

"Okay, okay. Action, everybody," the violinist answered back.

Clint ignored this one and turned to the rest of us and the crew and called for playback and action. We got through the song again, and it was time for the dialogue between Forest and me. I began, and it was going well for a few lines, and then it happened again—that now all-too-familiar sound of the violin bow tapping on the music stand accompanied by the whiny call to cut from an unwanted source. It was the same guy doing the same thing. This was shocking, and a few of the crew members started walking in toward the guy like they were about to throw him out. Clint coolly stepped in.

"What is it now?" he half hissed.

"Well, Clint, I'm looking down, and I notice that the wardrobe people gave me brown shoes." He pointed with his bow toward his shoes.

"Yes, so what?" Clint responded quietly.

"Well, I'm wearing blue trousers, and we all know that you can't wear brown shoes with blue trousers." He said this like it was a punch line in a Woody Allen sketch.

I don't think I was the only person in this room who was expecting Clint to pull out a .44 Magnum and blow this fiddler's head all over the incorrect sheet music. I would've done it if I had had a gun.

"Don't worry about it; the camera isn't going to a full-length shot on you. When it goes over the string section, I'm in a half-length shot, so your shoes don't come into the picture." Clint explained this all in a very professional, measured, calm sotto voce. No one could believe how cool he was. Then he leaned over, almost whispering in the guy's ear, "Don't do it again." There it was: Dirty Harry came out. It was perfect. He became Harry Callahan when he needed to. The little fiddle player was scared out of his wits, and everyone in the room felt a little fear. Clint called for playback and action, and I nailed my lines with Forest a few times in a row without incident. No way was I going to mess up after that. Clint called a wrap.

The crew got busy very fast in breaking down and loading up the massive amount of equipment onto the trucks parked out front on Melrose. I'm sure Electro-Vox Studios was empty and back to its faded glory within an hour or so. The musicians packed their instruments in their cases and left. I didn't see where the annoying fiddle player went. He probably went home to annoy his wife at dinner. I talked a bit to some of the crew and headed out. I looked back in the room, and Clint noticed I was leaving.

"Take it easy, Slim Jim; you did good," Clint said with a wry smile.

"Thanks, Mr.—um, er, Clint!"

There was another scene in a bar in downtown LA that we shot a few days later. That day was unmemorable. I was an old pro by then. That was that—my first, last, and only appearance in a major Hollywood motion picture. The film came out the next year to great critical acclaim. Forest Whitaker was amazing, and he would go on to win his Oscar a few years later. We stayed friendly for a while. He had a loft in Chinatown before it was trendy to move to that part of town. He's a cool guy, and I go to his movies whenever he does a new one. I've learned that Clint really loves all music and jazz in particular. It shows in *Bird*. I could tell he knew about and dug Charlie Parker's music. I'm thrilled that my one IMDb credit is acting in a scene with and being directed by these very talented Academy Award–winning cats. TJ was born courtesy of SAG insurance, and I've kept my dues current; I'm still a card-carrying member. *Bird* is shown on cable, and I get a check for forty-seven dollars once in a while. I think I was pretty good for a first timer. I'm ready for my close-up now, Mr. Eastwood.

14

A Quick Flight with John Lee Hooker

We were in San Francisco. Britt was doing the morning city show, and I had tagged along for the night and went to the taping. I left back for LA after the show, and she stayed for another afternoon show. I think she was promoting a book. We did these kinds of little trips a lot. Any time she had an appearance, we'd ask for two tickets and make a mini vacation out of it. Those promo people gave good hotel, and if I was off the road, why not? I'd always liked San Fran. We would walk around and go to the art galleries, eat somewhere nice with some drinks, maybe see a gig, sometimes just go to the hotel. San Fran and Vegas are fun overnight trips when you're in LA. Paris from London is a good one. We used to go all the time.

So I was on the morning flight back home carrying a painting we had bought, and there was a long holdup getting on the plane. I was a little hungover, not so bad after an airport beer. As I stepped onto the plane and walked toward the first row of seats, a cane blocked my way. The cane was attached to a hand with rings and a gold watch, attached to an arm in a ruffled-sleeve shirt, attached to an orange suit, and inside this fantastic outfit was sitting John Lee Hooker. I had originally been really into the blues, and I admired John Lee as one of the legends. You don't often get a chance to meet one of those cats, so any chance encounter is cool. He wore his signature big hat and sunglasses, patent leather shoes, and neon socks. He looked exactly how he was supposed to. The whole ensemble was complemented by a wildly patterned wide tie and gold chain around his neck. As I was taking in this scene and wondering why he was blocking my path with his cane, the whole planeload of people being held up behind me was starting to get impatient and grumble. While I was trying to figure it all out, I couldn't help but notice a huge gravy stain right smack in the middle of his tie. He finally spoke, like a Buddha:

"Yoo da boy marry-ed to da movie stah?"

"Excuse me?"

"R yoo da boy marry-ed to dat moovie stah?"

There is always a little panic that happens to everyone with a conscience when you know that you're holding up an interior airplane line. *Think, man, think.* I was blanking out and didn't want to make an old cat repeat himself again, especially since on the last one, he was almost yelling. It hit me—he was asking if I was the boy who was married to the movie star. He must've seen the morning show while he was getting ready to leave his hotel and saw Britt's interview, and now he was recognizing me on the plane.

"Yes, sir, that's me," I said, trying to be cool but sounding as if Wally Cleaver were from Long Island.

"You play, son?"

"Drummer."

He smiled, flashing a gold tooth, and he jabbed his minder with his other hand. His man reached into a bag and handed me a yellow John Lee Hooker T-shirt. John Lee produced a Sharpie pen and wrote his name in a childlike scrawl across the front under his picture and handed it to me. He finally lifted his cane like it was a tollbooth, and I passed. I flew home, and that was that. Pretty cool story to tell the others: I met John Lee Hooker on the airplane, and he gave me a T-shirt.

That night, everyone was home, and it was a regular night. I was watching the ten o'clock news, and the local anchorman presented a piece about the first night of the Playboy Jazz Festival, opening that night at the Hollywood Bowl. There was my new pal John Lee Hooker onstage sitting in a chair playing the blues in his unique, real McCoy style. "This is so cool; I just saw this guy on the plane today!"

As the newsman talked over and John Lee was belting it out, the camera panned in on him for a close-up, and there it was—that big old gravy stain on his tie, coming in loud and clear. Now, that is a real bluesman.

15

Live from the Sunset Strip

We opened the Cat Club at 8911 Sunset Boulevard in June of 1999 and were open every night with few exceptions for the next fourteen years. There were five bands a night, seven nights a week, rain or shine. It can never be said that I have not done my part to keep live music alive in LA. As is true with most clubs, the path to how certain players all come together as partners on a team is unorthodox. The Cat Club was no exception; certain factors lined up, and it just shook out with these guys. Everyone involved came from the nightclub business, had experience, and came together on this deal. I had three partners: Steve Scarduzio, who knew the nightclub business—I had worked with him in the past when we had a club together on Hollywood Boulevard in the 1990s; Sean Tuttle, who had the original lease and is the grandson of Mario Maglieri; and David Klass, the South African jeweler who was a popular club promoter in the 1980s and 1990s. The address, liquor license, and start-up money are all factors in how these places happen. We all got along well enough and had varying percentages of ownership and different responsibilities. I was the face of the place. Steve did most of the clerical, day-to-day juggling of bills and running of the place. I'll always be thankful to him for keeping the boat afloat, especially while I was away on tours.

There were a lot of legendary nights and good times at the Cat Club, but like everything else in my life, it was slightly more diffi-cult than it appeared, and it was definitely more famous than rich. In the bar business, the owner is the last one to be paid, and you're way down at the bottom of the list. The real winner is the landlord; he's guaranteed to be paid every month. The bar owner managed to attach a liquor license to his property, which is no easy deed, espe-cially in West Hollywood on Sunset Boulevard, and it's usually a low-maintenance property. The vendors who sell the beer and booze need to be paid, or they stop delivery. A bar with no booze is about as useful as an unloaded gun. The bartenders and waitresses need to be paid, or the booze goes unserved. The list goes on. The electric company is an important one—air-conditioning bills and the juice to power the amps and PA are big in a rock club.

The maintaining of the gear is also an important cost, because if the general word around is that the club has crappy gear, it makes it more of an uphill battle with the bands. In this case, we were lucky in that I got most everything on endorsements. The drums, amps, microphones, and sound system were put in by the equipment com-panies who thought it was good advertising for their gear, and the sales reps liked that they could also come and be taken care of at the bar when they were in town. It's a fact: everybody likes being involved in a bar. I've never met a regular guy who didn't like being recognized and treated well at a bar. There's something that every guy likes about being able to walk into a bar and have his order be on the house. The truth is that a drink costs a bar fifty cents, but it can buy a lot more in goodwill.

These mundane parts of operating a rock club still need to be taken care of and maintained; it's another constant expense and headache, but someone has to stay on top of it. The hardest part of the whole thing was the California State Board of Equalization, which is a fancy name for the state sales tax storm troopers. A lot of the bar business is cash, but for those who are unknowledgeable and think that the bar owner can just pocket money all night long, the reality is that the tax is due quarterly and estimated, and when it's time to renew any license, if the sales tax is not paid up, you're in trouble, and the state is relentless. They will keep at you. It's probably similar in other businesses, but this is the one I know a little about.

Like rock and roll, operating a nightclub looks cool and easy to the untrained eye, but it's damned hard to make a buck out of it. There has to be a certain amount of love of the unconventional hours and an ultimate resistance to a normal life involved. It's not for everybody, but I always liked the life. I had already stopped drinking for almost ten years by the time I got involved at the club, so it wasn't about that. There's a certain comfort and outlaw cool to operate your life out of a bar instead of an office. We had the keys and a liquor license to a joint on Sunset, and it felt like a natural place to have as a base of operations.

When we first opened, I lived right on the corner of Sunset and Doheny Drive. TJ and I shared one of the coolest apartments in town, in a vintage 1940s Regency-style building tucked away right off the main street. True pal Jimmy Ashhurst, bass player from the excellent local band of the day Broken Homes, lived in the high-rise across the street. We had his spare key and used the pool and mod cons of his building, so we had the best of both worlds. Girls came and went, some stayed longer than others, but mainly we were two bachelor boys and led a pretty normal life for quite a few years. I coached Beverly Hills Little League, and we would sit on the floor for hours at a time, cracking the codes on the latest video games and eating Mama Celeste frozen pizzas and deliveries from Greenblatt's. We sat at the little table in the kitchen of the Rainbow or at the sushi bar at Tenmasa most nights. I walked to the club every day and walked home at night, dropping the money off in the night deposit at City National Bank. I never felt threatened walking along the Strip, although at 3:00 A.M., I'd walk right down the middle of the street for two blocks. When you walk down the middle of the street, it takes away the chance of anyone stepping out from behind one the buildings. There's not much traffic at that hour, so I found it less nerve-racking.

TJ did his homework in the office of the bar, adding to his alternative upbringing. He pretty much grew up on the Strip. At ten years old, he was already an experienced jaywalker and had gotten his candy at Gil Turner's liquor store for years. TJ learned to ride a bicycle and throw a baseball in the parking lot behind the old Scandia restaurant. His brother, Nicholai, owned and ran the Roxy; we'd known everyone at the Whisky and Rainbow for twenty years already, so we were around family. We had two rescued pit bulls that lived in the apartment with us; they were very protective and would guard TJ, in his bed, if I had to run down to the club for a few minutes on a night off.

Living in the middle of town presented certain challenges, too. Walking two pit bulls who didn't like other dogs was like mounting a major military operation three or four times a day. TJ would help put muzzles and thick chains on the beasts and do a quick reconnaissance on the street behind us to make sure no one else was walking a dog at the same time. We'd take them for a few walks every day. We played basketball at the West Hollywood elementary school. We would jump the fence, and the pit bulls would squeeze underneath, and on the weekends, we had the whole field and courts to ourselves. Our back gate opened up onto Harratt Street behind the 9000 Sunset Boulevard building, Lemmy was a neighbor, and we'd holler up to his window. If he was home, the skull and crossbones pirate flag that served as his curtains would move back, and he'd pop his head out and we'd catch up. This was our routine life, and it never felt particularly strange.

I had met Julie McCullough at the end of 1992. True pal Jamie James was playing a gig at the Troubadour, and I walked down Doheny Drive to see him play. Jamie's girlfriend at the time was Kelly Coleman, daughter of the fantastic character actor Dabney Coleman. She was a gifted singer, and Jamie was backing her in a rock band playing her songs. I had known Jamie since the 1980s. He's the singer and front man of legendary band the Kingbees. He and I had a band in the late 1980s with Lee called the Rufnex. We played around LA during a hiatus taken by the Cats. He was there when TJ was born, and we've stayed best pals ever since. I believe we would have gotten a record deal. But Brian called me and wanted to get together, and the Stray Cats started to get busy again.

Kelly Coleman's band was good, and Jamie is a talented guitarist, writer, and singer. At the time, Julie was a regular on a TV show called *Drexell's Class* that Dabney was the star of. He had invited Julie to watch his daughter's gig, and Jamie had invited me. Harry Dean is a longtime friend of Dabney's; he was at the gig, too. I think he got up and sang with the band. We all went next door to Dan Tana's after the gig. Dan Tana's is a very famous restaurant that has been next door to the Troubadour on Santa Monica Boulevard since the 1960s. Dabney, Harry, and a few others held court at a back table, and we were welcome. It was the first of a hundred nights that this gang of people would sit around Dan Tana's.

Julie is a very talented comedic actress and a full-on American 10. She was a Playboy Playmate and had been unceremoniously fired from a successful sitcom called *Growing Pains* after the star of the show was born again and thought he was making a statement. This was all before I met her.

If you believe in love at first sight, then that's what happened between Julie and me. She gave me a ride home and her phone number. We made a nonverbal, perfunctory agreement to go out once or twice to make sure. I had really only split from Britt about six months before. These types of things come along maybe a few times in your life, but there's no telling when it will happen. There was no rebound or quick fix attached to this one. We connected on every level. There was some interest in us as a couple from paparazzi types but on a much smaller level than with Britt. If we had played it up, it would have been more. Within a week or so, she would wind up living with us at Doheny Drive.

The Stray Cats were making what would be our last album at Virgin Studios in Beverly Hills with Jeff Baxter producing. Julie came to visit and helped me by watching TJ, who immediately loved her. I can admit to being very proud to have her show up at the studio and showing her off to the others with no real explanation. I know it's immature; it probably stems from some insecurity, but I have always been and still am that guy. Part of my charmed life has been that the few times I was really loved and in love, it was with women that could stop traffic and make the others jealous. I do enjoy it, too. It's part of the original rock-and-roll dream. It may seem shallow on the surface, but it is deep in my heart.

I wasn't ready for the commitment it was going to take with Julie. We were very close for a quite a few years. She traveled with me to Massapequa, and the whole family loved her. Everyone thought we would eventually get married. I can't exactly remember why we never did. She was totally cool, not driven by money in any way, and we were definitely in love. We broke up and got back together three times. She moved in and moved out. I had never gotten a divorce from Britt; it had something to do with insurance. I could've done it if I had wanted; it was some type of safety net to protect me from a commitment. I accept it as my mistake. I don't really believe in predetermined fate, but everything in life happens for a reason. Maybe I need to chalk the whole thing up to bad timing. For a drummer, it's not a good excuse, but it's honest.

At this point, I've developed a coping mechanism where I tend to better remember the positives and have trouble remembering the negatives when it comes to important life milestones. I tend to embrace it as a gift, but I understand that there is a little selective memory and cluelessness involved. I can't guarantee that the other people involved are as willing to understand this way of looking at it all. If I said that I have no regrets in life, it wouldn't be truthful. I've learned that it's how I accept and then deal with the regrets that have been the real test. Moving on is always the hard part. But somehow everybody does it. Better things do come along. I can easily go crazy from the what-ifs. So I've learned to remember the good stuff and be fuzzy on the bad. I stay in the exact now. It's the only way I stand a chance.

Julie and I had fun; she had a lot of friends, and she was very friendly with the people who lived in my apartment house. There were only a few flats in the building, and each of the tenants was a character. It was a real-life version of the TV show *Melrose Place*. Courtney and Natasha Wagner both lived there, and their dad, Hollywood legend and leading man Robert Wagner, came over sometimes. He was Hollywood royalty and a big presence. There was also a crazy tenant with a terminal disease who purposely clogged the old furnace and almost blew up the building. He had embezzled money from the homeowners' association. He was slowly going crazy from impending death and medication.

Julie and I went out and had a lot of friends and people stopping at my flat for coffee and just to hang out a lot. Julie booked the Roxbury Club on Friday nights with her friend Tia Carrere. We played there with the Cheap Dates every week for a year. It was the mid-1990s, and we went to the Gate, Hollywood Athletic Club, Tattoo in Beverly Hills, and Viper Room and always went to gigs at the Whisky and Roxy or drove out to the Palomino. I did my own gigs and did much smaller jobs than I had done in a while.

It was a good time, and by then I was used to life without either the Cats or Britt. TJ spent a couple of years back in London before his mom moved back to LA. I went back and forth a lot. It was all hard; the Cats didn't play at all and had quietly without fanfare broken up again. If I had been earning even a little with them, it would have made the whole thing easier. I did prove that I could lead a full life without them. I played with a lot of good musicians during this time.

Julie moved on and got married. We tried another time to get it together. We had a genuine, special time, but we couldn't close the deal. Sometimes a ship sails and it never comes back to port. I hold on to the positive memories of a certain era of my life that she was an important part of.

TJ was always a gifted drummer and played in the school orchestra; I helped them get extra equipment through the companies I worked with. I went to every school event and sports practice. I also took TJ everywhere I went. We made it work. He was comfortable in clubs, dressing rooms, and recording studios. At a session I was doing one time, the bass player on the date was trying to make small talk with him.

"Hey, little guy, do you know what this is? This is a bass," the guy said.

"I know," TJ answered matter-of-factly. "My friend is Bill Wyman. He plays bass in the Stones."

The guy really didn't have an answer.

We called it "two guys together." For as wacky as our lives seemed to the casual observer, I spent more time with my kid than anyone else I knew. During the five years that I coached Little League, there were a number of kids I had on my teams whose parents I rarely or never met. They were probably nice people but were so busy hustling in Beverly Hills or Century City that they had no time for their own kids. One misperception about rock and roll is that you're away on tour for months at a time and don't see your kids. The flip side is when you're home, you're really home. I know a lot of musicians who have tight relationships with their kids. Britt had moved back to LA and lived right there on Alta Loma Road, so TJ spent some nights and good quality time with her, too. This was extra helpful when I realized I wasn't going to make a million as a club owner and needed to go back on the road a little to keep us in our relative luxury.

I liked having the Sunset Boulevard address attached to the club and the whole concept of a clubhouse, but at the end of the day, you have to remember that regardless of where it's located, it is a business and needs to be looked after.

The Cat Club was a classic hole in the wall, a dive bar in the true sense of the term. It was located in a little row in the 8900 block of Sunset. Our neighbors were the famed Whisky a Go Go and Duke's Coffee Shop. Anyone who was around in LA at that time has probably been to all three. In the past, the same address had also been home to Sneaky Pete's, a bar and grill that was a hangout for the original Rat Pack. In the 1960s, it was the Galaxy, a folk-music-based coffeehouse and bar. All the history appealed to me but didn't help pay the rent. The club itself was long and thin with the bar on the side toward the back. It had a small upstairs that we used for guests, and there was a small office attached, where I spent thousands of hours sitting at the desk. I liked the base of operations that the club provided; I took any appointments there and let all my friends do the same. Over the years, I let countless people do interviews and photo shoots in the club and in the alleyway in the back.

When we first opened, the Cat Club was almost swanky. It had been a little restaurant and a computer store in the last two leases and needed a spruce-up. We managed to get a liquor license attached to the address; that in itself was a big accomplishment. I just made the place into what I thought the perfect dressing room should be:

simply elegant but functional was the plan for the Cat Club. The place was the perfect size for a great party; the legal capacity was eighty-seven people. Black velvet couches and leopard-skin carpet was the theme. The industrial leopard-skin carpet handled at least ten years of dirty boots and spilled booze and still looked good in the dark. I made a deal with some local rock photographers I had worked with over the years to hang their framed works on the walls, and I played music from my own record collection. I borrowed a few ideas from some places I'd been in over the years, but I strongly believe that the Cat Club became the template for a certain type of rock-and-roll bar that has been copied many times since we first opened it. My personal favorite part of the whole place was the black-and-white awning in front that read in a classy, cursive font "The Cat Club 8911 On The Strip." It was a landmark on Sunset for years and made it easy to give directions. We were forced to take it down in another example of corporate small-mindedness. The landlord wanted the whole strip of businesses in his building to be painted the same to make it easier for a big refinance he was doing on all his properties. He felt the sign and leopard-skin door made it too hodgepodge for his report to his bank. It was the turning point of my disillusionment. It broke my heart a little.

We almost accidently once had the whole concept franchised, and dozens of producers approached me about reality shows. For a few months, the whole place was wired for sound and live on camera over the Internet like a TV channel, and it was used for location filming many times. With a few of these ideas, we were ahead of the curve. I could have little charity events and use the place for showcases and record releases for any bands we liked or were friendly with. I never had that much juice in LA, but we could help out with the use of the place. The Cat Club was there for bands to play too loud and for bartenders to sling drinks, for another generation to live the dream, trying to make it in LA while trying to get laid along the way. I was the celebrity babysitter and punk rock patron for another watering hole, serving the would-be rock and rollers of a certain time period. I understood this. I just wanted to pay the rent and keep our little joint open as long as I could. This was my lot in club life, and I accepted it.

We were open for six months and struggling to keep it all going. At that point in time, the western end of Sunset Strip was the rock-and-roll side. The fancier, high-end nightclubs and hotels were farther east. One night we made a fateful decision to make a change and turn the place into a live-music venue. Over the past few weeks, I had been inviting true pals Bernard Fowler, Stevie Salas, and Carmine Rojas to sit in with me and do a bunch of cover songs for a bar tab and some fun. We just moved the couches out of the way, set the gear up right on the floor, invited friends to jam, and did live music once a week. All our friends turned up, and word of mouth spread; it turned into a successful night. Again, it wasn't the first all-star-type rock jam night ever, but come hell or high water, every Thursday night for the next fourteen years, there was a band with a couple of guys everybody knew on that homemade stage at midnight, slaughtering the FM classics. Since then, a lot of clubs have tried to capture that scene and that vibe. I know of a couple of places that had brief successful runs with a jam night, but the one at the Cat Club was special, maybe in the fact that I was playing myself in attempt to keep the business open. There was a certain honesty and necessary practicality to the whole thing.

After the first few times, the writing was on the wall about what to do with the club. It wasn't going to make it as a chic, snazzy rock-and-roll cocktail lounge like I had hoped. This is when, in the lingo of club land, the club tells you what to do with it. Steve and I went to Home Depot, bought plywood and nails, and along with longtime faithful bartender Kenny Merrill, we built a six-inch-high stage down one side of the room. We stapled the remnants of the leopard-skin carpet to the frame, and the infamous Cat Club stage was born. I brought a drum kit in and cobbled together a little PA from some small stage monitors we bought cheap with the sweetheart deal from Guitar Center, a few microphones I had in storage, and a couple of borrowed amps.

We slowly made the change to a live-music venue and hired band bookers with varying levels of success. We could only do door deals, but the bands that could draw some fans always made money. Any club owner will tell you that he or she will happily give the bands the door money if they bring the bodies. Bars want to sell booze; that's how you earn in this business, and you will do what it takes to get the people inside.

I kept the Thursday-night jam going when the other guys went on the road or just got burned out on it. I had more at stake and thus more inspiration to keep it going. We hit a stride and started to get a buzz around town when Gilby Clarke, of Guns N' Roses fame, Tracii Guns from LA Guns, and Swedish bass man Johnny Griparic—who played with Slash—started doing it. Teddy "Zig Zag" Andreadis was a staple on keys. I've always said Teddy has more soul than any of us by a mile. Everyone is somehow connected, one degree of separation, two at the most. Tracii came up with the name the Starfuckers, which stuck and became the de facto name for the whole night. The whole thing changed one week when the reclusive Axl Rose came in and did a few numbers with Gilby and me; Jimmy Ashhurst was sitting in that night on bass.

It wasn't even that busy on that particular night and has become the type of legend where more people recall being there than actually were. By the time I came into the office the next day, the word was out, for apparently Axl hadn't been seen at all in public much lately, let alone been seen jamming onstage at a bar on Sunset. I had a bunch of messages on the answering machine, including one from *Rolling Stone* magazine, asking for a comment on why the normally camera-shy Axl chose to jump onstage that exact night and so willingly launch into a few numbers with the house band. I still don't know the answer, and the why is not important. The secret to anything organic is that there is no secret. That's what makes these things impossible to create, let alone duplicate. You can't force it; it's gotta just happen. I'm eternally grateful to Axl for choosing to turn up that night. I've only met him a few times, and he's always been cool with me. His appearance that night definitely upped the ante at the Cat Club. Thanks, buddy!

The next few weeks were crowded, as everyone hoped that they would catch another appearance by a famous rock star cat. *Rolling Stone* magazine had run a picture that a customer had taken that night. The caption mentions the scarcity of the sighting, my name, and the name of the club. The snapshot shows Gilby, Jimmy, and Axl on the little stage. After that, the Thursday-night jam became internationally infamous, and rock-and-roll tourists, who visit the Sunset Strip from all over the world, started turning up to maybe catch a glimpse of someone they recognized. Axl never came up onstage again, but a lot of others did. For a brief moment, it became trendy, and some Hollywood types would turn up. But this never lasts, and eventually only the real fans and tourists remain. True pal and former record executive Michael Lustig signed Gilby and me to a record deal on the V2 label based on the Thursday-night scene and sound we were getting on that little stage. Teddy and Thursday-night regular Muddy Stardust joined on that album, recorded under the band name Colonel Parker. Over the years, there was a cavalcade of rock stars who had a blast just turning up, plugging in, and cranking out some classic rock and blues tunes, including Brian May from Queen, Bruce Dickinson from Iron Maiden, Rudolf Schenker from the Scorpions, Slash, and CC DeVille from Poison to name a few. Rod Stewart and Jimmy Page both turned up on different nights, and Ike Turner made an appearance and danced with a couple of his background singers. Lemmy came on multiple occasions, and he, Danny Harvey, and I cut a live record there one New Year's Eve.

One of the local steady customers worked as a producer on the TV show *Monster House* and pitched us for the show. *Monster House* was a reality show where a team of workers would do major improvements to a house and surprise the owners. In the episode before ours, they fully handicap equipped a house for a war veteran coming home from Iraq. About ten years into our being open, the network came and remodeled the whole club. There were some much-needed physical repairs that we got included into the remodel. Rikki Rockett, the drummer from Poison and a good all-around dude, is also a master craftsman and was hired by the network to do the work. He did a great job. We unveiled it on TV, and it boosted the business again. Then we slowly replaced all their interior design ideas back to how we wanted it.

Dee Dee Ramone did a Saturday-night residency after sitting in on a Thursday night. True pal and bass man Stefan Adika was a longtime member of the house band and played with Dee Dee right up until the end. Stefan and I both played on Dee Dee's last gig in LA. Although offered, Dee Dee didn't want to sit in the office between sets and insisted on standing in the little-used kitchen at the back of the club. One night he put his coat down on top of the stove, and it caught fire from the pilot light. There was always a funny side adventure going on at the Cat Club. In the moment, I was just trying to get through the night.

The lineup of the Starfuckers changed a few times over the years, but there was always a major-league team up there. One of the best and longest-running lineups featured talented buddy Eric Dover from Alice Cooper and Jellyfish, Ryan Roxie from Alice Cooper, and Dizzy Reed from Guns N' Roses. There was an especially good feeling to the place for quite a while with this lineup, and we packed the place out most weeks. There were a lot of characters who came around, including a few infamous homeless hoboes who lived up and around Sunset Boulevard. When it was cold out and the place was rocking, I didn't mind admitting them and letting them dance. It added to the whole crazy scene.

We used to take this outfit on the road once in a while, too. The drum chair seemed especially desirable. When I was out of town, Eric Singer from Kiss, Clem Burke from Blondie, Tommy Clufetos from Ozzy and Sabbath, and Brian Tichy all subbed for me over the years. On a great night for drummers, Carmine Appice, Simon Phillips, and Narada Michael Walden all played on the house kit. Truth be told, most Thursday nights during the fourteen-year run were just solid gigs by a crackerjack house band who were there for $100 a man and a good time, but the fact that over the years so many rock stars dropped in and jammed unexpectedly kept the fans coming in.

Everyone was afraid they would miss something if they didn't turn up. In the meantime, the Thursday jam night put the club on the map as a live venue, and we were booked every night with every different type of music.

We had a good run with the Cat Club and were in business longer than 99 percent of the clubs, bars, and restaurants that open in this town. The end was a boring, long, slow boil. At a small place like this, the only way to make it is with consistency. It's not enough to do one giant night and make the whole month's nut. There is a certain skill to balancing the rent, the bills, the inventory, and the staff. Steve was very good at this, and his ability to do this kept it open for a long time. I couldn't be around as much as I could in the beginning, but I spent as much time there as possible and always managed to organize a band for Thursdays from wherever I was in the world. We had been there close to fifteen years; the rent and the cost of running the place had gone up by 20 percent, but the business had not, yet we were hanging on. I saw it as a punk rock public service. I had been part of the inaugural organization committee for the Sunset Strip Music Festival, and we were part of the landscape.

The long and short of it was that a petty lawsuit filed by a one-time-only customer, who was backed up by a bloodsucking, ambulance-chasing lawyer, led to the ultimate demise of an LA institution. The insurance company had to settle a $250,000 judgment against us and dropped us as clients. There was nothing we could do about it. We had to scramble to find a new company that would cover us, and it raised the rates to an unaffordable monthly payment. You need to have insurance to keep a bar open. The personal risk is too great without it. So some awful woman who allegedly claimed she was allegedly injured and sprained her ankle on the actual back steps and allegedly had a major injury definitely made more money out of the club than any of the owners ever had.

My own feeling is that this unfortunate incident just hastened the inevitable end. The Cat Club suffered the same fate that most mom-and-pop businesses do in America these days: whether it's the hardware store, the corner candy store, the drugstore, the ice cream parlor, or the gin mill with rock bands, it needs the support of the neighborhood locals. Everybody wants to say and think they support small businesses, but few actually do. In our case, if you want the experience of live music, you have to support it on a regular basis. I grew weary of the yuppie guy who would turn up once every six months with an out-of-town friend or family member in tow. He'd want to find a parking spot on the street, be recognized at the door, get in free, watch a few bands, get his round of drinks on the house, and show off to his hick buddy from back home how he knew everybody in this cool bar on the Sunset Strip. It made me crazy, and by the end it became harder and harder to hide my contempt for this type of customer. I'd be playing the drums and notice this type hanging around, taking up space, and not spending a dime. I'd get on the mic and try to embarrass them. Cheapskates who think they're rock and rollers may be the worst kind. The truth is that if all these fair-weather fans just turned up once a week, paid for parking, paid for their drinks, watched the band, and tipped the bartender, we'd still be there today. It's easy to complain about the death of local live music, but it's got to be supported by the people.

This goes for the bands, too. They're not the innocent victims; most were lazy. You'd be shocked at how many bands can't draw ten of their friends to come and see them play. I feel a little bad for the bands that did work hard and promote. It's tough to find a small place to play. Why bother rehearsing and calling yourself a band when you're incapable of bringing anyone to your gig? I told the same thing to the *Los Angeles Times* and the *LA Weekly* when they wanted to talk about the closing of the club. Where were you all when I needed you?

There's no denying that I miss the place, and I don't want to convey the message that my time there was a bummer in any way. It was a unique time and place that I don't think will happen again. The place was sold to out-of-town restaurant operators who have changed the whole look and format and made a go of it so far. They're good guys; I like them and wish them well. I kept a few shares, but it's not the same. I go in there once in a while, and the place is packed, but I don't know one single customer. I didn't think that it would ever happen that I'd go into any bar on Sunset and not know one out of a hundred people.

I don't kid myself that the street won't continue without me; I'm sure the old-timers who were there before I was thought exactly the same thing. It was a major part of my life and of TJ's childhood. There are thousands of good memories associated with the place. I see a lot of rock bars around the world and a few in LA that have definitely taken their inspiration from us. I don't miss the panic and nervousness on the thirty-first of the month when I knew we didn't have the rent. I don't miss the phony-baloney customers, the landlords, or the idiot bands. I do miss having a bar at my disposal for charity events, parties, or just a place to go in the daytime and read the paper. I do miss the clubhouse feeling and having those extra few keys on my key ring. I do miss the camaraderie of the staff and the whole gang up on the Strip, although a lot of things have changed up there since then. Maybe the Cat Club was ahead of the curve again.

16

The Candy Man

On Tuesdays in the late 1980s, there was a jam night at the Central, a bar on Sunset, where the Viper Room now sits. I'd start out at the Rainbow for a few drinks and walk up the street, maybe stop along the way if there was a show at the Whisky or go into Gill Montie's Sunset Strip Tattoo Shop for friendly conversation. There was usually someone in there I knew getting inked. Gill is one of the original biker tattooists and was a character up on the Strip in the 1980s. I'd leave my car behind the Roxy with the key under the floor mat; I knew the valet guys there, so if I didn't make it back by 2:00 A.M. to pick up the car, they'd just leave it, and I'd just pay them next time. We lived at the top of Doheny Drive, so even after a little partying, I could sneak back up the hill, driving very slowly, only having to go one short block along Sunset. For the true enthusiast, there is a route that will take you all the way from

Bel-Air to Laurel Canyon where you only have to drive on Sunset twice for a total of three blocks. It takes a long time and is very winding and easy to get lost on, but it can be done, depending on how much you've been drinking and how well you know the turf. At this point in life, I recommend a cab.

The Central looked pretty much the same as the Viper Room does now. The stage, bar, and tables are in the same places. There's only so much that can be done with a bar. Over the years, different owners or promoters may come and go and change the name and décor, but these places along Sunset were carved out long ago. These spaces can't change too much, and besides a coat of paint once in a while, most clubs are the same as they ever were.

The Central was a cool spot. It had been called the Melody Room in the 1950s, and original West Coast jazz musicians played and hung out there. The one-of-a-kind, ultrahip Chuck E. Weiss and the Goddamn Liars played there every Monday night, and it was a staple LA rock-and-roll event for ten years. We all went to that. At some point, Johnny Depp famously took the place over. There is an excellent documentary simply titled *The Sunset Strip* (which I was proudly a producer on), that gives a whole history on all the joints and legend of the Strip. There's a section of the film where I interview a few original members of Mickey Cohen's mob and associates and friends. One friend, gentleman Joe DeCarlo, was Sonny and Cher's first manager. He wasn't muscle; he seemed more business minded, but he certainly knew everyone in Chicago and LA. He was one of the first cats with a vision to bring entertainment to Las Vegas. He and I got along very well. I went to visit with him in his condo in Beverly Hills, and we got sandwiches from Greenblatt's Deli on Sunset. I also interviewed Anton Giordano Hosney, who was a member from Chicago who came to LA in the 1940s to keep an eye on the rackets here. He was with Mickey when he was shot by a member of a rival gang in front of Sherry's Restaurant—which became Gazzarri's, which became Billboard Live, which became the Key Club and is now One Oak, where there was a shooting recently at an awards ceremony.

Full circle—you gotta love the Sunset Strip. There's another scene in the documentary where Sex Pistol and true pal Steve Jones and I talk about the shenanigans along the Strip in the 1980s while sitting in my old bar the Cat Club.

So there was a nice little jam at the Central on Tuesdays. Al Kooper used to come, Jeff Baxter, and even Tom Petty a few times. There was a house band comprised of all working LA cats, and a bunch of friends and other musicians would come by and jam on rock and blues standards. This was in the days before these jam nights were en vogue, and some nights there would be only musicians hanging out. This night, I don't exactly remember who was there, but I'm sure it was good. At 2:00 A.M., Bill, the owner/bartender, locked the door, and I stayed a little while after hours, talking and drinking with whoever was there.

I walked back down the street heading to the parking lot behind the Roxy to retrieve my car, taking deep breaths and chewing gum. I had a system. As I was approaching, I saw a really big guy trying to get into On the Rox. He was ringing the bell and pulling really hard on the door handle. No one was answering, and he was banging and yelling to be let in. It was not my place, but it was my hangout, and I felt some loyalty, so I quickened my pace a little to reach the guy to tell him to knock it off and go home, that the place was closed. I never felt threatened up there and didn't think too much of the fact that even from half a block away, this was a mountain of a man. The street was hushed, quiet at 3:00 A.M., and this guy was making a raucous racket. If a West Hollywood sheriff had driven by, he definitely would have stopped and checked this guy out, which would have also blown my routine plan of getting my car from the back and going home without a fuss.

Boom, bang, bang, boom on the steel door. "I'm the Candy Man! I'm the Candy Man! Let me in!"

I approached, slowly and calmly—there were, still are, and always will be nuts up on Sunset. So I gently said, "Hey, man, what's up? The place is closed."

Bang, bang on the door again. "I'm the Candy Man! Open up!"

At that point, I realized that this was the actor John Candy. He was truly a big guy; he had to be three hundred pounds. He was a gifted actor and comedian. I had seen quite a few of his films and TV shows. He stopped banging and gave me a bleary stare. He was holding a Big Gulp cup and rocking back and forth on his heels. If this guy bit the dust, I couldn't catch him—no way I could hold him up.

"Who are you? I'm the Candy Man!"

"Hey, buddy, I recognize you from your movies. My name is Slim Jim; I play with the Stray Cats. I know them here; the place is closed. We gotta go. Do you have a ride? Maybe we can hail a cab," I suggested. The street was empty, but a cab went by now and again.

He eyed me warily. "I know them. Which one are you, the drummer?"

I nodded. A big, meaty handshake and bear hug followed. "Call me Candy Man. I'm the Candy Man. Let's have a drink!"

He plopped down on the step and pulled me along with him. He pulled a pint of Bacardi's rum from his inside coat pocket. He took the lid off the Big Gulp soda cup and poured half of it out on the sidewalk. He refilled it with the rum and swirled it around. He took a good sip and passed it to me. I took my swig and passed it back to the Candy Man. Maybe it was Coca-Cola, maybe it was Dr Pepper or some other redneck soda, I don't know, but it was half-filled with demon rum and went down smoothly enough. We sat on the step in front of On the Rox for twenty minutes, passing this Big Gulp rum and Coke back and forth, the Candy Man pulling out the pint and topping it off until the bottle ran dry. He had his arm around me, and we were like two old hobo drinking buddies, chatting away about nothing. When the cup was soggy and empty, it was time to go home. By this time, I was properly wasted.

"I gotta split, Candy Man. You shouldn't hang out here, either. Want me to call a cab?" I asked. There was a pay phone in front of the Rainbow. I would've waited with him. I struggled to help him to his feet.

"No, you go, kid," he answered, and he staggered off down the street. A few stumbling, zigzag steps, later, he lifted his head to the sky and again started bellowing, "I'm the Candy Man! I'm the Candy Man!" to the deserted street, lampposts, traffic lights, and sidewalk.

I headed to the back of the club to get my car. The key was under the mat. I started her up, made sure the lights were turned on, and eased out of the parking lot, making a right onto Sunset, looking both ways about five times. I was driving a 1985 Corvette with illegal mufflers and straight pipes, so it was really loud, anyway. The coast was clear—there was no sign of the cops or the Candy Man. I took the first right turn on Wetherly Drive, cut over to Doheny, and putted along slowly toward the top of the hill.

17

Life with Harry

"Hey, buddy. It's Slim Jim checking in."

"Hey, man. You watching the Game Show Network?"

"Hold on a minute. I'm changing the channel now."

"Well, get it on! Hurry up!"

"Okay, okay."

"Call me back when you've got it on!"

Thirty-three seconds pass, and my phone rings.

"*You got it?*"

"Got it."

"This guy is brilliant, one of the smartest guys I've ever seen. When he's on, no one can beat him. He may be a genius!"

"I agree. He's awesome!"

"What did you get for seven across?"

"Let me go back to the newspaper; I did the puzzle earlier, and I need to bring it back up."

"Bring it back up! What the fuck are you talking about?"

"I do the crossword puzzle on the *LA Times* Web site. I've told you this before—it takes two seconds to reload the page."

"Call me back. I just want to fill the motherfucker in; it's taking too long today!"

Click. Twenty-seven seconds later, the phone rings again.

"*Well?*"

I give him the answer.

"That's a made-up word!"

"I agree, but that's the answer."

"That's bullshit. Where did they get that from?"

"It's a pop culture term."

"They're really fucking stretching it!"

This goes on for an hour or so. There could be anywhere from ten to fifteen back-and-forth phone calls. The gravelly, three-pack-a-day-timbered voice belongs to Harry Dean Stanton. This is a conversation we've had a thousand times and could be from any time zone. If I'm out of town, the conversation is limited to just the crossword, as I can only get the Game Show Network when I'm home. We trace current world history not by who the president was but who the host of *Family Feud* was at any given time.

Harry has become a little trendy in recent years. His truly impressive career and personality have been acknowledged in a documentary. You'll recognize Harry as the father in *Pretty in Pink*, and he's had roles in *Godfather, Part II* and cult classic *Repo Man*. He has hundreds of credits. He's been doing interviews for all sorts of magazines from all over the world. He loves the attention, and I'm happy for him. It barely scratches the surface, though. He'd much rather be doing the crossword puzzle over the phone with a few deep inside confidants than be at his own screening in Cannes. I feel flattered to be called. I've done the crossword with Harry over the phone from dressing rooms and hotels all over the world.

I first met Harry Dean in 1982 at On the Rox. He was very friendly with Lou Adler, and we became fast pals. We bonded over music and history, trivia and word games, and the love of just hanging out. The longer I know him, the more I find out. He is a brilliant actor who doesn't have to do much on the screen to be effective. Whether it's playing the drums or acting, less is more, and the best ones can say a lot without overdoing it. A lot of heavyweight actors, directors, and writers know this about Harry, and he's rightfully one of the most respected guys in his game. I've spent a lot of time at his cabin in the canyon just watching TV, doing anagrams on his little 1980s Game Boy, and listening to music. Marlon Brando would call his house, and he would put him on the speakerphone while holding his finger up to his lips. They, like us, would talk about nothing with a few insightful, brilliant one-liners peppered in the conversation. We'd go to Dan Tana's, the Roxy, the Mint, and sometimes Mouses's, an old after-hours club down on Pico. He would come over when I lived in Stone Canyon, and we'd play pool and watch my fish tank. We would drink, but like all my real friendships, it turned out not to be based on getting wasted.

In 1992, we'd form a true cult classic band that played around in LA and on one notable road trip. We called it the Cheap Dates. We had Jamie James of the famed Kingbees on guitar, Tony Sales from Iggy and Bowie fame on bass, my brother from a different mother, the fabled Jeffrey "Skunk" Baxter on pedal steel (confidentiality agreement with Jeff prohibits me from getting deeper into his life, but he is my adopted big brother and TJ's godfather). We all sang, and it made for a whacked-out bluegrass, rockabilly, country sound. We played every Friday night for a year at the Roxbury, which was not known as a live-music venue and which added to the nuttiness of the whole thing. My girlfriend at that time, actress and former Playmate Julie McCullough, and her friend Tia Carrere were the promoters, and it made for some memorable gigs. After the first few gigs, *Rolling Stone* magazine did a half-page feature on us, and we eventually went into the Paramount Studio and cut a demo. I still have it on a cassette. We were going to try making an album and touring, but Harry got a movie, Jeff got a production gig, and it just never happened that way.

We did take a road trip to San Francisco to play a few shows. We rented a van, and we hired a roadie type who drove and did the gear. We had a movie star and four musicians who hadn't been in a van with the equipment for a long time. The concept was noble: we wanted to bond as a band. It was all going fine until we hit a little traffic about two hours into the trip. Everyone turned quickly into Diana Ross, and we regretted not flying. Tony Sales called his dad, legendary old-school Borscht Belt comedian Soupy Sales, who was in New York.

"Dad, it's Tony. I'm stuck in a van with some guys, and we're bored. Tell us some jokes."

He put him on the little speaker of an old cell phone, and we huddled around, looking for something to beat the boredom of that mind-numbing traffic.

"What do you get when you mix a Dutch impressionist painter and a New York City cabdriver?"

We all gave up.

"Vincent Van Gogh Fuck Yourself!"

This went on for a half an hour, and the distraction was greatly appreciated. We made it to San Fran and played the gig. We unanimously agreed to fly home. The van ride was fun but not fun enough to do it again. Harry got the senior-citizen discount at the airline ticket counter. That was nineteen years ago. I hope I want to do a gig when I'm that age.

Harry invited me to go with him to a barbecue at the home of Edward Bunker. He's a gritty ex-con, a street-style writer from LA, a real character. Harry had done a movie called *Straight Time* based on one of Bunker's books. I had read the book and was excited to meet the writer. Harry drove along Mulholland. There was a stub from a valet parking ticket stuck under the windshield wiper. It was really annoying him. I suggested pulling over and I'd take it off. He kept driving and put the windshield wipers on. While steering with his right hand he used his left to try to snatch the stub off every time the wiper brought it close enough. We weren't slowing down, and Mulholland is the trickiest of roads at the best of times. We were sliding around a few turns while Harry was becoming more intent on plucking this ticket stub off, without slowing down. I was thinking of Eddie Cochran and James Dean and decided that driving off Mulholland Drive in Harry Dean's Acura was not a fitting rock-and-roll legendary ending for me. Maybe the wind helped, or maybe he got a finger on it, I don't know, but the ticket flew off the windshield, and we slowed down and had a nice drive into Hollywood. He was listening to "Margaritaville" by Jimmy Buffett over and over. He wanted to learn the words and try to play it at a gig. The car had a cassette player, and each time he tried to rewind the tape, it flipped sides, and it was a whole process to get the song back. There were quite a few snarls of "Goddamn it, Slim!" of varying volumes and intensities flying around the inside of the car. We were sitting in front of the house, and I could smell the barbecue and hear the guests talking, but we sat in the car playing that song over and over, discussing the finer points of that song. I was going crazy; I wanted to go in, but it was his friend's house, and an introduction from Harry would be better than me walking in cold. We eventually went in, and I had a memorable time with a favorite writer of mine and an assorted cast of eccentrics. Thanks again, Harry.

The phone rang while I was trying to write this story. It was from a blocked number. It was time for *The Chase,* a game show that features a three-hundred-pound English trivia genius nicknamed the Beast, so I knew who it was.

"What's your middle name?"

"Thomas."

"Full name?"

"James Thomas McDonnell."

"Wow, I've known you all this time, and I never knew that. To me, you'll always just be Slim."

Like I said, I'm flattered to just be called.

18

Come with Me, Kid

I was a bit of a late bloomer when it came to being a Bob Dylan geek. It makes the few little experiences I had with him fonder, because they were organic and unplanned. There are a few classic backstage photos that are very dear to me, and they captured moments that won't be repeated.

Dave Edmunds was playing a gig with his band at the Palace on Vine Street circa 1987. The Cats were not working, and I was of course upset by it. Lee and I had done a record with Earl Slick, and things were going pretty well with that, but it wasn't the Cats, and I missed the whole thing of being in the band. Dave is a very important player in the whole Stray Cats story as the producer on the best Cats stuff. He knew what we should sound like and was aware of the need for making it modern and vintage all at once. I stayed in touch with him. He was the musical director for the *Carl Perkins and*

Friends TV special in 1986 that would become so legendary. I think that the TV people probably wanted the Stray Cats as a band, but we weren't doing anything together, and it was a case of them needing a rhythm section to back everybody up. Carl had come to see the Cats play in the past, and Lee and I had done some recording with him with Dave as producer.

Dave's show with his usual band in LA was not too long afterward, so everyone was still in touch. We were all invited to the gig. Brian and I showed up. We sat as a group in the Abe Lincoln balcony box off to the side and above the stage. George was there with Bob Dylan, Jeff Lynne, and Duane Eddy. Brian and I were friendly, and he went up and did a number with Dave at the end. The audience loved it. A great unrehearsed rock moment and a bonus if you had been taken along to see that Dave Edmunds's gig.

We all wound up in the dressing room after the gig. The classic picture that exists from that night was taken by talented photographer Robert Matheu from *Creem* magazine, who had done a Stray Cats album cover, worked with a lot of people, and was an experienced rock paparazzo. It was the early days of Corona beer being trendy, and it should have been an advertisement; everyone in the photo is holding one. I have a few other fly-on-the-wall shots of everyone chatting, looking relaxed, real dressing room stuff, and a great portrait with Britt that we posed for. Looking back, I think that was one of the moments that contributed to the Cats working together again the next year. Maybe it was an ice-breaking moment for Brian and me. He and I hung out, and I enjoyed seeing him. I felt then and still do that people like seeing us together. With George, Jeff, and Bob all hanging together, talking about music, I like to think that I was watching the loose formation of the Traveling Wilburys that night, too.

Dave was the natural choice for us to work with and would produce the Stray Cats' *Blast Off* album in 1988. We were back in action during December 1988 when Roy Orbison died. We didn't know Roy personally but of course knew his music, especially his early rockabilly sides, and we were honored to be asked to play on his tribute organized by his wife, Barbara.

The show was held at Universal Amphitheatre, and there were a lot of heavyweights on it: Bonnie Raitt, Emmylou Harris, John Fogerty, and Iggy Pop all did Roy songs. Chris Isaak collected autographs on original Roy sheet music. I wish I could think of those kinds of things. Everyone shared the dressing rooms and greenroom. It was a sad reason to bring this eclectic bunch together, but the vibe was really good and ego-free. Dylan was supposed to perform, and everyone was waiting on him. We took our turn in rehearsal; all was fine. We did "Rock House," a song from Roy's rockabilly days at Sun Records. I'm not sure how many of the audience or the other performers knew the earlier stuff; most everyone else did the more well-known songs from the catalog.

I didn't know all the famous stories about Dylan cutting things close and sometimes not showing when he was rumored to. One of the more well-known stories I've heard since include the supposed almost no-show at George's first-ever charity concert for Bangladesh at Madison Square Garden in 1972. The fabled rock-and-roll rumor is that someone close to him had to go downtown to a flat in Greenwich Village to collect Bob and bring him to the Garden with a sold-out crowd and full recording and film crews waiting in the afternoon. I don't know if it's true, but it's a good tale. It makes it even more memorable when he does show up for cameo performances at gigs that are not his own.

I was drinking pretty heavily at the time. Eric Gardner was the Cats' manager then. I liked Eric, and he had an interesting stable of clients, including Todd Rundgren, Bill Wyman, and Cassandra Peterson, who played Elvira. We affectionately referred to him as a rock-and-roll Broadway Danny Rose. We were all friends and went to each other's events. He kept us working and really did care about each of us. He had given me a disappointed look when I started drinking so early in the daytime, and I wanted to be clearish for the gig. I knew I should slow down. I was standing outside in the back of the theater where the cars pulled up. Limos were coming and going, and a mini army of crew members and assistants with headsets and clipboards were buzzing around. I recognized some people. Stephen Stills came through, and I said hello. I knew him, and he'd come around Stone Canyon a few times and we played pool, staying up all night. Years later, I would be very friendly with his son, the gifted singer/songwriter Chris Stills, another full-circle mini story.

A long, white, '80s-style *Miami Vice*–looking limo pulled up. Bob Dylan half fell, half stepped out of the car, making a very skilled entrance clutching a bottle of Old Crow bourbon. Jack Daniel's would've been too ordinary; in real Dylanesque style, his brand of whiskey was even cooler and more rock and roll. He looked exactly how he was supposed to, elegant in an almost scruffy way. He and Keith have that ability to really be comfortable while the scene around them is frantic. I've always admired it and tried to emulate it in my own way. Maybe call it rock-and-roll grace under pressure. As he was being swept in by a minder into the backstage area, he looked up and saw me. He must've remembered me from our dressing room meeting. We had met and talked previously at Dave Edmunds's gig at the Palace where we had gotten along, talked about rockabilly music, and drunk eleven Coronas. He put his free arm around me and handed me the bottle in one motion while we were both whisked through the milling backstage area. I took a good swig. As I looked up, I saw Eric and gave him a shrugged shoulder wise-guy wink. What was I supposed to do? I couldn't insult Bob and refuse his drink. I was hustled with him into an empty dressing room.

"I can't believe these guys are hassling me about drinking. Managers are a pain!" I complained to Bob Dylan.

"Hey, kid, don't ever take anything in rock and roll personally," Bob answered quickly and dryly.

There it was. I had just gotten immediate, off-the-cuff, life-changing rock-and-roll advice from Bob Dylan. I still try to follow this advice. It was one of the most helpful things anyone ever said to me, and I'd like to thank Bob in print.

The rest of the time we just sat, and he talked about Roy, his greatness as a singer, how it was Sam Phillips who gave him his first shot, and about our shared love of rockabilly music in general. He liked the Cats. It was another one of those special moments where if I'd been a little older or wiser, I wouldn't have been as in the moment as I was. I think I'd be more nervous now to sit in Bob's dressing room on two folding chairs, just yakking away about rockabilly. After a while, someone came to get me. Maybe I had a buzz—nothing memorable about that part. We did our song, and it was all good. I can't remember what song Bob did. K.D. Lang did a version of "Crying," which brought the house down. I think the show was filmed, and it's gotta be available somewhere.

It was 2012, and I was on a festival in Spain with Robert Gordon and Chris Spedding playing drums. Bob Dylan was on the bill. We did a set of solid rockabilly songs. Both Gordon and Spedding are iconic guys who are very good at it. I was looking forward to maybe seeing Bob and saying hello. By then, I was a full-fledged Dylan fanatic. I'd worn out copies of *Highway 61 Revisited* and *Blonde on Blonde*. It came to me a little later in life, but I understood now how he had combined styles of American music and really invented something. He always did his own thing. He continues to make quality records, all paying homage to and reinventing American music. I get this now. He loves Gene Vincent, too. I'd heard all the stories and read a few bios and really dug *Chronicles*. I wanted to meet him again, armed with all this newly found fanboy stuff, maybe take a picture that I was aware of while it was being taken.

I had lunch in the festival tent with his band members, including guitar whiz and good guy Charlie Sexton, whom I was introduced to by mutual friend Stevie Ray Vaughan in 1984, when he was even younger than I was. At fifteen, Charlie was smuggled in through the back of a pool hall in Austin, Texas, where he got up on one of the tables to shred the blues with the house band while Stevie, Brian, Jimmie Vaughan, and I were part of the audience. He did just fine. He was now in Dylan's band.

Bob arrived two seconds before the show and was taken right on-stage. That was cool; I just wanted to watch the show. I was bummed out when I was told no one could stand onstage or at the monitor desk. I couldn't really go into the audience, and the stage was really high, so standing in front was not so good, either. So I sat in the area behind the festival-sized stage and half listened, thinking about taking a shuttle van back to the hotel. During the second song, a burly personal security guy who looked after Bob approached me, and before I knew exactly what happened, he had led me up the stage stairs and into a little nook that had been created out of road cases. I watched the whole show from this cave on the side of the stage. Bob looked supercool in a white cowboy suit with yokes and smiley pockets. He sang a few I didn't know and did alternative versions of the famous ones. His band moved along smoothly in sync with him, and I could tell he was improvising the whole time, relying and expecting the band to be with him. I know this feeling well. It's both a lot of pressure and a lot of fun.

At this point, I might be nervous with Bob, anyway. I would more than likely think about what I was saying. I never thought about anything before I said it in the past. Sometimes it worked, sometimes not. Harry Dean called me "youthful and hotheaded," but we stayed buddies. In a few cases, as with Bob and George, my youthful innocence mixed with the right amount of bourbon and natural attitude got me through. Nobody gave me that weird look and walked off. These guys didn't have to be nice to a young drummer if they didn't feel like it. I must have been okay.

I really enjoyed the gig from my custom-made perch. Bob was led offstage onto his bus and was gone while the audience was still cheering. The way it's supposed to be done, like Elvis. As I was walking down the stairs, Bob's guitar tech gave me one of his harmonicas, key of E. I keep it in my drumstick bag. I have it with me at every gig. It was a good exclamation point on a good night. I like to think that someone told Bob that I was there, that building the little niche for me to watch from and the gift of the harmonica was his way of saying hello. A very cool move from a very cool guy.

19

Do It for Johnny

Johnny and Linda Ramone used to have barbecues every Sunday. It was always an eclectic small group of people that would be brought together by Johnny. The gang included Vincent Gallo, Eddie Vedder, Rob Zombie, Rosanna Arquette, record executive and commissioner of our fantasy baseball league Andy Gershon, Rose McGowan, Steve Jones, Billy Zoom, Gerry Harrington, longtime rock-and-roll manager and true pal Michael Lustig, and a few others. I've stayed friendly and hang out with most of these folks, and some of us promise to get together, but we were all united by lunches with the Ramones.

The Stray Cats and the Ramones had the same business managers in New York, and we had met on a festival bill we were both on back in the 1980s. I have a very vivid memory of meeting the Ramones in the parking lot of a Holiday Inn while we were both on tour. They were in their usual tour transportation, the famed van, and John was riding shotgun reading his copy of *Baseball America*. We were in a tour bus, and I remember thinking, *Why aren't these guys in a bus, too?* Around the same time, we were on a festival bill together, and John, being an avid autograph and memorabilia collector, had Britt sign a few original movie posters from films she had done in the 1960s.

I had been a fan of their music since I was in school. They embodied the New York City punk rock scene and proved that a band of outsiders from the neighborhood could go all the way. The band was loud and fast, but the songs were catchy and always had a strong musical hook, a clever chord change, and a deceptively simple lyric. Looking back, I see now even more clearly that like all the classic bands I still like, there was always a reference and a nod to the original American rock and rollers.

The Ramones had very good musical taste and influences. I was too young to have seen them in the early days at CBGB, but I had seen them in the 1980s quite a few times. One memorable show at the Roxy stands out, and I remember pogo dancing with a visiting Swedish relative of Britt's and losing my keys. To be from suburban New York City and be able to tour the world was as much of a dream as I could muster, and the Ramones were living proof that it could be done. They were from Queens, and being from Long Island, I could relate to the whole thing. John and I had an Irish-Catholic New York upbringing and love of the New York Yankees and Elvis Presley as our common threads. We would become very close when he and Linda moved to LA.

We were part of a wacky fantasy baseball league that was very serious and important to us all. Our league included musicians, nightclub guys, a former DA from the Bronx, and a few other assorted characters. We had one season where two guys who shared a team sued each other. We had long catered draft days at Gershon's house where everyone came with some notes and a few magazines. One year, a member was in Rome on business and did the six-hour draft on a cell phone. The bill must have been in the thousands. We had the league for years, and John especially took it personally. He tried really hard to win every year and did so a few times. John came armed with stacks of paper with statistics, graphs, and any info to help pick the players, all notated with his tiny, perfect handwriting in the margins. He was a meticulous cat in everything he did. This was before everyone was online, and every league member would handwrite and fax the lineup into the commissioner every week. It's much easier these days, and I often think about John doing fantasy baseball in this day and age of instant scores, updates, and stats; I know he'd easily win every league. I don't remember how I got it done, but I always did. I fondly remember waiting on Monday morning when the fax machine kicked on and all the statistics for the week would come through on my old-school roll-paper machine. We had one member who had longtime ties to the ownership of the LA Dodgers and had four of the best possible field-level box seats right on the visitor's dugout at Dodger Stadium with a choice parking spot. Neither he nor John liked to drive, so I would get the call and bring TJ with me. So we went to a lot of ball games together. We drove downtown, listened to the oldies station on the radio, kept score, and ate peanuts, but never got a foul ball. TJ and John became close, too.

Everyone at the barbecues was somehow linked either by rock and roll, movies, or baseball. TJ was the lone kid in the mix. I didn't have a nanny, so I was the guy with the kid. He went everywhere with me. John and Linda's house in Sherman Oaks was a combination of Pee-Wee's Playhouse and Graceland done up in exact 1950s Palm Springs Rat Pack style. They hadn't really ever hung out with anyone in New York, and now that they had a house in LA, I think they liked entertaining their friends and bringing a certain group together.

There was a small guesthouse where the roof hung out over the pool. TJ, Eddie Vedder, and I would climb up the back fence, scamper over the sunbaked roof, and jump out and over the patio into the water. It was a bit challenging, ill advised, and dangerous. We did it until Eddie slipped and hit his head. They asked us to stop, and we did, but not before dozens of successful jumps were made over the years.

John and Linda were the perfect rock-and-roll hosts. They tried to keep everyone's favorites on hand. If someone mentioned a preferred brand of potato chips or beer, it was there the next week. There were vegetarian and fish options available off the grill. The ball game was on the TV, some vintage rock music was on the stereo, and everyone chatted away and got along well. This was a punk rock So-Cal version of a salon. Everyone there had been through it all on their own time and had lived to tell in a nonpreachy way. There was no darkness, no drug vibe, and no one was there to pick anybody up or do any business. I think that after years on the road and living in cramped quarters in New York City, they genuinely enjoyed being in sunny LA, entertaining and bringing together interesting groups of people that they were friendly with. Britt and I had done this when we lived on Doheny Drive, so I related and respected what they were doing every weekend. I also appreciated the good home-cooked food that TJ and I would get without going to the Rainbow.

Linda was the queen of her pink-and-green castle. She would cater and serve everyone while always tooled up in classic designer miniskirts and boots under an apron like June Cleaver–meets–Nancy Sinatra with a twist of Debbie Harry. The queen's accent and expressions never softened.

"Wadda ya need, Slim? Yoo got wot ya want?"

"All good."

I liked ginger ale, and TJ liked root beer.

"I got Canada Dry and Schweppes."

"Whatever. They're both fine."

"Well, which one?"

"Um, Schweppes."

"Coming up."

A glass full of ice and ginger ale complete with lime wedge would appear with a cocktail napkin underneath.

When it came to the root beer and dealing with TJ, John got really involved. He liked root beer, too. Each week he would stock a new brand, and he and TJ would sip and compare like wine connoisseurs. TJ had a Ramones-style pageboy haircut, and the sight of the two of them in their bathing suits comparing notes on root beer is a classic image in my mind. These afternoons were good for me to unwind, as TJ would swim with the others and hone his skills of being able to hang with anyone.

One time, John asked TJ what he thought of that week's selection.

"It's okay, but last week's was better," TJ answered as he shrugged and slurped.

"It's the same kind; you said you liked it last week, so I got the same one this week," replied John in his clipped tone.

"No, it's not; this one is different," answered TJ.

"The same," said John.

"Different," said TJ.

This went back and forth a few more times, and it was starting to get like a school yard argument. I saw this from across the room and stepped in to tell TJ to back off and not argue with an adult. Linda had also seen it and told John, "Leave the kid alone, John. Who cares?"

There was one last round of disagreement before I glared at TJ, and he told John he was sorry and that he was thankful for any root beer. John accepted the apology, and we moved on with the day. John was forty-seven, and TJ was eight.

Next week, we turned up as usual for a barbecue and a swim. There were a few of the gang already there, Dion and the Belmonts were on the record player, all was cool on another sunny Sunday. John greeted us, said hello, and then gave TJ the come-here motion with his finger. TJ obeyed and followed John to the kitchen. John went to the counter and presented a tray with a white napkin over it. He pulled the napkin off like a magician doing a flourish to a trick. On the tray were three Dixie cups, each with two ounces of root beer in them. Each had a little index card to correspond to the cup.

"Drink this one," John said as he handed the first one to TJ.

This was repeated three times, and after each one, John asked TJ to identify the brand of root beer and then turned over the index card to reveal the brand name, written in his perfect little printing.

"A&W," TJ said.

"Wrong; it's Dad's," answered John dryly.

Next one, TJ guessed, "Barq's, definitely!"

"Wrong again; it's Hires!" John confidently answered.

Last one, TJ sipped and offered his expert opinion and guessed wrong again. John defiantly stood in front of TJ like a prosecuting attorney who had just gotten the criminal to confess and said, "I rest my case; you don't know the difference!"

TJ was momentarily flabbergasted, as were Linda and I. Then I was flattered that John had gone to all this trouble to prove his point to my kid. I think that TJ was the first, last, and only child that John ever interacted with. He needed to prove his point even to an eight-year-old. That was who he was. TJ said, "Okay, you win," and went off to jump in the pool.

John had a two-toned blue-and-white 1957 Ford convertible with a retractable hard top. This car was heavy and hard to stop, start, and steer. It was a real beast to drive. I have always driven old cars and am familiar with them. John, being a native New Yorker, didn't like to drive in general, but this car was supercool, and he liked being in it. I would get the chauffeur's job, and we'd all pile in for cruises along snaky, scenic Mulholland Drive.

When John got very sick, a few of that gang would go and visit him. We sat on the leopard-skin couch and watched baseball games and talked about everything except the fact that he was terminal. He just wanted to spend as much time as he could in the house that he loved, to pursue his hobbies, go to baseball games and good restaurants, and entertain some friends on the weekends. He looked at rock and roll as a job, saved his money, and wanted to retire in a civilized way. He was one of those cats who, like me, is very happy and proud to be from New York but really understands and loves living in LA. You can turn on the New York when it's needed but have had most of the rough edges rounded off by traveling the world. It's unfair that he worked on the road for so long and brought such great music and attitude to the world only to have his retirement spoiled by illness.

He was a special guy, one of a kind, and I'm very honored that he was a close friend. I'm still very close with Linda. Every year, there's a tribute where she celebrates Johnny's life at his graveside statue at Hollywood Forever Cemetery with the showing of an old horror film on a drive-in movie screen, a little gig, and some remembrances. This past year was the tenth one, and it's turned into a fan favorite, drawing a couple of thousand people. All the old gang helps out, and it's a chance for everyone to be in the same place at the same time. A little bit of a sadder occasion than a poolside barbecue in the sun, but it's a good charity event that raises money and awareness.

John's early passing made everyone feel a bit more mortal. He was the strongest, most rigid guy I knew, and if it could happen to him, it could happen to anyone, including me. It seemed like a bum rap for him. Unconsciously, I felt that every day in Beverly Glen, every ball game, every drive in the hills, every box score in the sports section should be appreciated a little more and not taken for granted. I was definitely affected by his death. It was the first time I had ever experienced the slow passing of a friend. I had known a few people who died suddenly from drugs or a car accident, but this time, we sat on the couch together, and I watched it happen slowly. We still go up to the Ramones' ranch for the occasional barbecue, where we inevitably talk about the fabled root beer incident.

20

Whatever I Can Do to Help

I was standing around, drinking coffee late at night next to the van with Captain Sensible and the crew members, at a truck stop somewhere in England, when Mikey Boy Peters came back over to the van and calmly told us, "My cancer has come back."

There was a collective gasp. How do you respond to that? This was one of my truest pals ever and the singer in a band we were currently on a tour with. No one spoke. We were all bundled up, shifting from foot to foot, trying to stay warm, and even in the cold, no one was anxious to get back into the van. I remember getting very hot under my heavy overcoat; my scarf was pulled up around my face, and the steam from my breath was fogging up my glasses. It was English weather—damp, cold, and windy in the parking lot—the nearby motorway traffic was whizzing by, and the whole scene was lit by the usual fluorescent streetlights and signs in an English roadside services stop parking lot at 2:00 A.M. We had just finished a show, and we were driving overnight to the next one. More luxury and glamour, but with this gang, I didn't mind; we were all pals and equals.

The Jack Tars is a good side project. We each bring a few hit songs to the table, and the fans like this combination of musicians. We continue to do this band with Captain Sensible, Mikey Boy in remission from his cancer, and current permanent member Chris Cheney from the Australian rockabilly/pop/rock band the Living End. He sings and plays guitar as good as anyone I've ever worked with and is a true pal. We first met when his older sister had to smuggle him into the shows on a Cats Australian tour in the 1980s. My son, TJ, later discovered his band, and we stayed reconnected. The Jack Tars is a bunch of beloved characters. Sometime guests and members include true pal Billy Duffy from the Cult, true pal Glen Matlock from the Sex Pistols, good buddy Duff McKagan from Guns N' Roses, Mick Jones from the Clash, Rami Jaffee and Chris Shiflett from the Foo Fighters, and good buddy and super-talented fellow Long Islander Fred Armisen.

Fred's the creator and star of the fantastic sketch TV show *Portlandia*, and he did a long, successful stint on *Saturday Night Live*. Fred and I have a good connection. His childhood train stop on the LIRR was in Valley Stream, not far from ours in Massapequa. He's a longtime musician and fan; it turned out that he had seen the Cats play very early on. Besides being a real drummer, he has an act where he sings and plays a perfectly researched, invented punk rock character called Ian Rubbish. He is a perfect fit for the Jack Tars. I'm happy to know him.

Captain Sensible is almost indescribable, a one-of-a-kind, unique character. As a founding member of the original punk rock band the

Damned, he's become a British institution. He's reinvented himself a few times along the way and is now a punk rock elder statesman in the best sense of the word. I'm fortunate to count him as a true pal and a bandmate. We've piled up a lot of road miles and sound checks together. One of our tours in the UK coincided with his attempted run for Parliament, as the Blah! Party representative. It didn't seem to me to just be a stunt. The guy is passionate and knows his stuff. It's not easy, punk rock and antipolitics.

There are tales around him of legendary bad punk rock behavior. I've only had positive times with the cat, although I did have to hold his hand a few times on bumpy flights and once had to read to him during some exceptionally rough turbulence on a flight from London to New York City. At the end of the day, he's a wicked good guitar player and a lovely bloke.

Mike Peters and I go back thirty-five years. His band, Seventeen, would later become the Alarm. They were the opening act on the first Stray Cats UK tour in 1980. They turned up at the gigs and pretended they were the official opening act. It took ten shows until anyone realized there was no official opening act. By then, we all liked them, and they did the rest of the tour. The last night of the tour was in Blackpool, and we whooped it up at the show. It was Christmas 1980, and the Cats had a top-ten hit record on the British charts; "Runaway Boys" was at number nine when they froze the charts for the two-week Christmas break. We had followed through with everything we knew we could accomplish and had been shooting for.

In a tragic coincidence of that tour, we were in Liverpool on the day John Lennon was killed back in our hometown of New York City. I was and am a Lennon guy. I can't even say how much I love and respect the man and his music. I can get choked up every time by thinking about it for too long. Liverpool was a mythic musical place to me like Memphis or Lubbock. The club we played was called Erik's, and I think it's been on the club circuit a long time. Everyone has played there. It's right in the section of town where the Beatles had played the Cavern Club a hundred or more times. At the time, this place was the closest thing to playing the old Cavern Club, which was across the street but closed down. We were looking forward to visiting a music mecca. No one we knew had ever been there, for sure. The pile of flowers in front of the club was ten feet high. People were just walking by and throwing bouquets on the pile. There was a heavy vibe in the city, but we didn't cancel, and everyone was nice to us, and we had a great show. We did an encore of "I Saw Her Standing There" with Seventeen coming up to sing along. Lennon was a well-known Gene Vincent fan and a rockabilly at heart. I've always liked to think he would have dug the Stray Cats.

After a high-energy show and big encore, I was in a bathroom stall doing a little powder when the door was kicked in and flew off the hinges toward me. I was dragged out and knocked to the floor by some angry security guards. They kicked me over and over again. I tried to crawl away and hide under the sink. With the help of crew member and buddy Bobby Startup, I got to my feet and out of the bathroom. There was a full-scale riot going on in the club and in the parking lot. I later found out that a girlfriend of one of the security guards was in the dressing room. All of this happened over the un- true and mistaken idea that some awful drunken woman was in our dressing room. One thing led to another, and the security guards stormed the bathroom where I was. This led to someone in the club getting a foot stepped on or beer spilled, which led to someone throwing a punch, and it was game on, and the audience was involved, too. People were just fighting each other, and the club security was going at it for no good reason other than it was Saturday night in Blackpool. These were the classic tuxedo-clad, no-neck or -brains gorillas that worked in the clubs in the north of England. These are horrible characters and would even be funny caricatures if not for their violent nature and quick tempers. I was unaware of this sort but have seen them a lot in the years since. They seem to propagate in club culture. This time it was not my fault. A few of our crew guys were caught up in the melee and were busted up pretty good. Lee and Brian were both uninvolved and unhurt. They had gotten out of the dressing room and into a car and avoided any injury.

The police arrived, and a few of us were being taken to a local hospital and then to the police station for questioning over our part in the riot. On the way out, I slipped a plastic bag with my stash to Mike Peters and told him to hold it for me. I had a chipped tooth and was bruised, but nothing was broken. At the police station, I called a copper Barney Fife and compared their town to Mayberry after they were interrogating me and treating me like the bad guy. They didn't get the reference, which was good. We all drove back to London.

The other two guys flew back to Massapequa for Christmas. For some reason I can't remember, I stayed in London by myself. After a few days of sitting around, I started to get a little antsy. There was not much going on, and BBC television just showed the picture of the girl holding the balloon for fifteen hours a day. On top of it all, I was out of blow and a bit lonely. Not being a proper drug guy, I was never very good at getting the stuff, and no one was around to help this time. I called around a little, but it was Christmas, and even dealers take off for the holidays. I remembered giving the baggie to Mike. So I somehow got to one of the main stations, probably Victoria, got the right train, and made the right connections on British Rail to arrive in Rhyl, North Wales, on Christmas Eve 1980. I then asked around at the taxi stand and found a driver who knew Mike, who took me to his mom's house, where the family was having dinner. I managed this, I'm pretty sure, with no or very little money, wearing a T-shirt and leather jacket in the middle of a harsh winter.

Christmas in Wales—the whole extended family was there around the fireplace. It was a scene right out of a movie. They were understandably surprised when I turned up unannounced. Everyone greeted me and took me in as a member of the clan. They all knew Mike had been on tour with the Cats and were all proud of him and armed with questions for me. I had a few drinks with the folks; I seem to remember an elderly woman knitting by the fireplace, but I was trying to get Mike's attention.

He sensed this and took me to an upstairs bedroom where he had the baggie stashed in his sock drawer. Mike didn't use the stuff, so it was intact. I went to the bathroom, did a healthy whiff, and went back downstairs to Christmas in Wales. The whole gang was lovely, and I was more talkative now. The only slight wrinkle came when it was time to eat. I had gone back and forth a couple of times to the bathroom and had been steadily drinking wine and beer since I'd arrived. I was feeling just fine, but in that state, I didn't have an appetite and didn't want to appear rude or ungrateful. These people had just taken in an uninvited, rough-looking, 120-pound, frozen, greasy-haired, leather-jacketed New York stranger to their family holiday dinner. So when the Christmas goose arrived with all the trimmings, I had to keep pushing it around the plate to make it look like I had eaten it. It was real home cooking, and I'm sure it was amazing.

After dinner, Mike and a few others took me around their village, where I met all the locals at the pub and neighborhood disco that was a having a special do that night. Word spread fast, and in the pub there were quite a few people who wanted to meet me and say hello. The Cats were currently on TV and the radio, and it was a small town; Mike's band being on the tour was big news. One guy, who thought he was the town mod and tough guy, wanted to start some aggro with me, the visiting teddy boy celebrity. With the day I had just had, I couldn't even muster my usual vitriol for any comeback or response. The guy was so disappointed by my lack of interest that he wound up just walking away in the end in a kind of disgruntled defeat. The best way to win this fight turned out to be with pure indifference. I made it back to London the next day and carried on with life.

Mike's band changed their name to the Alarm and went on to have success. We always managed to stay in touch, as I have with a few true pals I still have from those early days in London. I saw the Alarm do their most famous show at a huge open-air concert at UCLA—I think it was televised on MTV. We lived in Stone Canyon at the time, which is close to UCLA, and the guys came over to my house after their big show. On a different occasion, Brian and I got onstage with them at the Palladium.

Sometime in the 1990s, Mike was diagnosed with cancer. The prognosis was not good, and I believe the doctors told him to get his affairs in order. He opted out of traditional treatment and got heavily involved with a self-healing method. I don't know all the ins and outs of it, but he continued to play gigs as a casting-out type of therapy and fought the cancer like an enemy within. He miraculously went into remission and stayed that way for ten years. We continued to stay in touch and would see each other's bands when we could.

Sometime in the early 2000s, he contacted me with an idea for a new band. After a few lineup and name changes, we've become the Jack Tars. The band is a loud, acoustic, traveling jukebox playing the hit songs from our respective bands. Each guy sings his own songs with accompaniment from the others. The gig is peppered with stories about the genesis of the songs and clever banter and brings some big onstage personalities. It makes for a good show and a fun night out.

It was during the early days of doing gigs with what would become the Jack Tars, with the overwhelming support of the others, I had the confidence to try to sing a few songs. I'm not a real singer, but I love singers and have always envied real singers. The natural ability to sing is a great gift. I've always been pretty good at playing the drums and can comfortably play anywhere, anytime, in front of anyone. Singing is another story, and I found it hard in the past. At Mike's insistence, I sang the Cats songs during the set. The audience accepted me doing my own songs, and it made sense to me right away. I earned the right to sing these songs a long time ago, and the fans excuse my lack of vocal expertise because they want to see one of the Cats do those songs. I like to compare it to Ringo doing a Beatles song. I tell the audience that I was the third-best singer in the Stray Cats. Now I can sing quite a few and have learned the most important thing is to pick the right songs. I'm not going to try to do Otis Redding or Elvis. I owe it to Mike for encouraging me to just do it.

True pal and original Sex Pistol Glen Matlock was very helpful on this front, too. We've known each other since the early days of the Cats in London. The first official bonding act of our new rhythm section was Glen offering to pay the dry cleaning bill that I incurred from an old drinking incident with him at the Venue in Victoria at some gig years before. I told him I appreciated it but that the jacket in question was lost long ago. Glen and I used to drink together, and now we don't drink together. Unbeknownst to me, he gave it up, independently, around the same time as I did. Everything else is the same. The love of rock and roll and the need to pay the bills win every time. Glen and I have driven in his car to and from gigs all over England. We had a blast stopping for cream teas and visiting historic monuments on the way to the shows. A Stray Cat and a Sex Pistol, stopping and making detours involving heavy map reading, for a cream tea lunch in an English country village? What has the world come to? Glen's hospitality and friendship over the years have helped me beyond words. Having a luxury suite waiting in a good part of leafy London is a great relief when trying to hustle up a rockabilly life. In a spooky small rock-and-roll world coincidence, Glen had a similar incident at the same club in Blackpool the year before our adventure there. It was through his encouragement that I decided to write this book in the first place. We've recently done a record with mutual true pal Earl Slick, confirming my sneaky suspicion that there are really only twenty-seven people in the world and they're just running around all over the place.

So back in the van, Mike had dropped this bomb, and we were all speechless. A bunch of old rockers were crying in a van at a motorway services truck stop. We drove to the next place in silence. The sound of everyone's thoughts was loud. Sometimes silence can be the perfect form of communication. Everyone knew what everyone else was thinking without the use of words. We were near the end of this run of dates, and Mike got through them. I went home and didn't hear from him for a while. I've since learned that he did a few rounds of chemotherapy and radiation then.

Mike has always been that "rock and roll can save your soul" kind of cat. No negativity is allowed to ride on him for free. This is real heavy stuff, but he's the type of guy that does beat this. He's also the type of guy that does something about it. When he told me he was going to start a charitable organization, I told him I'd always help, no matter what. Be careful of what you agree to in advance.

The new charity was to be called Love Hope Strength and would do rock-and-roll type events to raise money for cancer research. I figured I could handle that. The first event was a climb of the interior staircase of the Empire State Building on April 16, 2007. We were set to play a little gig on the observation deck on the eighty-sixth floor. I was born in New York City and walked past the Empire State Building a thousand times but had never been inside. I figured I'd kill two birds with one stone—do a good deed and do a little hometown tourism.

A few of us were on the stair-climb event, including longtime true pal Billy Duffy from the Cult. I've known Billy since 1981, when he had an after-school, pre-rock-star job with another true pal, Lloyd Johnson, at Johnson's Clothing on the Kings Road. Everybody shopped and hung out at Johnson's. BD has gone on to make a dozen great albums; I've seen his band play twenty times, and he's a current buddy whom I see all the time. We are charter members of Hike Club, a loose affiliation of idle musicians who stay marginally fit by hiking Franklin Canyon in Beverly Hills just about every day. He has known Mike almost as long as I have, confirming the twenty-seven-people theory. Other stair climbers included true pals—the excellent bassist and longtime neighbor Jimmy Ashhurst and the Pontiff, original Sex Pistol, and king over us all, Steve Jones. He's one of my best pals ever, and I continually blame him for just about everything I've ever done. He's the guitar player on *Never Mind the Bollocks, Here's the Sex Pistols,* an album that is very important and influential to all of us. Along with Elvis Presley's *Sun Sessions* and *Gene Vincent Rocks! And the Blue Caps Roll,* it made up the three records that really shaped me as a musician and style-conscious cat. I got into rockabilly around the same time as I did punk rock, and that record was an influence. I feel honored to have both Steve and Glen as true pals.

Billy and I were in pretty good shape for the Empire State Building climb, and once we got into a rhythm, it was very doable and kind of cool to see the skeleton of the most famous building in New York City's skyline. I met LHS cofounder James Chippendale that day, and he and I were to become fast true pals. BD and I blew away the competition on the stair climb. He had a little burst at the end to pass me in a friendly race. There was a major storm that day in New York City, so we did the gig in the old gift shop on the eighty-sixth floor. This place is in a time warp out of the 1950s, complete with old souvenirs and original employees. We set up and played with producer Tony Visconti recording the whole thing. Later that night, we played a show in a club in the Village. My daughter, Madison, joined me on the first of our adventures together. No problem. Little did I know that this would turn out to be the easiest one we would do.

How could a drummer from Massapequa possibly conceive of hiking to the base camp of Mount Everest? Mike had planned the next event to symbolize conquering cancer by climbing the mountain and doing the highest concert ever performed. I had agreed to be on the team that was going to attempt this in October 2007. Team members were to include Mike; super-talented guitarist, singer, and songwriter Glenn Tilbrook from Squeeze, whom the Cats had done shows with in the 1980s; Cyril Curnin, singer; and Jamie West-Oram, guitarist from 1980s hit makers the Fixx. Cy is a spectacular classic English front man, and we would become close friends. The eclectic lineup was complemented by English whiz blues guitarist Nick Harper, whose mother had passed from cancer a year before.

When it comes to charitable endeavors, I'm best served by a small-picture, get-directly-involved type of approach. Some of these guys like Geldof—and, in this case, Mike—are able to look at a very big picture, but I don't have the head for it. LHS is easily researched, and they're doing a lot of big stuff. All these things we've done and they continue to do is readily available to see. I would like to think that I climbed a couple of mountains to help cure cancer, but I really did it because my true pal Mikey Boy Peters asked me to do it. I always say that I'm glad he didn't ask me to go deep-sea diving to find a cure. It may be the same mind-set that makes you part of the rhythm section. Drummers don't often write symphonies, but they will get their hands dirty and hang out with the crew.

I had no real concept of how hard this trip was going to be. I just did my daily hiking with my dog, Lucy the golden retriever, and tried not to think about it too much. When events are booked so far in advance, I tend to think the world will end before they arrive. So far, this hasn't happened, and we're all still here, but everyone has his or her process.

I flew on my own to Bangkok, stayed overnight at the airport hotel, and the next day flew to Kathmandu, Nepal. I was the only one coming from LA. Most of the thirty or so other people on this trek were from Dallas, where cofounder James Chippendale is from, or Denver, where former LHS director and fantastic woman Shannon Foley Henn is from. The rest were from England; I didn't know anyone until the UK contingent arrived.

This place was the first time I had ever seen the real third world, and I was unprepared for what I saw. There were open sewage and trash dumps everywhere, wild packs of dogs, and seemingly feral children in torn clothing roaming the potholed streets. People holding up traffic, leading farm animals around in an urban environment, crossing the streets in front of taxis beeping at them. No one seemed too stressed, but there was a general feeling of built-in despair, and the quest seemed to be about pure survival. I thought it made Tijuana look like Beverly Hills. We were in the one Western enclave of town where the embassies and government buildings were housed. We stayed in a nice hotel, aptly named Hotel Yak & Yeti. It was comparable to the older mid-level Holiday Inns.

I had managed to cajole another true pal into taking this trip with me. Garrie Renucci is a former Scottish Professional Football League player turned business tycoon and one of my best pals ever. In the 1980s, he was a rising star in pro soccer, and through the classic combination of booze and anger, he got himself kicked out of the league after an incident involving swearing at the coach and referee, removing his shirt, and storming off the field, all on national TV. I could relate. With some perseverance, a little luck, and sobriety, he turned his luck around and is now a partner in an international building and construction company that does everything from shopping malls in Dubai to hotels in Hawaii, the New York Times Building, and all the Topshops, to name a few. I met Garrie at a gig

through longtime mutual friend Clem Burke, the rock-solid drummer from the great Blondie. We've always stayed very close. I have
visited and stayed with him in Glasgow and London, and he's in LA
a lot on business. I talked him into leaving his comfort zone in
Knightsbridge, London, SW1, to join me on this crazy adventure.
His company also made a very healthy donation to the charity.
Garrie and I would share a room and a tent for the next few weeks.
I hadn't shared a room with anyone since Lee and I shared one on
the first Cats tour. He hadn't shared one since his playing days with
Dundee United. Garrie was cool, and we didn't have a problem.

Mike had found the only recording studio in Nepal. We went in
and recorded an on-the-fly version of a song Mike had written for
the event—a cool little anthem called "Give Me Love Hope and
Strength." The others strummed, and I banged a little, and we all
sang the chorus. It's a very catchy number. The next day, we all were
introduced and left from the hotel in buses. Everyone was all loaded
up with brand-new, top-of-the-line camping and climbing gear, provided by Nike, North Face, and Marmot. James and Shannon had
worked long and hard and had gotten all this gear through spon-
sorship and endorsements. Mike's lovely wife, Jules, was along too
and was very helpful with everything. I left most of it behind and
took only the bare essentials to make my backpack as light as possible. I did bring a top-shelf pair of hiking boots, which I can now say
was the most important part of the whole thing. There would be the
real stars, the amazing Sherpas, to help with the big items, but each
person was responsible for his or her own basics. We were headed to
the Kathmandu airport to take shuttle planes to Lukla Airport, from
where we would set off on the trek.

At the airport in Kathmandu, there was a ceremony where we

were all draped with the local flower necklace and prayer scarf, and everyone had a red thumbprint applied by a local woman. This whole thing reminded me of a Nepalese version of the Hawaiian tourist send-off and greeting. It was the first of five thousand times I would hear "*Nah mas te*," the Nepalese version of "Aloha." For all the similarities, this place was literally ten thousand miles away and five miles higher in the sky than Maui—no beach, either. I would later deduce that this was more of a "good luck landing in Lukla" than a "good luck on Everest" ceremony. Lukla is among the world's most dangerous airports. There is some technical info about how altitude and air pressure meet the steepness angle of the landing strip, but it's just plain terrifying. I'm not a bad flier, and I long ago accepted that it's part of my life, but this one was different. The first giveaway was the duct tape stuck on the wings, and the second was overhearing the story of how Everest conqueror and history's most famous mountaineer, Sir Edmund Hillary, had lost his wife and daughter in a crash at this airport. This man is officially the first Westerner to summit Everest, and he continued to go back there his whole life, building schools and trying to help the locals. His name is everywhere in Nepal. If this guy couldn't get a break from the mountain, no one could.

We flew in shifts of about ten at a time, and there was the usual gallows humor from those who were nervous and talked on airplanes. I think Garrie and I just kept quiet. It was truly scary; everyone has been on a bad flight and can relate on some level, and nobody likes turbulence, but this one was magnified by the rickety plane, desolate location, and knowing that you wouldn't be landing at LAX when it was over.

I can't fully express how difficult this climb was. Imagine walking straight uphill over loose gravel for twelve hours a day with a pack on your back, while every molecule in your body hurts, you can't breathe, and every thought you have is telling you to quit. The only real thing preventing you from stopping is the overwhelming but basic knowledge that if you stop, you die. There is nowhere to go but to the next lodge. You must carry on.

We had a memorable standoff with a horse on a rope bridge at about five thousand feet. There wasn't enough room for both sides to pass, so we were waiting and negotiating while the bridge was swinging, high up over a gorge, with the nerve-racking overriding idea of us being dashed onto the rocks below. I began thinking about how many people and animals had crossed this bridge since it was last repaired. We squeezed past after careful calculation, and I think Garrie got a slight mule kick on the way around.

There were a few professional mountain climbers who were very helpful. Jake Norton is a dashing pro climber who has summited Everest and was a big help in getting me up that mountain and patched up when I had a yak-induced fall into some sharp rocks. His wife, Wende Valentine, works for Water for People, an important charity I've done quite a bit of work with in the past. They help local communities build water purification facilities and dig wells. Jake and Wende are both genuine charitable people and a great couple. Alan Hobson is a Canadian cancer survivor turned mountain guide and motivational speaker. He was the biggest help to getting Garrie and me up that hill. We stuck together the whole time, and we owe a debt of gratitude to him.

We stopped at all the lodges and camping grounds along the well-mapped and historic route. The Sherpas were somehow always ahead of us, and when we reached the next stopping points, the tents were already set up. These are the most efficient, skilled high-altitude workers in the world, and without them, none of this would ever happen. One of the stops was at a monument of piled rocks that was in memorial of the Sherpas and climbers who died on this quest. Those guys got quiet, and it was clear that it was a sacred place for them. All along the entire route, there are thousands of colorful prayer scarves tied to just about everything. How I understand it, the idea is to say a prayer for a specific person and tie the scarf around an object, and with this, the memory of any pain is taken over by the mountain and is continually blown away in the wind. I'm unreligious and uncomfortable with all ceremony on most accounts, but this is a positive action, and it makes for a brilliant, moving, multicolored art installation. The locals sell the scarves, and it's a little cottage industry. I'm all for local economies. It's a nice thought. Some religions light candles. It's hard to light a match up there.

We stopped at the highest monastery in the world. The grounds were very stark but impressive. It was carved out of the mountain, with Tibetan mastiff guard dogs roaming everywhere, while acolytes and monks did the daily chores and routines of a monastery in a completely relaxed and chilled way. We met the guy second down from the Dalai Lama and had an audience in his private, dark chambers. A little funny detail is that in his room, he had exercise equipment from the 1950s, complete with Indian clubs, dumbbells, and one of those old-fashioned reducing machines where a belt goes around the waist and a little motor jiggles you to fitness. It looked like a small gymnasium where Jack Dempsey would have trained. I kept thinking of a *Three Stooges* sketch the whole time I was in there. He seemed like a serious man and would be very helpful with advice and wise words, but I'm sure he didn't know who we were or what we were doing. I envy the way these guys must be able to tune out and meditate. I've never been able to slow my head down long enough to give it a good try; maybe it's in my New York DNA. If I haven't done it by now, after this exceptional opportunity, I probably never will.

We started each day with a song. We would all take turns singing and playing every time we stopped. I believe there is a definite healing and unifying quality to music. The trekkers looked forward to the music and seemed to get some strength from it. It's the best distraction and mood changer ever invented. Personally, watching Glenn Tilbrook shredding on an acoustic version of "Goodbye Girl" with his pants around his ankles at daybreak made setting out on a ten-hour uphill hike almost seem like the right thing to do. A real treat and head changer to see one of the most talented cats I'd ever known to be acting the court jester, lightening everyone's mood before the brutal yet majestic day of climbing ahead of us. We played around campfires, and when we stopped for lunch on the trails, I had a pair of drumsticks in my backpack, and I played on water bottles, logs, and rocks. It always worked, and I've now confirmed that I can do a show on anything. The performance really is in the spirit and soul.

There is a natural, majestic beauty to a mountain, and every now and again someone would point out that the peak of Everest could be seen in the distance. There are plenty of other peaks to astonish on the way up. The air was crisp and thin, and it was hard, but I could manage. Every person's body reacts to high altitude differently. Some people's oxygen levels in their blood get low, and they feel more fatigue. I was fortunate my blood produces oxygen nearly the same as at sea level. I was lucky my blood oxygen level never got too low. The footing was very difficult, and it was hard to get into a groove because every step was different and needed to be measured. The whole trek can't be done without two walking sticks, which become extensions of your body. Sometimes you'd be going on for a few hours and never be able to look up to see the magnificent surroundings and scenery.

We had a great day in Namche Bazaar, an ancient trading post where we shopped for Nepalese trinkets and small gifts. I brought home Nepalese prayer scarves in every color. We met in a local tavern and played an impromptu gig that ended in a conga line around the village where the locals and visiting tourists got an extra treat. We slept in a lodge with actual walls that night. There was a cold-water shower in the room, and Garrie and I dared each other to go in, lather up, rinse, and repeat. We howled so loud during the ice-cold bracer that the other trekkers came out of their rooms to make sure someone wasn't getting killed by a yeti. We formed an on-the-spot Himalayan polar bear club, anything to keep you going. It was a real luxurious treat. How many memorable cold showers do you have in one lifetime?

A week or so into it, we reached the goal of the base camp. There were a few international expeditions waiting for the all clear to do the summit. To summit requires a different skill set and equipment needs. We had done the extreme hiking trek to base camp, but some other crazies were going to climb the peak. Our own form of insanity was the other part of the mission, to play and record the world's highest gig and get into the *Guinness Book of World Records*. So we took a little rest at base camp and then headed up one thousand feet more, straight up the side of the mountain to Kalapathar. My memory is that it was a ledge sticking out of the side of the steeper mountainside and that we somehow got some guitars, thirty fans, and a drum kit up there and played a few songs. It was very cold and windy; the gusts chilled you to the bone and knocked over the snare drum stand. The whole trek was filmed by a cool young pro camera-man named Stash Slionski, who was, in true small-world fashion, from Massapequa. His uncle had seen the Cats play in bars back on Long Island. He did the same trek as we did, but he did it walking backward to film us. He's a good guy, and we're close friends now. CNN International had a satellite flying over, and ten seconds of it went out on the air, live. We were playing "Rock This Town" when it went on the airwaves.

We climbed back down to base camp afterward. We had done the highest-altitude rock show in history. Some wiseasses did a gig in an airplane a year later and technically overtook us, but I personally don't count it. We did it for real with no loopholes.

The whole week, Garrie and I had been planning a side adventure and an easier way back down the mountain. We had heard a rumor that there was a helicopter service that went from base camp all the way back to Kathmandu. One of the Sherpas was a real fixer. There is one of these guys in every community and walk of life, and I can usually find them. If you wanted to buy a Cadillac or score a little weed in Nepal, this would be the guy who could hook it up for you. We had been asking him the whole time we were climbing about the rumored helicopter. After the trek up, the achievement of the gig and conquest of the hardest part of the trip, the idea of going back down through the same yak muck for three days was unappealing and anticlimactic. We were sitting around a picnic table in the big tent back at base camp when the fixer told us it was possible to get a helicopter back to Kathmandu the next morning, in a small village about four hours' walk from base camp. We would need to set out at dawn and be prepared to give the pilot $1,500 that could be charged on Visa. Miraculously, I had my wallet in my backpack. We agreed, and it was set.

At that point, we got a new player on the team. A woman, a friend of Chippendale's from the Dallas contingent who was on the trek the whole time and we had seen but had not gotten to know that well, approached us and said she couldn't help but overhear us and that if we're doing the copter ride, she was in for one-third. This true gal pal was Rini Andres, and I think of her now like a sister. Rini is a successful businesswoman in her hometown of Dallas, a mother, wife, and all-around cool person. The next morning at dawn, the three of us set off to meet a helicopter in an unknown village with a Sherpa guide leading the way.

After four or five hours of moderately hard walking, we arrived on the outskirts of a tiny village with an adjacent field that, we were told, was used as a landing space for choppers. The guide left us, and we were standing around in a dirt field talking to some local kids, sharing the last of our granola bars with them. There was a certain amount of faith involved here, because if the helicopter didn't turn up, we really had nowhere to go and no gear to even camp out with. Another one of those "How did I get here? Why did I agree to this?" moments was upon me.

We waited for a couple of hours, really doing nothing in the middle of nowhere. With no warning and out of nowhere, a brightly painted, shiny orange-and-blue military-looking Russian-made medevac helicopter appeared and landed in front of us with a great roar of the rotors, creating a huge dust cloud. We threw our little bags into the back and climbed in.

The crew inside of the helicopter consisted of a big military-looking pilot, a local-looking Nepalese woman as copilot, and an average-looking guy, who I would later learn was a medic, sitting in a jump seat behind them with a doctor's bag open and ready on the floor in front of him. All were wearing headsets and were very focused. The rest of the large interior was empty, and I figured it was originally built to transport tanks and that a private company had bought the old Soviet-era military helicopter and retooled it for a service for injured climbers. They didn't know why they were stopping here and looked a bit relieved when they saw it wasn't a medical rescue emergency situation.

We had a breathtaking ride through the mountains. The pilot was really driving, and it was in no way a walk in the park for him. It seemed like we were very near to the sides of the mountains a few times, and I could see the powdery snow being blown off the cliffs when we got close. The whole ride took an hour or so, and the relief of not having had to slog back down the mountain was intense. We were three happy campers. A taxi into town found us back in the comfort of Hotel Yak & Yeti.

The first hot shower and shave in two weeks was a relief and a treat. A soft bed was welcome, too. We had a good nap, and when we woke up, we went for a stroll around the neighborhood around the hotel. There's a big U.S. embassy and the palace grounds, but it's surrounded by squalor. We found a place to eat pizza and went back to the hotel. We had been living on power bars, bananas, and cooled-down boiled water for two weeks. Many of the trekkers had gotten sick, but Garrie and I didn't eat the local fare and toughed it out with near starvation. Maybe it all hit us at once, but that night we were both violently ill. I was worse—this was a time when sharing a room was uncomfortable. It was the sickest I've ever been, and I asked Garrie to call the fixer guy, get a gun, and shoot me. I spent two full days either on the bathroom floor or in bed, in a fevered daze. We finally called the hotel desk and asked for a doctor.

An hour later, a young guy in a tracksuit knocked on the door. The doctor was a local guy who had trained in England and returned to his hometown to help the locals. He rode a scooter all over town and treated the poor. He had a little black bag and a lot of knowledge. I trusted him right away. I had no choice. He gave us a couple of injections and charged twenty-six dollars. He must have had the right stuff, because we both got much better by the next day.

The others returned three days later, and by then, I was in tip-top shape. We had a visit to the cancer ward of the Kathmandu hospital. The money we raised on the trek through donations had been used to purchase the first mammography and internal radiation machines in the country. There was a ceremony where we met the doctors and the mayor. We then went to Durbar Square in the middle of the city, where the police held up the traffic in the city's biggest square while we played a thirty-minute concert on a ramshackle makeshift stage. This kind of thing may happen all the time in LA or London, but in Kathmandu, it's a major, unique event.

We were there for one more day, and I still had a small personal itch that hadn't been scratched. James, Stash, and I went to the very local and underfunded Kanti Children's Hospital for a visit. This place is a haven of hope that everyone should see once in their lives before the next time you complain about not having a good parking spot or having to wait in line at the supermarket. A whole small neighborhood has sprung up in the parking lot and surrounding area of the hospital. The parents and siblings of the sick children move to be near them and visit every day. Many of them are from the countryside and cannot go back and forth to the city every day. They take jobs that allow them to stay near the hospital and some have market stalls in the parking lot that cater to other families of the sick kids. No child is abandoned by his or her family, and the whole gang comes every day to visit the sick one. We did a tour of the hospital, and it affected me like nothing else ever has. The conditions were appalling, and although the doctors, nurses, and staff are trying very hard, the poverty of the whole country pervades everywhere. They didn't have enough paper towels or soap for the doctors to wash their hands as often as they wanted. Dirt showed through part of the floor, and they couldn't keep the electricity on all the time. Still, the kids had positive energy and were thrilled when we brought some simple coloring books and small toys to the ward where the sickest kids were undergoing chemotherapy. I gave them some of my T-shirts. We had a good cry in the lobby and organized some steady shipments of basic stuff by encouraging our friends to go to a bulk store and send the stuff to the hospital. It's harder to organize this than you'd expect, and I hope it's still going on to some extent. I know it was happening for a while, because we were getting pictures sent to us. It fulfilled my own need to see things up close, to make a small, relatable personal difference, and to give one toy to one kid, as the whole concept of a radiation machine is way over my head.

I came back to LA and had a strong gratitude vibe going for a while. I made a bond with the new people who were on this trek and reinforced an existing bond with a few of the others. I was happy I did it but said I'd never do something like it again. This was true for two years until I got another call from Mike, James, and Shannon saying we were doing Kilimanjaro, the highest peak in Africa. All of this over again, with rhinos and giraffes, too? Sign me up for another adventure.

21

A New Chapter

In 2009, at Brixton Academy, London, there was a life-changing incident for me. The Stray Cats had played a show and were saying good night to the audience. We had a scorching gig, and as is often the case with a gig in a major town like London, there was much relief on the stage when it was finished. The next week was to be easy, gravy shows in Manchester and Glasgow, and we were going to finally make it to Ireland.

I had already jumped off and over the drums, ran around the stage, and had an all-around fun show. The drill was the same every night. I'd walk to Lee's side of the stage, say good night to those folks, walk to my side, and say hello to my people, and then we'd all meet in the middle, take our bow, and be gone. Everyone does it in a more or less similar fashion.

On the way back to the middle, a combination of things

happened in a split second that would change everything. An audience member tried to hand me something that I reached for—this never happens; I ignore this type of thing 99.999 percent of the time—the front of the stage curved a little on the right side, and the heel of my boot caught a groove in the wooden floor. I remember a brief sensation of falling before I hit the floor. I had fallen off the stage about ten feet straight down. I must have put my right hand down in an attempt to break my fall. I broke my arm instead. I remember a couple of security guards helping me up by pulling on my arm, and at that point, I knew something bad had happened. I got back onto the stage and took a bow with the others. Brian remembers me saying, "I broke my fucking arm."

Once I was in the dressing room, my wrist and hand really started to swell up. Another original buddy, punk rock legend Charlie Harper from the U.K. Subs, took his bandana off, got some ice, and wrapped my arm up. I had the feeling he had done this before. A rock-and-roll medic came to the rescue. A bunch of true pals were at the show and had already made their way to my dressing room. Glen Matlock, Captain Sensible, Mick Jones, Mike Peters, the late, great Gerry Harrington, and Peter Golding were all waiting for me. I'm told it was the first time that a member of the Clash, the Sex Pistols, and the Damned had been photographed together. I think I was in a mild shock. I did think that this was an excellent rock-and-roll who's who moment, and Gerry took a classic photo of all of us in my dressing room. What is out of the frame is my right wrist, swelling up like in a cartoon, wrapped in Charlie's bandana, the ice quickly melting, soaking my sleeve and leaving a little puddle where I stood.

I took a taxi with Pete back to his house in Chelsea, where I've stayed a hundred times. The plan had been to go by train to Manchester the next morning and do the gig at the Apollo, which was sold out in advance. When we got back to Pete's, I unwrapped my wrist for the first time in a few hours. It didn't even hurt that much, but I could tell things were not right. It was very bad and a bit shocking to look at. We walked down to the Chelsea and Westminster Hospital on Fulham Road. I had walked past the place a thousand times before but had never gone in. I must have cut an odd-looking figure having my hair piled high and still wearing stage makeup. I signed in at the emergency room desk, and we just sat. After a little while, I was taken for x-rays; Pete stuck with me the whole time. The results were not good. My wrist was broken in three places, and one bone had been reduced to dust. By then, it was about 4:00 A.M., and I was exhausted and bewildered by what had happened in the past few hours. The doctor wanted me to come back at 8:00 A.M.; he would do the operation then. I told him I couldn't do it; I needed to get to Manchester and turn up at the hotel. In hindsight, I should've just stayed in London and done it that way. He was a respected surgeon who was on rounds that night and wanted to help me. He put on a temporary cast and told me that I needed to have it done soon to avoid any permanent damage. So now I had fear on top of shock and disbelief.

I had never been in a cast before, and the whole thing didn't seem real. I stopped at the desk on the way out and asked about the payment. I told them I had a USA-based credit card, but I could get the tour manager to wire cash or that my buddy, who was English, could pay them with his credit card. They told me there was no charge and that if I were to have chosen to do the operation with my admitting surgeon, the whole thing would have been on the cuff. I told them again that I was American; the nurse told me it didn't matter. One thing I had to give the British: they were prepared to take care of me even though I wasn't one of their own. Can you imagine an English guy coming into an American hospital at 2:00 A.M., wearing makeup, and telling them a story about falling off a stage and wanting help? There would be cops and questions within two minutes, and the guy would still be sitting there with a broken arm. They never grilled me about my story or even asked for ID. In a typical light rain, we walked the three blocks back to Pete's house and sat in his kitchen in silence.

I had spoken with the tour manager and told him to tell the others. I still had to go to Manchester the next day and be examined by an approved doctor sent in by the promoter to affirm that I couldn't play. This would guarantee that the cancellation insurance for the tour would cover the accident. I was also holding out hope that I could somehow do the last few shows.

The next morning, Mikey Peters, who had stayed in London and lived in the Manchester area, picked me up in a taxi and took me to Paddington Station to catch the train to Manchester. Chris Monk, the Damned's European agent, who was at the show the night before and had also stayed in London, was along, too, and was a big help to me. The whole train ride, I was trying to think of ways to do the show. I thought about taping a stick to my casted wrist or wedging a tambourine in there. Mikey just smiled and nodded. He knew the inevitable truth that there was no way I could do a show in that condition.

We made it to the station and then the hotel. Apparently, there had been some announcements on the radio telling the fans about my accident in London and about the probable cancellation of the show that night at the Manchester Academy. At the hotel lobby and bar, there were fans crying and asking me if I could play the show in the cast. A doctor had to push past the fans; he came to my room and confirmed that I had a broken arm. He was a little embarrassed, as his diagnosis was obvious, but there was red tape to get through to make sure everyone, besides us, would be paid for the last part of the tour. This thing was officially over; I could not do the remaining gigs on this tour.

The plan was to go back to LA and get the operation there. A doctor friend of mine had arranged for a top-notch surgeon to do my arm right after I landed. The original ticket was booked with us all leaving from the last tour stop in Ireland. I still had to make it to Dublin, where I had a first-class ticket to take me back home. When I hit the floor back in London, we had each lost a lot of money, so to book a whole new decent ticket through Manchester was financially impossible. A couple of the crew guys who were going back to LA helped me with the luggage, and I made it to Dublin for the final leg of my long, arduous journey.

I was sitting in my seat on Aer Lingus when the last interesting part of the story happened. Through my haze, I recognized the guy in the seat next me. It was the actor Colin Farrell. He definitely looks and carries himself like a movie star. He looked at me like a lot of people do. He knew I was somebody but didn't know exactly who. After I introduced myself, he knew right away, and we quickly discovered five people we both knew. He asked me about my giant cast. I told him the story. He thought that if it had to happen, it was a pretty cool way to get a broken arm. That members of the Clash, the Damned, and the Pistols were all there and that it happened in front of a live audience were all mitigating details. I appreciated the positive spin. I would try to remember it in the darker days ahead.

About an hour or so into the flight, my wrist really started to hurt. The broken bones had still not been set, and as the doctor had warned, the air pressure caused a little extra pain. They had given me a couple of painkillers at the hospital and encouraged me to take them while I was there in the emergency room. I had kind of forgotten I had taken them. The first batch was beginning to wear off, and the pain started to well up. I'm a sober guy, but this was an extraordinary situation, and it was doctor's orders. I popped the last one and washed it down with a nice cup of tea. Twenty years ago, I would have boozed it up a bit, too, but now the drinking doesn't ever really enter into it.

I started to get a little goofy before falling asleep. There was a Colin Farrell movie playing on the screen. I don't know if it was a coincidence or maybe they show Irish actors on Aer Lingus, or maybe he has a deal with them. I saw him on-screen and started to say out loud, "Hey, man, you're in the movie!" I was busting his balls just a little. He asked me to not draw attention to us, and I stopped right away. I fell asleep five minutes later and woke up for breakfast. Colin and I talked a lot about regular stuff. He's a big punk rock fan, and I told him a few Captain Sensible and Steve Jones stories with good rock value.

When we landed, he was very helpful. He carried my carry-on bag and went with me to the baggage carousel and waited for my luggage to come off. He got my stuff off, loaded it onto a cart, and wheeled it all the way through. The paparazzi were waiting for him. He made a big deal out of telling them to leave me alone, to give me my space and respect my moment of privacy. It was really him they wanted the whole time, but he played it well and got himself off the hook at the same time. I never saw him again. He's a genuinely cool guy, and I thank him for being a positive part of this story.

Cherie was waiting for me, and I went straight to a hospital in Marina del Rey, where I went through a two-hour operation, which rebuilt my wrist. The doctor put in fifteen pins, one-sixteenth of an inch apart. They put a new cast on that went from my fingertips all the way up to and over my elbow and almost up under my armpit. It must have weighed twenty pounds and had to stay on for the next ten weeks. I went back to my house, sat on the couch, and thought a lot.

Cherie and I had met a few years before and lived in a house we'd bought together in a good part of town. It was the farthest away I had ever been from my beloved Sunset Strip, and I still miss my grand old flat on Doheny Drive. I thought TJ would benefit from a more normal environment. Cherie had a daughter, Madison, who was four years old when I met her. She would become my daughter, and I love her more than words can express. We have a very deep connection and have always loved the same things and each other's company. She is thriving now at an ivy-walled university back in New York.

As the weeks went by, my arm must've been healing up under the giant cast, but the inside of my skull and my soul felt broken. When I hit the floor in London, it was a big financial drag for all of us. Without getting too much into the economics of the rock-and-roll business, the last four or five shows of a tour pay for the expenses of the first twenty and are also where the band's profit comes from. Especially with the Stray Cats, where much of the profit for the band comes from the sale of T-shirts and other merchandise. We have historically done very well from this part of the biz. The Cats' head logo and overall imagery of the band has always been a unique and strong part of our whole game. Because of my accident, we missed out on four or five very lucrative merchandising nights. That would have been a good chunk of our profit on that tour. Everyone else had to still be paid. Trucking costs, crew, equipment being moved all over the world, hotel and air fares are but just a few of the dozens of expenses on any good-sized rock-and-roll tour. The cancellation insurance pays for that stuff but does not pay the band for lost income. The other two were very understanding on this issue, and neither of them ever said a cross word to me regarding my costly misstep. I appreciated that, because I was sitting on that couch, beating myself up over it, rerunning the incident over and over in my head until I thought I'd lose it. The "what might have beens" and "if onlys" were a constant companion in my throbbing head. I couldn't drive, I couldn't have a shower, and I certainly couldn't play. It was my right wrist that was broken, and I'm a funny type of ambidextrous. It's called cross-dominance. Certain things I do left-handed, like play drums, throw a baseball, or play tennis. Certain things like handwriting, brushing my teeth, and changing the channel, I do with my right hand.

There wasn't much I could do except sit there and think. About six or seven weeks into it, I had a big day out on the town, when I went back to the same hospital in Marina del Rey for a doctor's visit. After an x-ray that told him my bones had healed perfectly, he took the cast off, knocked me out again, removed the pins, and put a new, even bigger cast back on. Good news on the bone-healing part, but a further six weeks or so with a different giant cast lay ahead. I got better at life with a thirty-five-pound right arm with no fingers. I fashioned a functioning sling out of a big old pirate scarf with skulls and crossbones, so I did make it my own.

The whole time this recuperation was going on, the house we lived in was under major construction. The roof had been removed from a whole section of the house, and a new staircase was being built, along with an addition of two new rooms. It was a job that had been planned for months and in a case of perfectly bad timing started just as I was a prisoner in my own home. Every day, there was a different team of workers there, making all different sorts of deafening noise with heavy machinery. Drilling, banging, hammering, and dust that started every day at 8:00 A.M. were my daily visitors. I would have been on tour for another week or so, and I had planned on staying in Dublin with Madison for another week after the tour. I usually would've at least been able to drive to the Cat Club and kill time in the office or on Sunset Plaza with my gang every day, but in this new routine, I didn't go anywhere, and—understandably—no one really wanted to visit me in a construction site with a couch in the middle. My head was off to the races with the first nail being driven each day, and I knew that when it was over, I wouldn't be able stay in the house any longer. The accident caused a loss of funds on the tour, and escalating construction costs combined with the financial crash and housing debacle in 2008 really got me down. The bank had canceled the line of credit attached to the house, and we had to start paying for the whole thing directly out of pocket. I had to get out from under the house and all the panic and despair that went along with it.

Meanwhile, the U.S. insurance company would call me constantly to question the treatment and charges that were fully covered by the tour and extra workmen's compensation insurance that I had personally taken out on myself, as is the norm on a tour of this size. All sorts of people would call and ask trick questions about the accident details. I kept calm and told them that I had five thousand witnesses and that it was all on film. They just didn't like having to pay out. Never mentioned was the fact I've had every type of premium, platinum insurance since I was twenty-two years old on cars, health, and touring. I never took one penny off them for over twenty-five years. I had the feeling a few times that someone was watching me to make sure I hadn't been faking this injury. I never saw a bill, but I've been told by a few people in the know that the whole thing cost the insurance company over $300,000. A few hundred grand versus a new arm for a drummer—it still boils my blood that they put a price tag on it and made a hard time even harder.

In the face of all this, Cherie and I broke up. It was sad in the moment, but it was over on both sides. I moved into a small house in Beverly Hills and stayed virtually by myself for a year. I went about my business, did gigs, and tried to hustle up a living. We sold the house in the middle of the housing bust and took a bath. During this time, I didn't use the club to pull a lot of girls and without thinking too much went into monk mode. I stayed in touch with all my true pals, but on the whole, I didn't want to talk to anyone, and nobody pushed advice, which is part of why someone is a true pal in the first place. I stayed close with Madison, and we worked out a way for everyone to get along.

During this self-imposed quiet time, I did do quite a few other things. When the cast came off, I did twice-a-week hand therapy and reacted well to it. I started to practice the drums and felt no pain with that type of motion. I had a few gigs with Head Cat, which were perfect warm-ups for the bigger tour that the Cats had coming up later in the year in Australia. Lemmy was very supportive, and in his own way, he admonished me by telling me, "The drummer shouldn't have been in the front of the stage, anyway!" I played the gigs with him and had no pain. Turning a doorknob or getting the gas cap open caused more distress than playing the drums. I can live with that. As long as I can play the drums, carry the luggage, and type, I stand a chance; none of the necessary activities were affected in a long-term way by my accident. Having said all this, I can say it still aches but has never stopped me from doing anything since.

In October 2009, with the Love Hope Strength charity crew, I did climb and peak Mount Kilimanjaro. By that time, my arm had healed up just nicely and didn't prevent me from doing any physical activity. We all reached the summit, Uhuru, the local Swahili name for the mountaintop. Another true pal joined on this one: I shared a tent and toothpaste with Robin Wilson of the Gin Blossoms. He was a positive and helpful tent mate, and we had a gas climbing and singing the whole way up Kilimanjaro. In accordance with tradition, I can now call it Kili. The local legend and pro mountain climber code mandates you cannot use this nickname unless you've peaked it. It fulfilled a longtime wish of mine to go to Africa.

I visited the cancer and children's hospitals in Arusha in Tanzania. I brought a bunch of swag, and there are now kids in Arusha wearing Slim Jim T-shirts, and one lucky one is sporting a Yankees baseball cap with a World Series patch on it. We stopped in villages and clinics all along the way. I enjoyed hanging out with locals and always get gratitude shots when I see kids who are happy with what we think is so little. I have a lot of respect and admiration for Shannon Foley Henn, who was the head of the charity at the time. She has since moved to Arusha full-time to help with the newly built cancer ward and really deserves a more than honorable mention in the charitable sections of my story. I really dug the whole African experience and on one day was especially glad to be a vegetarian when the big chief of one the villages served roasted goat for lunch. No matter what anyone may say now, nobody liked it then.

We went on a once-in-a-lifetime safari, too. I had been telling our excellent guide James for two weeks that I had better see a rhino on the safari or I'd be very upset. It became a running joke. I made out I was serious, and the guides gently insisted that rhino sightings in that part of the country were rare and almost unheard of. At the end of the breathtaking safari where we saw every possible animal except the elusive rhino, the joke was on me. We rode the safari in open-topped Range Rovers and just saw nature at its finest. Actually seeing the lion take down an antelope is spectacular, frightening, awe-inspiring, sad, brutal, and vicious all at once. It was really right out of the *Wild Kingdom* show we watched as kids and could never imagine it would ever really happen in front of us. The only way I have ever been able to travel anywhere is when there is a gig attached at the other end, and a gig in this locale is unlikely for anyone. So this opportunity was even more special, because I knew it was a one-off chance to see some things I had never seen before and may never have the chance to see again.

Near the end of a long day in the sun, while we were driving over an immense open plain, heading back to the final camp, the guide guys were looking at me with disappointed long faces. I was almost ready to shrug and tell them it was all a gag and a coping mechanism for the last two weeks, when someone in the lead car cried out while they circled back to us and handed me his high-powered binoculars.

Off in the distance, sitting by himself, was a huge black rhino. The tour guides and locals were amazed, and a few of them had never seen one before. With the special binoculars I could see him vividly, could count the wrinkles in his massive neck, see the flies getting swatted off by his tail, and look right in his eyes. He just sat there, motionless, and everyone was patient with me while I just stared at him through the field glasses. Although I was captivated and would have stayed a little longer, I could feel the group unease and knew everyone wanted to get going. I understood that not everybody was as into the whole rhino thing as I was. We had a nice base camp waiting, but it was still a few more hours' drive from there.

Even among the wonder of nature, a five-hour drive in a Land Rover with five people per vehicle is a tough one. As the convoy was getting ready to start pushing on, my rhino stood up, shook himself off in a big dirt cloud, and started running around, stopping, turning, and starting again. He was putting on a show that everybody was surprised by and enjoyed. After a few passes, he ran off past the horizon. I've read everything that Hemingway ever wrote but proudly admit that I never even once thought about shooting him. I'd kept up the act that I was confident and knew my rhino would turn up. The trekkers who were along with me and even the guides and locals couldn't help but wonder if I hadn't summoned up this beast through sheer will.

When I got back from this adventure, I went back to regular life. A few months later, I had another short, fun series of dates with Lemmy; we were doing some easy ones up and down the coast in California. I was not looking for it, but I found another rarely spotted wonder of nature. There are not many six-foot-tall, super-gorgeous, twenty-two-year-old, rockabilly-loving true California blondes out there. I saw one and didn't let her get away. I met Christy Lynn Nelson at our gig in San José. She was a platonic friend of Danny Harvey's and was coming to visit him. I saw her in the audience and knew I couldn't miss this chance. I was introduced to her after the show and was just honest about my feelings. She started to visit me on my home turf, and the rest is history. We are still together, and she's my girl. Another example of how if you are open and let it come to you, the extremely rare things in life can happen.

22

The Boys in the Band

Alot of guys have sold more records and had more money, more girls, and more drugs, but not with the same combination of varying adventures as the Stray Cats. Country guys stay with country guys, rock guys stay with rock guys, actors stay with actors. The Stray Cats and I in particular have straddled all these fences.

The other two have never been close. Lee thinks that Brian has tried to rewrite history to make it seem like the Stray Cats was all him and we were like a backing band. Brian thinks Lee has an over-inflated opinion of his own place in rock-and-roll history. I don't care about any of it. It's a hundred years later, and people still care about something we came up with when we were kids. There are still new fans every year. At this point, I just want to play, earn, and have fun—back to the basics. On any given night, there are three different bands on a stage somewhere in the world, each with one member of the Stray Cats playing a different version of "Rock This Town." I'm sure they are all pretty good; they are excellent musicians and full-on pros. But I feel in my heart that none are as good as if we three were doing it together. I really do love my guys and want nothing more than to play with them, earn a good payday, and cement our legacy as the best rockabilly band ever.

I like to remember everything in a positive light. Let's be honest: if anyone can find any way to complain about the details of being a rock star, it's pretty sad and petty. We are one in a million, and if you add rockabilly to the mix, we are one in ten million. I try to keep the early hunger and excitement as close as I can. I know none of this would have happened exactly like it did if we hadn't all played those gigs and gone to those record stores and thrift shops on Long Island in 1979. No one can tell, maybe the others would have made it on their own, but not in the legendary way the Stray Cats did. I do not live in the past, nor do I deny it. I embrace the memory and move ahead. I am proud of our achievements. I do think we should take the old car out for a spin once in a while; it still runs great and looks cool. In the long-term sense, we blew it a long time ago.

The other two are more gifted in a technical, musical way than I am. They always have been. I have never been a soloist, but I do feel that my style of drumming and spirit helped them both get to their best. I feel it was a total team effort, but I love the team the most. The others would never have done anything they didn't want to do. We all benefited from the band, but I think I did the most to hold it together and was the most hurt when it split up in 1985. I think that's part of being the drummer.

I was devastated, personally and in a career sense, but quickly moved on. Lee and I got busy right away. Then we reformed it in 1988, but it was never the same. We had lost valuable momentum, and although we did some of our best songwriting and live shows between 1988 and 1992, the real opportunity to become a truly important band had passed. We could have really rewritten the book with the right record after *Rant N' Rave*. At the time, in late 1984, Brian didn't think I was up to the task, although I don't think he gave me the right chance. He had a vision at the time for what he wanted to sound like and I feel was looking for a way to do it on his own. After everything we had been through and achieved, he was ready to pack the whole thing in after a few very impromptu coke-and-booze-fueled rehearsals. He seemed to almost want it to go badly so he could break up the band with a clean conscience. He had me feeling that I wasn't musically up to his new vision. I think he has always wanted to be a solo artist. He's not a band guy, and the time spent with the Cats, which had equal voting rights, did not come naturally to him. It's frustrating to me to have wanted to tell him for thirty years that all I ever wanted from him was for him to be in his own band. He is older than I am by two years, and it doesn't matter now, but when one guy is fifteen and one guy is seventeen, it does matter, and it stays with you. Since we were kids, I've always looked up to the guy and wanted his approval. He was the best guitar player in New York, and he was from my same school and Little League. And as a kid, I always wanted to play with him. When we discovered rockabilly around the same time, I got the chance to work with him as an equal.

Lee and I had played together since we were twelve years old and agreed on most things. In that regard, the two-against-one vibe was definitely created by Brian. Lee and I would have never broken up the band. We would have both ridden out any bumpy patches. I felt Brian was open to listen to the first people who got in his ear and told him he should go solo the first time. We should have circled the wagons and have been closer at that time. I accept my part in it but would have never left the band. It's a common hindsight, but we should have just taken off a few months.

Brian and I have the same horoscope sign, and Lee and I were born in the same year in the Chinese zodiac. So that throws astrology completely out the window. We are all very different characters. We agree on how great Gene Vincent was and how good we are. I wish we discussed these more positive things more often.

I don't follow either of their solo careers. I'm not very computer savvy. A funny contradiction I've noticed with the whole rockabilly scene is that for a bunch of people who crave the lifestyle of a bygone era, they have really embraced the Internet and all modern ways of gossiping, snooping, and snarky commentary. In the past, a disgruntled fan would have to write a letter and lick a stamp and an envelope in order to express some clumsily veiled jealousy toward a band he or she secretly worships. We three do all agree on this one. The rare times I speak with them, I enjoy talking to each of them. We inevitably wind up talking about something or someone from when we were growing up in Massapequa. There is always one time in every conversation where I genuinely crack up with laughter, and when I hang up the phone, I always wonder what happened and what could be so bad that we don't do this more often. The other two tend to remember unhappier moments. Maybe it's my drummer's naïveté and glass-half-full optimism.

I have rarely ever listened to a solo record by either of them. It's too hard for me to be objective. When I do hear a track, I recognize their styles immediately and know their records are going to be good if for no other reason than that they are both super-talented guys. For me, the records I've heard lack the X factor of the Stray Cats, regardless of how many copies have been sold. I don't think they are as good as the records we did make or the records we could have made. These are very unspecific regrets, I know. I won't talk about their personal lives. I was very hurt when Brian called to tell me the band was over by a phone call. I thought then and still believe it was a shabby way to end it.

In 1985, I didn't have the life skills or technique to navigate this properly. I was twenty-four years old and had spent my entire adult life up until then in the Stray Cats—it was all I knew. I slammed the phone down and yelled. I didn't speak to Brian for two years. I know he felt at the time that I couldn't musically handle his vision for his new musical direction—which in the end was straight-up rock music that I could've easily handled. I wish we had given it more of a chance, because the next record would have been the one that really proved something to the world and us. If we had combined what would appear on both his and our solo records, it would have pushed rockabilly forward again. I think I proved on the *Phantom, Rocker & Slick* record that I could handle regular rock music. I felt insecure about my playing for a while, but I haven't for a long time. Perhaps I had to make that album to prove something to myself. I have learned to embrace my own style and technique, but am not sure if I would have got there without doing that first *Phantom, Rocker & Slick* album. Further proof for me that although sometimes unwanted, everything happens for a reason.

From 1979 to 1985, I can never remember a serious band meeting type of discussion in the Stray Cats. When we reformed in 1988, we had a few talks, but nothing too serious. It's a real New York trait to not talk about anything personally uncomfortable or serious. It spans all types of people and I think is a regional phenomenon. The eight-hundred-pound gorilla is a common guest at many dinner tables in New York. Reforming seemed like the obvious thing to do, so we did. The three of us are still, at the end of the day, instinctual guys, the others even more so than I am. I was thrilled, and it was one of those rare times in life when you really know your life choice is the correct one in that exact moment. There was no doubt for me in this instance. It all happened when we started communicating a little, and we reunited without much fanfare or "I love you, man" moments. I think some of our best work was in this time period. Any live performance that I happen upon is blazing and musically a bit more sophisticated than the performances from the early 1980s. We made a groundbreaking album with *Blast Off*. Dave Edmunds was back in the producer's chair. It holds up against anything today. We were upset when it didn't do better in the charts. We expected to pick up right where we had left off. We left EMI and did two more albums without the chart or radio success we were looking for. Nile Rodgers, who I became close with, produced one. It was during the making of this record that I quit drinking. The live shows were always strong, and in Europe we did big festivals.

I find the other two guys to be more similar than either of them would like to admit. They are both concerned mainly with having their own names on the marquee. Besides the Cats, neither of them has ever been in an equal band situation. I've always preferred the band/gang mentality; maybe it's part of being the drummer. Most drummer guys I know have similar feelings. I'm not an elevated Zen guy. I'm still the "youthful and hotheaded" guy that Harry Dean told me I was. I've acquired more calm along the way, but it's still New York peeled nerve right below the surface. It may be deeper now, but it's still there. I did quit drinking and drugging about twenty-five years ago. There was no spectacular last flameout; I just hit the wall and couldn't do it anymore. Ten years of constant partying and maintaining a buzz had worn me down.

When I bottomed out, I knew it; it was very clear, and it wasn't that hard to continue not drinking after the initial first month or so. Now I don't know another way of life. I've accidentally developed some life skills and don't get wound up in traffic. Sometimes I wonder how I got along. I did have my adventures in partying and kept up with the best, but I am ultimately happy that I got out when I did. I could not have done the things I've done since if I had continued drinking. I sometimes think I wouldn't have made it to thirty, but I had my fun and got out with no lasting mental or physical damage.

With no intended irony, I had my last drink, by myself, at On the Rocks in September 1990. In one last drunken act of choreography, I fell down the stairs, hit the door handle on the way down, and rolled into the street. The next day, I didn't drink. I called a rock-and-roll buddy who I remembered didn't drink and still seemed to have fun. I stopped going to bars and, after a month or so, knew I couldn't do it again. My life changed for the better. I have experienced every type of setback in sobriety, but I do believe that if I continued the way I was going, I wouldn't have been able to handle any of it. Regular, everyday life is hard enough, as it is for everyone I know. There have been breakups with bands and girls, financial highs and lows, broken bones, and broken hearts, but these too will pass. There is the chance of not even making it that far. It doesn't have to be a health issue. Drinking and drugging puts you in strange places and situations that you'd not normally be in. You can only roll the dice so many times before you crap out. I would've walked in front of a bus or driven off the side of Mulholland Drive or slipped in the shower. A few partying acquaintances fell by the wayside, but I'm still friends with 99 percent of the people that I was friends with when I drank, plus a few new ones; a true pal is a true pal.

The Stray Cats have gotten back together a few times and have had real positive reactions to the gigs—a 2004 European tour that saw us sell out Brixton Academy in London twice, the Zénith in Paris, the Heineken Music Hall in Amsterdam, and the Helsinki Ice Hall in Finland, where we set the single-night house record for merchandise sold. I saw these as triumphant returns to the world capitals that we had played and conquered in the early 1980s. Maybe now we could get paid and not sweat the small stuff. We could enjoy a more relaxed time with just a great show to be concerned with. In the past, we had TV and radio station appearances on the day of the show, harder travel, and constant partying to worry about. We really did cause a stir both onstage and offstage in these places.

A USA tour in 2007 with ZZ Top and the Pretenders was the best summer anyone could remember. Hootenanny in LA in 2003 was an affirming show, as we headlined the biggest rockabilly-themed festival at the time in the USA. TJ, Madison, and the other Stray Cat kids were all at these shows, and it was great seeing them all grown up and hanging out together on the side of the stage during the gigs. This whole event had sprung up around the scene we had created. An oversold Orange County Fair in 2009 was a memorable one for the band and fans. This was the last time we played a show in California. I thought a sold-out tour of Australia in 2010 was the beginning of a more frequent reunion that would happen when the offers and everyone's schedules matched. I never thought we were going to make a new record or start a third part of our career; I know that ship has sailed, but I did think we could take the whole thing out every few years. There is a brand-new generation of rockabilly fans, and we are still the best. A new counterculture has blossomed in our absence from regular touring. There is a big hot-rod, 1950s-based lifestyle scene out there on every continent. Other bands and promoters have stepped in to fill the gap, and a few do very well at it. I firmly believe the Cats have always been and continue to be the main inspiration and best representation of this movement. We did the heavy lifting and made it safe to bring this music and style back into the mainstream. Now it should be easier to benefit from all that hard work, but that has not been the case. We have still been unable to fully commit to a new project.

It's come close a couple of times. The 2004 Rumble in Brixton is a perfect concert captured on film. We recorded one new studio song for the release of the DVD. We didn't promote it enough or give it a fair shake. I was into going for it. There are many reasons we didn't that are unimportant. I think it's always there if we want it. Like the original artists we looked up to and were influenced by, we have become timeless. The Stray Cats name, logo, and legend are strong. No other rockabilly band from the last forty years has become a household name.

The other two do not get along, and there is no communication between them. I have always been in the unenviable position of being close to each of them individually and always trying to be the peacemaker. I think now, more than ever, the need to be friends with someone in your band is unnecessary. We have traveled separately for a long time, and besides doing the gig, we don't see a lot of one another, anyway. There has never been a problem on the stage, and at this point, everybody in the audience loves it, and we have nothing left to prove. There is precedent with many other acts, and from my experience, no band that stays together goes to lunch or hangs out. There is the common bond of the history and legacy of the band; I think that should be enough. Anything else is personal, and at this advancing stage of my golden years, personalities do not enter into it. We should be reaping a little of what we sowed thirty-five years ago. I think the hard part was finished a long time ago. One member = one vote; this is just my feeling. Maybe someday we'll get three out of three votes and do something fun and important. I hope so—that's my vote.

23

Full Circle

Looking up, I noticed I was late. The lyric from the song was stuck in my head. I had just gotten out of the shower; Christy and I were toweling off. We had a gig with Head Cat at the Roxy that night, and the sound check was looming. I had to pack a little bag and get out of the house. Christy had to get ready, and I had learned a long time ago that you cannot rush a woman getting ready. Another line from the same song was telling me that I still had to drag a comb across my head. TJ was helping me, but I was bringing the drums in my car. Trying to save a few bucks on the cartage of the gear seemed like a good idea at the time. Luckily, I had loaded up my car in the morning.

I still had an hour of Game Show Network watching with Harry Dean ahead of me. I had it all timed out. I would get ready while keeping an eye on the TV in the mirror. I could do it all over the speakerphone and use the hair dryer only during the commercials. Harry would not appreciate anything less than my undivided attention during Chain Reaction. The fallout for nonparticipation on a weekday while I was technically in town was not worth it. I operate well in a slight state of chaos and am able to multitask, so I can handle it. I do understand that the situation is self-imposed, but at this point in life, this wackiness is my reality. Of course, I can just say no to anything at any time, but it's easier to just go along with my own quirky life than to try to change the details. I get a legitimate pass from Harry Dean if I'm actually out of town. The choice between being late for the sound check and facing Lemmy or ducking out early and missing a game show session and dealing with Harry Dean is a no-win situation. The gig is, of course, more important, but I try to accommodate everyone, and I'm still flattered that these are my biggest problems.

What I really wanted to do most was relax a little after shower time, but you can't have everything. I had already not gone on my daily hike in Franklin Canyon with Steve Jones, Billy Duffy, and Jimmy Ashhurst. They were very understanding. My little dog is our de facto mascot. He was disappointed. The daily midmorning constitutional through the hills is the highlight of his day. Being a vintage TV enthusiast (addict) with thousands of hours of my life invested (wasted) in reruns, I'm still thrilled every day to walk along the pond and trail where the intro for *The Andy Griffith Show* was filmed. It never gets old for me, and hiking it with a few true pals whose records and gigs I still enjoy makes it even better. A good lunch in Bev Hills or WeHo and back home in time for the Game Show Network with Harry Dean, which takes me right up until it's time to tune into MLB .com for the Yankees games during baseball season. Every now and then, I need to go and play the drums to keep this idyllic lifestyle going. One hundred years later, doing it with Lemmy at the Roxy was a pretty cool, truly fun, street-credible, and legit way to pay the bills for a month. If Division Avenue and Merrick Road in Massapequa were the crossroads and the devil had asked me to sign on the dotted line, telling me that in exchange for my eternal soul, this would be my life in rock and roll, I would have signed right then and there. I have no regrets. I would've liked a little bit more money, but it wouldn't really change anything. I don't believe in that hocus-pocus stuff, anyway.

The problem with local shows is that it's hard to be in the on-the-road mode. When I'm on the road, it's a little easier to tune out everyday life and concentrate on the show. Anyone in a band will tell you the same thing. There are always a few scattered guests in every town, but when you're playing where you live, it's usually the deep gang members that come to the shows. My real pals don't insist on having their hands held, but I put a little pressure on myself to make sure that everyone is taken care of as well as can be in the situation I'm in. TJ is very helpful with this. He's grown up in this life and knows the drill. I moved off Sunset Strip a few years ago, and for those who know LA, just a few miles at the wrong time of day can mean an hour's worth of extra driving. I'm in Beverly Glen now; we could've walked to the Roxy in the past, but now, even knowing a few shortcuts, it's a pain-in-the-ass drive if you leave ten minutes past the optimum time. So I was late to the sound check.

"Slim, can you please give me the full hour today?" implored Harry Dean.

"I'll try, Harry, but I've got this gig at the Roxy tonight with Lemmy. I have to get to the sound check; it's just today," I harriedly answered.

"Lemmy? Who's that? Anyhow, the Roxy is only ten minutes away!"

I didn't want to get into the whole thing of explaining Lemmy to the one guy in the world who doesn't know who he is, and it's true that the Roxy is only a ten-minute drive, if you don't leave Beverly Glen at 4:00 P.M. I just did the whole hour over the speakerphone while frantically getting ready.

We went down Deep Canyon to Benedict, cut through on Lexington, a few blocks on Sunset, and a quick left onto Foothill to get up to Doheny Road. No matter what, between 4:00 and 7:00 P.M., when you run back onto Sunset at Doheny Road by the old Hamburger Hamlet, it takes fifteen minutes to go the block and a half east to the Roxy. I got a few calls from TJ that Lemmy was upset that I was late. He still lives across the street. I know I'm in the wrong, but if it comes down to it, my excuse is ironclad. I've gained calm in traffic over the years, and I know it's only a sound check and that the gig is four hours away, but a little rock-and-roll anxiety still lingers in my bones. It's ingrained early in a musician's life that being late for the gig is the worst of all behavior. The Cats rarely, if ever, did a sound check. I know that Lemmy is old-school rock and roll. Even if it's just a quick line check, he likes doing it, and this was a real gig. Christy is a very chilled California girl and is a perfect counterbalance for my naturally slightly stressed New York state of mind. I've done a hundred sound checks with Lemmy, and it's always the same. Watch the excellent documentary done by Wes Orshoski about Lemmy's life and you'll see a classic Motörhead sound check scene. It's the same with Head Cat. It takes loud to a new level, and he inevitably tells the soundman to take out all the bass of the lead vocal. We run a song, maybe half of a second one, and we're done. It's timed out perfectly to make sure that I can't go back home and will have to spend three hours hanging around the dressing room at the Roxy.

We go next door to the Rainbow, where we'll hang out. Lemmy will sit in the back of the outside bar, smoke, and play the video games. I'll say hello to everybody, sit with TJ and Christy, and have my one thousandth bowl of minestrone soup. I'm grateful for the gig. At that point in his career, Lemmy didn't need to do club gigs with me, but he loved rockabilly music and knew these songs inside out. We got a special sound when we mixed his style of bass playing with my drumming, and when you added Danny B's ace guitar playing and a long, strong friendship, a certain cool sound happened when we played together. We tried to find a few good gigs every year and make them special events. We always talked about doing more and about doing another album. Every musician also welcomes a little bit of extra bread. Sadly, late last year, Lem hopped the bus to the great gig in the sky. He was the last of a breed. I'm happy that I knew the guy the way I did.

The gig sold out and went off without a hitch. There is a type of rockabilly magic that happens when talented, big-personality guys do the music they really love. I have been fortunate in that I've had the chance to play this music my whole life. The cats like Lemmy, who are well known for doing other types of music, really embraced the chance to do the old rockabilly numbers.

Being the drummer, I'm always faced with the reality of the "who else" question. Everybody loves me, but they want to know who else I'm bringing along to the gig. I've been lucky with the who else, but it's tough to constantly deal with it, and I become frustrated. Starting with Brian and Lee, I've continued to meet, become friends with, and work side by side as equals with some of the finest musicians and characters in our business, so necessity is the mother of invention in my case. Whether it's Lemmy or Captain Sensible, Earl Slick or Glen Matlock in a band situation, and George Harrison or Carl Perkins on very special occasions, I'm genuinely honored.

Steve Jones came to the gig, and I appreciated him going out because I knew he'd rather have been home watching oldies TV. True pal, fellow Irish New Yorker, deep gang member, and House of Pain founder Danny O'Connor was there, too. Billy and Jimmy were in the audience. We missed hike club that day, but we got together at my gig. I was flattered by these cats coming to my gig.

I went with Christy and TJ to On the Roxy after the show, and we hung out with a few friends. I was a little quiet as I wondered to myself if this was a full-circle moment or a stuck-in-a-rut, never-moved-ahead moment. I had feelings that were beyond the standard déjà vu moment. I ultimately decided I was grateful to be surrounded by my son and a superhot girlfriend, after having played a sold-out show of the music I love with a rock star pal. Besides wishing that the Stray Cats were playing the next night at the Palladium, I couldn't think of a better situation. Hopefully, that will happen again, but I'm satisfied with what we've achieved, the legacy we'll leave, and the fact that it's allowed me to live this charmed life.

At the risk of being psychoanalyzed, I needed to do something that was just mine. The stories involve other people, but I don't know of anyone else who has assembled the same cast. Some of these adventures happened a long time ago, and sometimes it feels like it happened to someone else. I'm too old now to be consciously cool, to be cool on purpose; I've got to hope enough of it has rubbed off on me and I can cruise, a little bit easier, into the sunset. These are the only clothes I have.

Acknowledgments

· · · · ·

Thanks to Dana Newman, Stevie Salas, Eric Gardner, Glen Matlock, Bill Wyman, Ian Kilmister (RIP), Dickie Harrell, Charles Connor, Captain Sensible, Fred Armisen, Steve Jones, Paul Cook, Linda Ramone, Darrel Higham, Harry Dean Stanton, Jello Biafra, Gary Schwindt, Dixon Mathews, Peter Golding, Lloyd Johnson, Danny O'Conner, Jim McSorley, Mike and Jules Peters, James Chippendale, Stash, Jimmy Ashhurst, Frankie Madeloni, Bernard Fowler, Charley Drayton, Glenn Tilbrook, Nick Harper, Cy Curnin, Jerry Schilling, Carmine Appice, Chris Cheney, Chuck Labella, Clem Burke, Danger Ehren, Billy Duffy, Shannon Foley Henn, Dizzy Reed, James and Maureen McDonnell, Doris Tyler, Duff McKagan, Ed Begley, Jr., Elliot Easton, Eric Dover, Faith Cowling, Garrie Renucci, Vincent Gallo, Gary Haber (RIP), Gerry Harrington (RIP), Gilby Clarke, Glenn Palmer, James Fearnley, Jamie Evenstad, Bobby Sands, Mim Scala, Jamie James, Jeffrey Baxter, Jeff Stein, Jody Carson, Phil Carson, Matt Sorum, Michael Des Barres, Michael Lustig, Chris Monk, Andy Halligan, Mark Halligan, Dave Phillips, Brent Barnett, Jamie Henry, Ben Davies, Joe Testa, Kirsten

Matt, Mick Jones, Topper Headon, Muddy Stardust, Murphy, Nick Curran (RIP), Danny B. Harvey, Chrissie Hynde, Martin Chambers, Pete Farndon (RIP), James Honeyman-Scott (RIP), Peter Stormare, Phil Bennett, Phil Doran, Bob Rech, Anthony Bettencourt, Kim Graham, Chris Schiflett, Rami Jaffe, Jack Gray, Rhoda Neal, Stiv Bators (RIP), Rob Kirkpatrick, Steve Bonge, Jeanne Marie Giulianotti, Robert Matheu, Robin Wilson, Julien Temple, Ronnie Starrantino, Ryan Roxie, Spider Stacey, Stefan Adika, Stanley and Naomi Drucker, Andy Gershon, Boz Boorer, Terrence McDonnell, Josh Richman, Steve Luna, Virginia Karras, Steve Mona, Stuart Ross, Supla, Sonny Burgess, Robert Plant, James Rippetoe, Steve Strange (RIP), Michael Siddons-Corby, Wanda Jackson, Wendell Goodman, Susan Wiesner, Tayloe Emery, Franklin Canyon Hike Club, Jeff Porcaro (RIP), Teddy Zigzag, Tim Polecat, Tim Medvetz, Todd Singerman, Twiggy Ramirez, Lynn Swanson, Vic Firth (RIP), Fred and Dinah Gretsch, Wende Valentine, Jake Norton, Smutty Smith, Gerry Laffy, Dave Edmunds, Willie Nile, Victoria Sellers, Nicholai Adler, Lisa Socransky-Austin, Joe Sib, Tony Sales, Mark Fowler, Billy Zoom, Lee Rocker, Brian Setzer, Claudine Martinet-Riley, Ian McLagan (RIP), Ronnie Lane (RIP), Gavin Cochrane, Bobby Startup, Derrick Unwin, Joel Brun, Bob Roberts, Dennis Cockell, Steve Ferrone, Quentin Tarantino, Michael Madsen, Scotty Albenesius, Peter Joseph, Melanie Fried, Christy D'Agostini, Karlyn Hixson, and everyone at Thomas Dunne Books.

A Drummer's Dream

· · · · ·

I've never seen a drummer I didn't like. I can watch any drummer in any live situation and get something positive out of his or her playing. All drummers get along with one another, and there is definitely a universal camaraderie, unlike any other group of musicians. I always wanted to be part of this brother-sisterhood. The older I've gotten, the more I embrace my own place in and contribution to this special club.

I'd like to use this time and space to offer thanks to a few of my favorites. I'm very happy to say that I can count quite a few of these folks as real friends. Knowing and hanging out with certain people on this list were childhood drummer dreams come true. A young me would've signed any deal with the devil to have been guaranteed peerage with these cats. Dipped in blood and signed with a drumstick, of course.

Dickie "Be-Bop" Harrell

DJ Fontana

Charles Connor

Earl Palmer

W. S. "Fluke" Holland

Buddy Harman

Charlie Watts

Ringo Starr

Philly Joe Jones

Max Roach

Gene Krupa

J. M. Van Eaton

Chick Webb

Martin Chambers

Clem Burke

Paul Cook

Jim Keltner

Nigel Olsson

Jim Hodder

Buddy Rich

Jeff Porcaro

Bernard Purdie

Rick Marotta

Louis Bellson

Alan Dawson

Steve Gadd

Nicky "Topper" Headon

Jerry Allison

Clyde Stubblefield

Blair Cunningham

Billy Cobham

Tony Williams

Elvin Jones

Joe Morello

Carmine Appice

Cindy Blackman

Sandy Nelson

Mark Craney

Butch Trucks

Jaimoe

Monte Yoho

Paul Riddle

Joe English

Tony Thompson

James Gadson

Charley Drayton

Steve Jordan

Paul Thompson

Andy Newmark

Bobby Z

Mel Gaynor

Gene Riggio

Rat Scabies

John Farriss

Simon Phillips

Michael Bland

Larry London

Keith Moon

Carlton Barrett

Kenney Jones

Myron Grombacher

Gregg Bissonette

Tommy Ramone

Bun E. Carlos

Mick Fleetwood

Freddie Below

Willie "Big Eyes" Smith

Al Jackson, Jr.

Dennis Davis

Pete Thomas

Neil Peart

Sid Catlett

Dennis Wilson

Meg White

Jim Gordon

Gina Schock

Max Weinberg

Roger Taylor

Phil Taylor

Terry Bozzio

Jughead Jones

Chris Blackwell

Zigaboo Modeliste

Ray Lucas

Stewart Copeland

Eric Singer

Tommy Clufetos

Brian Tichy

Shelly Manne

Papa Jo Jones

Stix Hooper

Phil Collins

Rick Allen

Mousey Alexander

Terry Williams

Steve Ferrone

Stan Lynch

Roy Haynes

Chris Layton

Randy Castillo

Mikkey Dee

Chad Wackerman

Larry Mullen, Jr.

Mel Taylor

Mick Avory

Nick Vincent

Chris Frantz

Jimmy Cobb

Lenny White

Alphonse Mouzon

Thomas Pridgen

Alan White

Ted Reed

Jim Chapin

Nicko McBrain

Supla

Danny Seraphine

Ronnie Tutt

Jonathan Moffett

Ricky Lawson

Ian Paice

Bill Kreutzmann

Don Brewer

Bill Bruford

Art Blakey

Billy Gussak

Robert St. Judy

This list has no particular order. I've enjoyed and taken something from every one of these players, some of whom I've borrowed from more than others. Sorry if I've forgotten anyone.

SEP 2016

Riverhead Free Library
330 Court Street
Riverhead, New York 11901